CHILDREN IN THE FIELD

Anthropological Experiences

EDITED BY JOAN CASSELL

TEMPLE UNIVERSITY PRESS

Philadelphia

Temple University Press, Philadelphia 19122
Copyright © 1987 by Temple University. All rights reserved
Published 1987
Printed in the United States of America

Library of Congress Cataloging-in-Publication Data

Children in the field.

1. Anthropologists—Family relationships.
2. Children of anthropologists.   3. Anthropologists—Biography.
4. Ethnology—Field work.   I. Cassell, Joan.
GN41.6.C48   1987   306'.092'4   86-23160
ISBN 87722-477-3 (alk. paper)

Chapter 9 is reprinted by permission from
Human Organization, Volume 46, Number 1.
It appears with some revisions in that journal's Spring 1987 issue.

To my children,
Justine and Stephen

PREFACE

The contributors to this volume do not represent a scientific sampling of fieldworkers (although sociologists, who have impressive phrases for everything they do, might describe it as a "scope," "opportunistic," or "snowball" sample). I did my best, using friends, acquaintances, their friends and acquaintances, and every other source I could think of, to assemble articles that involved a wide variety of geographic areas, field situations, and family constellations. In the end, as with much of the data of fieldwork, the results are based on idea, effort, serendipity—and persistence.

The idea of the book was generated by a summer spent in Jamaica learning to do fieldwork, accompanied by two children (see Chapter 1). At the time, I had finished a year of graduate school, had no idea what to expect, and was terrified about the prospect of bringing children to the field. Since then, any number of equally panicked neophytes have approached me at anthropology meetings, saying, "I heard you did fieldwork with children. What was it like? Were your kids okay? Could you get your work done?"

I kept trying to convince someone—anyone—to assemble a book of articles by people who had brought children to the field, to offer information as well as practical and theoretical advice on doing fieldwork with children. Every fieldworker I talked with thought it was a good idea, a few agreed to contribute articles, but no one was willing to spend the time and effort to collect and edit the essays. Eventually, I decided to do it myself.

Renate Fernandez, one of the people I tried to convince to edit the book, promised an article and offered the names of a number of anthropologists who had done fieldwork with children. (As an anthropologist's wife, she had as much fieldwork experience before attending graduate school as most anthropologists have throughout their professional careers.) Fernandez also mentioned an article—one that I had read more than ten years earlier and never forgotten—about the death of a child in the field and told me how to get in touch with the couple who had lost their child.

In 1982, I began to contact potential contributors. I asked each to describe their family's experiences *in narrative form* (I have never understood why a work of theoretical value must be difficult to read). Each participant was asked to respond to a list of questions, in any order and form they wished.

Many anthropologists were invited to participate; some accepted; eight actually produced finished articles, and a ninth agreed to contribute a piece that had already been published.

In a session I helped organize for the 1982 meeting of the Northeastern Anthropological Association, Morton Klass, a former professor of mine at Columbia University, described how the birth of a child in the field had altered his relationship with the East Indian men he studied in Trinidad. He and his wife, a writer, agreed to contribute an article for the volume.

When I was in Jamaica learning to do fieldwork, Melanie Dreher, a friend and graduate school classmate, was studying a local healer in a nearby village. Dreher did her dissertation research in Jamaica, and subsequently returned with three children. When asked to describe her experiences for the book, she assented.

I had met Nancy Scheper-Hughes in Edinburgh, at a meeting of the Society for Applied Anthropology, where she received the Margaret Mead Award for her book on schizophrenia in Ireland; she was accompanied by her husband and three children, who had been in Ireland with her. When contacted, she agreed to participate in the project. Scheper-Hughes was the only fieldworker who planned her contribution *before* going to the field. After a summer in Brazil, she wrote:

> Since I was "forewarned" in advance of fieldwork of your volume I was able to incorporate family responses to the field in Brazil this summer as part of my general research task. I had each of my three children keep a daily journal of their reactions to Northeast Brazil (many of these, however, are unprintable!), I interviewed them from time to time on tape, and took some photographs of them in the field.

Patricia Hitchcock, who had published the haunting article on the death of her two-year-old son in the field, assented to its inclusion in the volume.

Renate Fernandez told me about Jonathan Wylie, an anthropologist who had been a child in the field. He was one of the first participants to finish an article; we have been exchanging letters, articles, revisions, ideas, and personal news since 1982. (We discovered that when Wylie and his family had Thanksgiving dinner at the U.S. Army base in Chinon, France, in 1957, I too was in Chinon, where I had just married Eric Cassell, who was doing what the French called his *service militaire* at the U.S. Army hospital there.)

An editor who was interested in the book suggested I get in touch with Stephen and Christine Hugh-Jones, at Cambridge University in Great Britain, telling me that they brought their children to live in a longhouse with an Amazonian tribe. The Hugh-Joneses agreed to participate in the project, and, Christine, who had left anthropology and was attending medical school, eventually wrote the article.

Two couples, the Nichters and the Lobbans, contacted me. During a group dinner, at the 1982 meeting of the American Anthropological Association, I mentioned the projected volume to the man sitting next to me, who turned out to be Mark Nichter. He told his wife, they expressed interest, I was encouraging, and they produced a piece for the book. The Lobbans learned of the project from Nancy Scheper-Hughes, after contacting her about a session I had organized on bringing children to the field, for the 1983 meeting of the American Anthropological Association. Receiving their inquiry, I remembered reading their article some years before on the reactions of Josina, age two and a half to three and a half, to their fieldwork in the Sudan. (The Hitchcock and Lobban articles were the only pieces I had encountered on children in the field.) The Lobbans were now able to compare the experiences of two children in two field sites. They were interested; naturally, so was I.

Like an angler, I still regret the ones that got away. One article, promised but never produced, involved a graduate student, too poor to afford a sitter, who brought her baby with her while doing fieldwork with black inner-city women in the United States: "They taught me to be a single mother!" she declared. Another anthropologist, who had conducted fieldwork in New Guinea with her husband, both before having children and afterward, adamantly refused to participate: "I was a bad fieldworker and a bad mother," she insisted. I tried to convince her that it was important for potential fieldworkers to learn of negative as well as positive experiences; she agreed, but said that the events were still too painful to recall.

I find all the accounts fascinating. But, then, I am a prejudiced audience. To me, the subjects—fieldwork and children—are fascinating.

CONTENTS

1   "Oh No, They're Not My Shoes!":
Fieldwork in the Blue Mountains of Jamaica   01
BY JOAN CASSELL

2   Children in the Amazon   27
BY CHRISTINE HUGH-JONES

3   A Tale of Simeon: Reflections on Raising a Child
While Conducting Fieldwork in Rural South India   65
BY MIMI NICHTER AND MARK NICHTER

4   "Daddy's Little Wedges": On Being a
Child in France   91
BY JONATHAN WYLIE

5   Birthing in the Bush: Participant Observation
in Trinidad   121
BY MORTON KLASS AND SHEILA SOLOMON KLASS

6   Three Children in Rural Jamaica   149
BY MELANIE DREHER

7   Our Ulleri Child   173
BY PATRICIA HITCHCOCK

8   Children and Parents in the Field:
    Reciprocal Impacts   185
    BY RENATE FERNANDEZ

9   A Children's Diary in the Strict Sense of the Term:
    Managing Culture-Shocked Children in the Field   217
    BY NANCY SCHEPER-HUGHES

10 "Drink from the Nile and You Shall Return":
    Children and Fieldwork in Egypt and the Sudan   237
    BY CAROLYN FLUEHR-LOBBAN
    AND RICHARD LOBBAN

    Conclusion   257
    BY JOAN CASSELL

CHILDREN IN THE FIELD
Anthropological Experiences

JOAN CASSELL

1   "Oh No, They're Not My Shoes!": Fieldwork in the Blue Mountains of Jamaica

Every night, those first two weeks, the rats would hold what Jamaicans called a "fete" in the living room. I would cower in my bed, listening to their creaks, steps, and squeaks, terrified that one of the children would call me and that I would have to walk through the rats to get to their room. At 4:00 in the morning, before the donkey brayed and the rooster crowed, I would lie awake composing imaginary letters to Margaret Mead:

Dear Dr. Mead:

I am in a Jamaican village learning how to do fieldwork, with a six year old, a nine year old, and a houseful of rats, who invite their friends to come and share the rat poison I put out. I can cope with the lack of electricity—Coleman

1

lanterns are bright enough to read by. I can cope with
spending the better part of a day driving to and from
Kingston to buy food—even fruit and vegetables grown in
this village. I can even cope (well, sort of) with the continual
breakdowns of my refrigerator, spoiling our meat and forcing
me to go into Kingston again to buy more. But I can't cope
with the rats. No one mentioned rats in my anthropology
courses at Columbia. What do I do?

The next morning, I would stop worrying about the rats and start
wondering how to set about doing fieldwork in the village of
Mango Ridge.

As a graduate student in a brand-new program in applied anthropology, I knew that one of the requirements was to do fieldwork for a summer before taking my comprehensive exams and
beginning dissertation research. There was talk, that first year, of
taking students to Jamaica for the summer, but funding was delayed. When Jamaica was discussed, I took it for granted that, as
a married woman with two children, I would be unable to go.
Fieldwork far from home seemed one of the luxuries reserved for
childless students—as were classes scheduled for Thursdays,
when I had no one to watch the kids, or time spent hanging out
with professors and fellow students. I attended classes, read the
reserved books at the library (when I was unable to get copies to
read at home), and rushed back to Brooklyn to make sure the
children were all right. They always were. But, when I telephoned—and I did frequently—they had a wonderfully wistful
way of asking where I was and when I was coming home that
always made me feel guilty.

In retrospect, I see myself as a somewhat uptight mother and
uptight graduate student. Part of this was situational: My husband, a physician, had evening office hours, and during the week
the children were usually asleep when he came home. I felt it my

responsibility to kiss them good night, to spend time with them, to be there with and for them. Part was temperamental: I am not particularly flexible or easygoing. Part was class and culture: Middle-class mothers worry about their children's welfare and development (and, in the folklore of mothering, Jewish mothers worry more). Part was historical: In 1968, my first year as a full-time graduate student, I had not been exposed to feminist notions of individual fulfilment for women. And part probably stemmed from a lack of role models: I knew no female professors or anthropologists with young children. My male professors with children had wives who stayed home to care for them. And the few female graduate students with children seemed as busy and harassed as I was. In my immediate neighborhood, I was the only woman attending graduate school; there was no one to discuss these issues with, and at the time they were not even defined as issues that could be contemplated, let alone discussed.

At the end of the school year, in May, the Jamaican fieldwork project was funded. And, at 2:30 one morning, inspiration awakened me: Why not take the children to Jamaica and have Eric, my husband, spend his vacation there with us? Eric thought it was a fine idea. And my adviser, when asked, assured me that lots of people did fieldwork with children.

And so, in June 1969, six students and a professor arrived at the University of the West Indies, on the outskirts of Kingston, the capitol of Jamaica, to live in the dormitories while getting settled. My children, Justine ("Justie"), age nine, and Stephen, age six, were in New York; Eric would send them to me when I found a place to live. Because the arrangements were made at the last minute, none of us had detailed research plans. We knew we were going to "do fieldwork," and one of my classmates could not wait to "groove with the people," but I, for one, was not entirely sure exactly what one did when one did fieldwork. (I had missed

the course my classmates had taken on studying small communities because it was scheduled for Thursday, the day when I had
no sitter.)

The university was beautiful, with brilliantly colored tropical
plants and flowers shimmering in a heat so intense it made everything seem unreal. The food at the student cafeteria was greasy
and highly spiced; the showers lacked hot water; the electricity
blacked out during frequent thunderstorms; and the women's
dormitories sounded like a tropical birdcage, with students singing, calling to one another with melodic cries, and using musical
expletives for punctuation and expression. I learned that I could
not just lift the telephone and talk with Eric and the children.
There were few telephones available, none in the dorms.

"Getting through," as they said in Jamaica, was a production.
You had to reach the operator and coax her for an outside line;
you had to dial local numbers several times before the call would
"take"; and you might spend an hour or two at the phone before a
long-distance call to the United States would go through.

"Getting through" was equally difficult in every other aspect of
life. We spent hours sitting patiently with our professor in government offices, making connections to help us get placed and
days driving around the island, looking for suitable locations.
The other students were going to stay with a landlady or family, a
situation that was relatively easy to locate. I was the only one
looking for a house, with a housekeeper or student to watch the
kids. We looked everywhere. There did not seem to be an empty
house available on the entire island. I did not want to live with a
family. I was not sure how the children would react to such an
abrupt and radical change in living patterns, nor whether I could
stand the lack of privacy; I was sure Eric would hate it.

All of us were nervous about starting fieldwork, the mythic *rite
de passage* that transforms amateurs into anthropologists. Added
to this were my worries about how the children were going to

acclimate to a place that I found hot, foreign, exotic, and intimidating. I started awakening in the middle of the night, wondering whether I had made a terrible mistake. It occurred to me that all the people my adviser knew who had done fieldwork with children were probably researcher-husbands, whose wives cared for the children, ran the household, typed their husband's fieldnotes, and studied the local women on the side. My adviser had no children. What did he know about bringing kids to the field? He probably thought they could be shipped as easily as luggage. How would children who had never been on a plane manage by themselves? Who would watch them while I did research? Where would we live? What would we eat?

At this stage, I was fortunate that long-distance telephoning was too complicated for me to pick up a phone and tell Eric to forget the whole thing, I was coming home by the next plane. I tried to think of a noble or even a legitimate-sounding reason for returning to New York. I could think of nothing that did not sound like exactly what it was: cold feet. I still do not know how much of my anxiety was related to fieldwork and how much to the children, but the combination was a killer.

A day before our professor was scheduled to return to New York, we heard of a house in the village of Mango Ridge, in the Blue Mountains above Kingston. We drove out to see the house. It looked rustic but comfortable, equipped with hot water—a welcome change from the dormitories—a kerosene refrigerator, and a four-burner gas stove. Behind the house lived an eighty-year-old caretaker, who said he had relatives who could help with child care, cooking, and cleaning. We learned that there were no buses into Kingston but that taxis and trucks brought people and produce to the city. We also learned, to my relief, that there was a local clinic, with a full-time nurse, and a doctor who visited twice weekly. Mango Ridge had no electricity—the lines were being put up that summer—and a single telephone located in the post office. The idea of being connected to Kingston, and to New York, in case of emergency, was a comfort.

My professor had left when I moved in two days later, so a professor from the university drove me to Mango Ridge. He was a jovial, considerate man, who tried to allay my evident nervousness by teasing, telling me I was not going to be doing "real" anthropology, since my food would come from the Kingston supermarket, and there was no savage "bush." I did not laugh; it seemed like bush to me. I had the feeling of jumping off into space, with the children being tossed after me.

The house really was lovely, on top of a hill, surrounded by trees, with a vegetable garden, an orange and a lemon tree bearing fruit, a wide verandah, and jalousied windows. It was far from the main road, with lots of space where children could play safely (an important consideration to a New Yorker, who thought of places away from home as unsafe). The caretaker had not expected me and went to get "the maid," a woman of about forty-five, with a paralyzed arm, who walked with a rocking gait. Gloria had thin arms and legs, a large bosom, and an air of intelligence; she wore a kerchief on her head, tied back, country-fashion. She brought Maude, her nine-year-old adopted daughter with her. The caretaker lit lamps and the gas refrigerator and moved cannisters of gas around for the stove and hot water; Maude swept floors and dusted; Gloria made beds. I felt as though I had a staff of thousands. Some bush!

Gloria told me she was willing to work every day but the Sabbath and that she made 15s. (shillings) a day, which made her wages £4 10s. a week—or $10.80. She would watch the children, clean the house, and cook meals; Maude and her mother would help when necessary. Subsequently, I learned that Gloria's salary was, by local standards, outrageous. The going rate was £2 a week, or at most £2 10s. From Gloria's point of view, I was rich, and, in fact, the salary was very low by New York City standards. I never did learn to cope with the problem that this difference in perspectives represented. To most of the people in Mango Ridge I was a rich white lady, and even if they liked me, I still represented a potential financial resource to be exploited by desperately poor people. Thus, I ended up feeding not only Gloria when she prepared our dinner, but also Maude—how could I let a hungry child watch while my children ate? I also frequently fed Gloria's mother and the caretaker and his wife. I resented this, but I also felt guilty about my relative affluence, and they were much better at getting food from me than I was at keeping it from them. When the owner of the house, a high-status, light-skinned civil servant, came to Mango Ridge, Gloria worked for her. This woman probably knew how to handle such problems. No doubt there are recognized patterns of interaction between Jamaican employers and household employees that cover salary, food, and "perks." I was unfamiliar with these patterns, however, and did not live in Mango Ridge long enough to work out a way of coping with what I perceived as a kind of financial exploitation. I understood it. I also resented it.

I feel less guilty about having people work for me these days than I did eighteen years ago. But the radical difference in resources would still be hard to cope with. Today, however, I would discuss the problem ahead of time with people who had employed household help in the field, preferably in a similar location. No real solution may exist—interfering with one's work and refraining from hiring desperately poor people who need the money is hardly an answer. But having some sense of the local rules for interaction between employers and employees, and knowing ahead of time what sort of problems you are going to face and how you intend to deal with them, would be helpful.

Three days after arriving in Mango Ridge, I took a taxi to the Kingston airport to pick up Justine and Steve. We had been separated for two weeks—the longest we had ever been apart.

When I said I was going to meet my children, the man at Customs and Immigration allowed me to break the rules and go through to the plane (love for children allows one to shortcut many rules in Jamaica). I arrived at the plane to find them embracing several doting Jamaican stewardesses. They had had a marvelous flight; the stewardesses had let them help serve food. This was the first, but not the last time, I learned that Jamaicans, who might seem somewhat closed and glum to a stranger, were open, loving, patient, and indulgent with children.

(Later, Eric told me that when he delivered them to the plane, they looked so tiny and vulnerable—six-year-old Stephen trustingly holding the hand of nine-year-old Justine—that he had to leave rapidly so they would not see tears streaming down his face. He spent several hours, until my cable came saying they had arrived safely, listening to the radio for plane crashes.)

Their first evening in Mango Ridge, the children were unable to fall asleep. I finally put them together in the big bed in Justine's room and sang to them for several hours. About a week later, I knew they were beginning to feel at home when their usual squabbling resumed, and I was able to move them into adjoining rooms. I continued singing to them, however. It helped make bedtime safe, cozy, and familiar. I found it as comforting as they.

Having children who needed care and reassurance was a benefit at this stage, although I did not then perceive it as such. The kids acted as an emotional anchor. I was neither willing nor able directly to confront my own fears about living in a strange place and carrying out fieldwork. Instead, I focused on the welfare of the children. Setting up a daily routine, trying to arrange for relatively familiar meals, and making sure the children were beginning to feel at home were ways of getting acclimated myself. Reassuring them reassured me.

The first few days, the children and I walked around together, exploring and meeting people. The village of Mango Ridge, about a third of a mile from our house, consisted of unpainted, tin-roofed, wooden "rumshops" that also sold groceries, a tailor, and a freshly painted stucco post office with adjoining police station—all strung along one side of the road from Kingston. The three of us walked miles, resting when tired in one of the rumshops, drinking sickly sweet "aerated water" and talking to anyone who would talk with us. And people on the road, in the rumshops, at the police station, and in the post office did talk, when not to me, to the children. Steve was shy, but would answer direct questions. Justine enjoyed the attention; she responded to questions and asked her own. We were followed by groups of barefoot children dressed in ragged clothing who seemed to find the kids enthralling. Before they knew us, they said nothing; they just followed quietly, giggled, and stared. Once, Justine looked back and loudly said, "Boo!" They startled and seemed unsure whether or not to laugh. Later in the summer, when I walked by myself, the children would poke one another to get up their courage and then inquire: "Where Justine, Mum? Where Steve?"

Justine reports that when walking to town the first week, a group of children ran after her, shouting, "Whitey, whitey!" This was one of the few unpleasant occurrences she remembers.

The day the children arrived, our refrigerator failed. It was a nuisance at the time—the meat started to go bad almost immediately. In retrospect, however, it turned out to be a splendid way to meet people. Almost everyone in town who had a refrigerator kept our meat at one time or another. And every man with a reputation for being mechanical spent some time under the refrigerator, trying to fix it. (When tinkered with, it would work for a few days and then fail again. It never worked properly until

Eric came and took the offending section into Kingston and replaced the entire thing, at a cost of £5. No man in Mango Ridge was capable of such extravagant, high-handed—well, American—behavior.)

Another way to meet people was more intentional: I did not rent a car. Instead, I relied on the kindness of the few people in town who owned cars to get into Kingston to shop for food and replace the meat that spoiled each time the refrigerator went out. The drive to and from Kingston was a good time to talk with people, to ask questions, and to answer theirs about who I was and what I was doing there. Here, the presence of the children was an advantage. They guaranteed not only my intent—someone up to no good would not bring children with her—but also my identity—a six year old and a nine year old will tell anyone who asks anything they want to know.

"People were so friendly," reports Justine, today. "Everyone was so interested in us. Everyone knew who we were. They were all interested in where we came from and how many Tonka Toys we had."

Sometimes the children would go swimming with Gloria and Maude. Maude had no bathing suit, so Justine, who had two, politely offered her brand-new bathing suit, which stretched to fit Maude's stocky figure. From then on—I am not exactly sure how—the new suit automatically went to Maude, while Justine wore her faded old one. This was the kind of thing I resented but did not know how to cope with. Gloria would prepare dinner— enough for us, herself, Maude, and (I suspect) her mother. Although Gloria would occasionally watch the kids in the evening, she did not want to babysit at night regularly. And I was afraid to leave the children alone in an isolated house, with Coleman lanterns that might start a fire, and no one near but an aged caretaker and his sick wife. Gloria offered the services of Maude, who was the same age as Justine, but not as quick-witted. I declined, and most evenings I stayed with them.

As a result, until Eric arrived in August, I missed most of the night life of Mango Ridge. This was indeed a loss. Had I been more flexible, I would have followed Mango Ridge custom and brought the children with me. Instead, I would sing the children to sleep and then read by Coleman lantern until about 9:30, when the rats would begin to scratch in the walls. I would then retreat to my bed, awakening before dawn to the sound of the rats. I put out poison, their bacchanalia intensified; there seemed to be more rats every night. One night, they rolled or pushed the tin of rat poison from the corner of the living room right into the center; pellets were scattered everywhere.

I never discussed the rats with the children. I think I had a superstitious feeling that unmentioned rats would go unnoticed. If a telephone had been available, I would have complained to Eric and perhaps even announced that we were coming home. If there had been a car, I might have taken the children to the university for a long visit or perhaps to a tourist beach at the other end of the island. No hiding place. So we stayed put. And walked and walked and talked and talked to everyone who would talk to us, since I could think of nothing else to do. Loneliness increased receptivity: I sat around with great patience and really *listened* to people. As we walked along the roads, Justine petted every baby goat she encountered, to the astonishment of all passers-by. Animals did not seem to be something one petted in Mango Ridge; the local children stoned dogs and killed stray birds. Perhaps compassion for small creatures is a luxury reserved for comfortable city folk.

In August, after Eric's arrival, the children rescued a baby bird that had fallen from its nest. With great excitement, they helped Eric lift it on a bamboo pole and return it to the nest, where it was eventually accepted by its parents. Our Mango Ridge acquaintances looked at us as though we were demented. Some local children told Justie and Steve that they ate birds.

Compassion was not the only luxury reserved for my children. I had been careful not to bring fancy toys: just a few storybooks, crayons, and paper. But in Mango Ridge, where barefoot children wore clothes with more holes than fabric, where the exposed roots of a tree were used as a swing and toys contrived from cast-off scraps, where to buy milk we had to send our own empty rum bottles to the man who owned a cow, my children were very rich. They had crayons, paper, books, flashlights, well-fitting shorts and T-shirts that had been bought just for them, bathing suits, shoes, summer sandals.

When Eric arrived, he made the mistake of buying a tiny metal car, truck, and tractor in Kingston; these scale models, with perfect moving parts, are irresistible to children, boys in particular. Groups of older boys started to arrive daily to play with the vehicles and with Steve, since it was clearly a package deal. Three times, a vehicle disappeared, to return with an adult, holding a shamed boy, who had been unable to resist the temptation. It was our fault. We had provided what I believe the law calls an "irresistible nuisance."

Our second Saturday in Mango Ridge, we attended the service at the Adventist church, where Gloria was a preacher. The service included a children's Bible class; the lesson concerned Moses crossing the Red Sea. Justine, with a number of Passovers under her belt, an excellent memory, and a tendency to show off, was the star pupil. About twenty adults and thirty to forty children were present, and clothes were clearly Sabbath-best: The women wore straw hats, rather than kerchiefs; the girls wore freshly ironed cotton dresses; the children wore shoes. During the intermission, Justine said in a loud voice, "Oh, look, Mommy, there's my shoes!" (We had given Gloria a pair of shoes that were too tight for Justie, and Maude was wearing them.) I elbowed Justine, who with flawless nine-year-old tact said in an equally loud voice, "Oh no, they're not my shoes. They just look like them!" The first half of the service lasted from 9:30 to 12:15. My children had never sat still so long in their entire protected, understood, progressively schooled lives. I thought Steve would explode. He complained of ravenous hunger and a stomachache at the same time. We left, instead of socializing and staying for the afternoon service, because I did not think the kids could take it.

Mango Ridge residents took church seriously. The Bible was quoted frequently to justify or criticize the behavior of others and to comment on current events. The Sunday when the first Americans were due to land on the moon, villagers were discussing the news as they left church. "Signs and wonders, that's what the Bible said, and that's what we're seeing, signs and wonders—the time is coming," proclaimed one woman. Another held that the Lord did not want to put a man on the moon and would not allow it. Man did not belong on the moon; where was it mentioned in the Bible? That I could quote suitable phrases from the King James Bible (having specialized in Elizabethan literature in college) seemed to please and impress villagers, as did Justine's biblical "knowledge" (her prowess in Bible class was bruited about by Gloria). People kept inquiring, "What kind of Christian are you, Mistress Joan?" They would look puzzled when I replied, "I'm not Christian, I'm Jewish." The right answer came in a burst of inspiration: Everyone seemed to understand when I responded, "We're the people of the Good Book, we're Jewish." (Justie caused a fuss in clinic one day when she refused to fill in a form with her "Christian name." "But we're Jewish!" she kept objecting.)

School was still in session when the children arrived, and Justine received permission from the head teacher for both of them to attend. The children spent two days at the school, which was near our house. The school consisted of one large room with no walls; there were too few benches, so some children sat on large stones. Most of the day was recess, said Justine; what lessons there were consisted of rote learning by the entire group of several hundred children. Children were disciplined by being "flogged." After the Mango Ridge elementary school, Justie and Steve's annual summer "*Yech, school*" routine was muted. The quantity as well as quality of schooling differed: At six, Steve had already attended school for four years (two years of nursery school and a year of kindergarten and first grade), while only a few of the Jamaican farm children had been lucky enough to attend "basic school" for a year before elementary school.

Perceiving the poverty of the Mango Ridge farm children—a poverty of possessions, schooling, opportunities—through the eyes of my children, and comparing it with the middle-class urban advantages they and I almost took for granted, sharpened the contrast and made it more poignant. Even Steve was aware of differences, while Justine was quite verbal about them. In her "field notes," which I reproduce verbatim, she contrasted her life and that of the pampered niece of the Mango Ridge postmistress with that of Maude, Gloria's adopted daughter:

> I live with a girl (Maude) whose live is different because she is poor. I live with another girl too (Cynthia). She lives more like me because she is well off. There is a difference between them, one can get things the other can't.

> You can tell Maude is poor because (1) of her clothes they are few and she weres the same clothes each day. (2) Because she eat the extras and a little of her own food.

> Our freind cooks here food on a camp fire . . . and one bed for three people . . . a shack really.

Of the school, she noted:

> The schools are different from New York there is about a
> hundred children in a room whith two teachers. When a
> child does something wrong she (he) gets whipped twice on
> there hand.
>
> People in school get whipped if they don't do a composition.
>
> This morning the teacher was flogging some children. She
> asked me "if they flogged in New York" while she said it she
> added another big smack with the belt she was showing off a
> lot for me.

This is not to say that the children or I spent our time pitying
the Mango Ridge kids. They were remarkably inventive and used
whatever came to hand to construct the most fascinating toys,
which seemed far more interesting and imaginative than the
mass-produced items Justine and Steve played with. To quote
Justine's field notes again:

> The children here don't have toys so they make them like
> making a swing out of a root and a pinwheel from a peace of
> wood and a motor car out of a peace of wood and
> type writer ribbon. . . .
>
> A popogun out of bamboo, a sling shot out of rubber . . . a
> roller coaster out of wood and leaves.

As the children and I walked around and talked to people,
went to church services, and attended any other occasion we
could find, I kept looking for someone who knew what was going
on, who would be able to introduce me to people and answer my
questions. Our second week in Mango Ridge, I finally located
Lucille Davis, who was what Jamaicans called a "volunteer social
worker." A light-skinned widow, Mrs. Davis distributed AID
(Agency for International Development) powdered milk to poor
families, bought pimiento from the local farmers for the Jamaica

Agricultural Society, ran the weekly lending library, owned the three largest pots in town (which were loaned out when people entertained), cooked for parties, baked for weddings, visited the sick, and was godmother to a number of local children. Almost everyone in Mango Ridge called her "Miss Mommy." (Her sister was "Miss Darling.") When walking through town, Mrs. Davis would greet everyone, including children, by name. "Miss Dora," she would say in a calm tone; a "Good afternoon, Miss Mommy," would come the reply. Passing children would be dispatched on errands, to fetch sugar, to deliver a message, to pick lemons from a tree; they obeyed without question; it seemed to be taken for granted that this was one of their functions. When we knew her better, she would send Justine on errands as well. She loved going—on returning, she was given a piece of home-made cake or something else good to eat. One afternoon, I was with Miss Mommy when she saw a stranger entering a cabin: "I don't know you!" she said in a loud voice. The woman hurriedly explained who she was. Mrs. Davis inquired where the stranger came from, whom she was related to, and how long she intended to stay. "Oh," she said, nodded, and passed on.

Mrs. Davis was a kind, capable, sharp lady. Once, after an outing together, Justine burbled enthusiastically, "I've been here so long, and I feel so at home that I can't tell the difference between black and white!" "What's the matter, child, you lose your eyes?" asked Miss Mommy. Mrs. Davis was bilingual, switching from English to Jamaican dialect as the occasion required. One day, when the two of us were strolling through town conversing in English, she saw a little girl with a bandaged forehead. "Pickney, is you drop off tree?" she queried. "Yes'm," whispered the child. "Know better next time," advised Miss Mommy. (When I inquired at the university about the term *pickney*, I was told that it may have come from the Portuguese slavers who brought the blacks to the New World.)

Life became livelier after we met Mrs. Davis, who acted as our
social sponsor in Mango Ridge. The children and I met people,
helped cook for "fetes," decorated wedding cakes, and attended
celebrations, commencements, agricultural fairs—all the cere-
monial occasions that gladden the hearts of local peoples (and
anthropologists). Life became easier our third week in Mango
Ridge when a friend gave us a skinny little cat; it immediately
mounted a formidable campaign against the rats, who soon
disappeared.

We learned that children were part of people's lives in Mango
Ridge in a way that was very different from our experience. We
found no occasion or location where children were considered
inappropriate or unwelcome. People brought young children to
celebrations that might last until 3:00 in the morning. If they
tired, they went to sleep on the nearest bed or in the nearest car;
if they cried, the nearest adult would hold them. The local children would spend hours sitting through programs consisting of
speeches, songs, and recitations; they were used to such cere-
monies and wriggled a lot less than my kids. When the brand-
new Community Center was dedicated, I left Justie and Steve
home, to their distress: I knew they would be bored by the long
program, extending past their usual supper and bedtime, and
fatigued by the two-mile hike in each direction, and I did not
want to cope with cranky kids. Yet the place was crammed with
children of all ages. One woman, who asked why my children
were not there, explained that everyone in Mango Ridge brought
children, and all the kids got tired and misbehaved, so no one felt
bad. Jamaicans were less uptight than I about children. They
took it for granted that kids were portable. Parents did not seem
concerned about the proper hour for children's meals, bedtime—
or anything else. Not surprisingly, the children grow up to be
Mango Ridge adults, who run on "Jamaica time," arriving an
hour or two late for appointments, if they arrive at all.

People in Mango Ridge emphasized the joy, the comfort, the company offered by children, as opposed to the middle-class American stress on the responsibility, stress, and work children represented. Grandmothers, relatives, and friends would take other people's children, for a day, a week, forever. Gloria, who was very poor, had adopted Maude; she spoke of her as a blessing, not a trial, and indeed Maude worked hard, helping Gloria and her aged mother. The postmistress, who was raising a seventeen-year-old niece and the five-year-old daughter of another niece, was looking forward to the arrival of the two-year-old child of another relative. She said of the seventeen year old, "She was given to me by my brother's wife before she was born. My sister-in-law said, 'Whatever I have, boy or girl, you can have it.' That's how much she loved me!" An old peasant lady, admiring my kids, lamented her childless state: "Poor me. Me no have none. Not even one little crab!"

Mango Ridge children were part of the adults' world of work as well. Unlike Justine and Steve, who knew their father was a doctor but had little idea of what he did, Mango Ridge children knew just what adult work consisted of, and most of them took part in it. My children were thrilled to help harvest the "pimiento" (allspice) crop; this was "real" work, not the children's make-work tasks they did in New York. Justine got a "job" in the post office: She sorted mail; made change in pounds, shillings, and pence; and gossiped with customers. Steve was so impressed that he asked if he could work at the local chicken farm. The owner, one of the few Mango Ridge women whose children did not have to work, was enormously amused, but assented; every day, six-year-old Steve (who was not allowed to cross the street by himself in New York) walked to work in town; there, he played with the owner's son, occasionally helping the boys who worked at the farm collect eggs. (I am not contending that Mango Ridge taught me the benefits of child labor. For one thing, my children had a choice; they could "play" at work and stop when they got bored. But I did learn that the gulf between the world of children and the world of adults, taken for granted by urban middle-class American families, is not present in rural Jamaica and that its absence offers certain social and emotional advantages.)

The children and I learned what it was like to live in a very small town. There were so few cars in the area that local people, sitting in our house above the road, surrounded by trees, could tell by the sound who was passing. Everyone knew Justine and Steve. They seemed to be minor celebrities among the village children, who would inquire after them when I was alone. I was worried one evening when it became dark and Justine had not returned from an errand in town; she arrived home, radiant, reporting that six older girls had walked her to town, five more had walked her back, one man had greeted her by name and rapped on the counter to get the storekeeper's attention, and the storekeeper had given her a bunch of fragrant white lilies that usually sold for 5s.: "You just can't be afraid at night when people are with you!" she said. One morning, when I fell while jogging on the hilly road, everyone in Mango Ridge knew, by afternoon, that I had hurt my knee and gone "to clinic," where "Nurse" had put a "dressing" on my scraped knee. (With the exception of an exceedingly itchy rash I developed a few days before Eric's arrival, which he medicated, this was the only medical problem we had during the summer.)

When Eric arrived in the middle of August, he reported that utter strangers would greet him as "Doc" and offer to buy him a drink at a local rumshop. People probably did know a great deal about him; they could and no doubt did ask the children everything they wished to know.

One evening, I arrived home with friends, after a day's outing, to find that Justine, with the assistance of Maude, was having a party on our verandah. Justine and Maude had what seemed to

me to be a remarkably harmonious relationship: Justie was enter-
prising and bossy; Maude, biddable and good-tempered. (Did
Maude see playing with Justine as part of her—and Gloria's—
job? The question never occurred to me at the time.) It was a very
Jamaican celebration, with a written program, speeches, songs,
and recitations. They had invited Gloria and the local butcher,
and served candy and soda. Justine was quite put out when we
joined her party without being invited (after all, she had managed to exclude Steve) and even more annoyed when her bedtime
arrived, was enforced, and the "party" went on without her. In a
moment of inspiration, I told my friends that I too was going to
have a fete, for my birthday, in mid-August. After that, the fete
had a life of its own; everyone seemed to know what to do, especially when directed by Miss Mommy. (By this time, the children and I called her "Aunt Lou," as did many of our Mango
Ridge friends.) Aunt Lou helped me invite people, including
three local men who sang reggae and played harmonica, guitar,
and a bass soundbox; the butcher killed "a nice little rammy"
bought for the occasion (watched by my fascinated children), a
campfire was built outside our house, and two of Aunt Lou's large
pots materialized; curried goat was prepared in one pot, and in
the other, a fiery soup, from every part of the goat that could not
be curried; soda and ice were borrowed from two local rumshops,
and quantities of rum bought. Aunt Lou directed; Gloria, the
butcher, and Justine served. Everyone seemed to get special pleasure from watching us drink, dance, and have fun—they said as
much. There was great approval, of themselves for having the
kind of party we could enjoy, and of us, for so obviously enjoying
it. Everyone danced with everyone, including Justine and Steve,
who, for once, stayed up, Jamaican style, until 2:30 when the
party started to break up.

I was unsure of what the people who helped with the party
expected from me. I had discovered that Mango Ridge ran, in part,

on a system of reciprocal favors: Many of the people who helped when I lacked a car and the refrigerator kept breaking down asked for various kinds of help when Eric arrived with a rented car. If we had not attempted to reciprocate, I suppose we would not have entered the system. We did, but there were some favors we could not grant. Two of the men in the little band that played for my party asked, in a tactfully roundabout way, whether we could sponsor them in the United States. We received this request frequently. Justine reported that she could not tell when Jamaicans were serious: Ladies in Mango Ridge were always asking her "jokingly" whether I could sponsor them in the United States, and what gift she intended to give them. One day, a friend who was visiting our house asked, in the same half-joking way, what Justine was going to give her when she left Mango Ridge. "What are you going to give *me?*" responded Justine. When promised a hand-crocheted purse, Justine emerged from her bedroom with a one-of-a-kind gift: a carefully polished tooth that she had lost the week before!

Justine, who saw me keeping scrupulous field notes, started collecting her own; these included the following—and again, verbatim—observations:

> When you receive milk in the morning, it has not been skimed, just milked.

> The children don't like the jobs their mothers give them but they do it anyway.

> At night it's very peaceful with a gas light burning next to you.

> It is very homely here.

> We watched a goat being killed first he took it by one leg and tyed both legs to a tree and cut its neck then he started

skining it then he cut its belly open and took out the
adamonen [abdomen] and intenstine, big and little, and he
took the rest of the stomach out and gave them all to a boy
who turned them inside out and washed them then he
wash everything else and started to make soup with them
then he took the head and took off the hair and horns and put
them in the soup he took one of the horns and cut the
bottom off and put leaves in then smoked it! then we went to
our house and ate them all.

On a flying visit to Jamaica, my professor came to Mango
Ridge. He admired Justine's field notes, which made her "red
with pride." After discussing my activities, we decided I would
concentrate on the upper strata in Mango Ridge: Aunt Lou and
her friends. These were the people who spoke English and, consequently, the ones I communicated with most, since we all had
difficulty understanding conversations when people spoke rapid
dialect.

Two days before we left, we were given a "sendoff" party at the
house of a man I had interviewed for my study. The fete included
copious amounts of food and liquor, and speeches from almost
everyone, including me. One man said how happy everyone was
that "Mistress Cassell and her two pickneys" had come to spend
time with them. The next evening, I walked through town to say
good-bye to people. I ended my walk at Aunt Lou's house where I
found Eric and the children, and several friends. More people
arrived, and it turned into a second, impromptu sendoff. The
local taxi driver made a long speech, detailing our entire association and expressing his respect and esteem for me and the children. At least three times, he mentioned with approval that
whenever he went into Mango Ridge, he was greeted by Justine
and Steve. Several other people had mentioned this.

Mango Ridge residents talked of my children with love and
approval. They were friendly, cuddly, well behaved—and white,

the only white children in town. In a country where social status is largely correlated with skin color, the children belonged to the group who control the money and opportunities denied the residents of Mango Ridge. The children represented status and power, yet they were utterly accessible, to be snuggled, questioned, played with, teased by the black inhabitants of Mango Ridge (see Conclusion).

I believe I would have been accepted without the children. But my acceptance was faster and warmer because of them. Their presence highlighted the relationship between adults and children in Mango Ridge. Having them with me interfered with my work at night only: Lacking a reliable babysitter, I stayed home, missing much of the night life of Mango Ridge. Of course, one reason it was comparatively easy for me to do fieldwork with children was that I did not have a complex and focused research design. I wandered around Mango Ridge, meeting people, talking to them, and asking questions. The presence of the children facilitated meeting people and making friends. These friends provided the data on which my study was based. If I had done fieldwork in the slums of Kingston, as did one of my classmates, or conducted the kind of research where I had to collect large quantities of precise data, the children might have been a hindrance, or at least a distraction.

When I look back, I realize how little the Jamaican flexibility in childrearing influenced my behavior; it simply did not occur to me to keep the kids up and take them everywhere at all hours, as did the people of Mango Ridge. But then, if I had been more flexible, I might have had fewer grounds for comparison and not connected the differences in rural Jamaican and urban middle-class American childrearing styles with the results. I believe my style of childrearing produces adults like Eric and myself, somewhat rigid, upwardly mobile, middle-class strivers. In rural Jamaica, where social mobility was blocked, the issue was not striving but *surviving;* what Mango Ridge children needed to develop was a tolerance for difficult, boring, and frequently meaningless tasks and the adaptability to exploit whatever resources became available in a limited environment.

Our final day, Gloria bid us a tearful farewell. She had gone into Kingston to buy us gifts—beautiful ones, chosen with care and taste. She kept saying sadly how much she would miss the children.

Two Mango Ridge friends came in to Kingston to see us off at the airport. They waited patiently the two hours the plane was delayed, and the last thing we saw was both of them waving.

Epilogue

About a month later, I was glancing out the window at the sidewalk in front of our Brooklyn house, where Justine and some friends had set up a lemonade stand. Down the street came a stylishly dressed black dude, walking "the pimp's walk"—every inch of him proclaiming, "Don't mess with me." I watched as Justine, with perfect trust, walked up and asked him something; I could not hear her words, but it was clear that she was asking if he wanted to buy lemonade. He looked down at her, and seemed to inquire, in astonishment, what she had said. She repeated her request. (After all, she had just finished two and half months of being admired and loved by an entire town of black-skinned people.) Slowly, the dude took out a bill, gave it to Justine, and walked on.

Many years later, my children remember Mango Ridge with warmth and pleasure. Both children recall people, places, incidents. Justine has a vivid memory of arriving at the house in Mango Ridge, going on the porch, and seeing that there were *lemons* growing on a *tree!* "And I thought, 'Wow, this is *wonderful.*'"

Although Stephen, who graduated from college last year, does not reminisce about Jamaica as much as his sister, he recalls the summer in great detail. (When he saw me writing about his "job" at the egg farm, he described how the older boys would pick him up to use as a shield in egg-throwing contests: "They figured no one would throw an egg at me," he explained.)

When I asked if he remembered the poverty, he said no; he just thought that was the way it was. How about the difference in skin color? I asked, and he answered, no, he thought that was the way it was, too. "I just remember it as super fun!" he said.

Nine-year-old Justine noted in her field notes: "If you were going to Jamaica you would be in a tourist hotel and you would see only the Jamaicans who serve you. But we are like citizens, we do our own things, get grocerys and *LIVE!*"

At twenty-two, when asked about the effects on her of the summer in Jamaica, she replied, "it worked so well there that it made me want to travel a lot more. It made my habituation period much shorter. I get used to a new culture very quickly and I fit in. I don't look from the outside, I look from the inside." She continued, "Maybe I learned not being scared of strangers. They were the first strangers—no, the first people who thought of me as a stranger. Before, we had visited people who were friends of the family."

After spending two years at a French university, Justine graduated from an American college, spent two years doing graduate work in Edinburgh, and is now a Ph.D. candidate in Chicago. Her field is children's language; she is particularly interested in bilingualism.

My subsequent fieldwork was carried out in the United States, primarily in the New York City area. I did not perceive the children as portable, and Eric, in fact, was not.

Had I been able to talk with parents who had taken children with them, I would have been less apprehensive those first days in Jamaica. I would have had some way to distinguish realistic fears from chimeras, to separate apprehension about attempting field-work from worries about the welfare of my children. This book has been designed to answer some of the questions I was unable to ask in 1969.

have to retreat from the social relations, ritual patterns, and economic structures back to the feels and smells and incidents of everyday life in another culture. Of course, there is a sense in which this is impossible because our memories themselves have been changed by the academic uses to which we have put them and, more important here, by the ways in which we have translated them to masquerade for answers to other people's questions. I am thinking of questions about what fieldwork was like and how our children reacted to it. I say *masquerade* because, from my own point of view, my replies are not answers. They share the quality of all my attempts, grudging or willing, to reveal the less concrete aspects of fieldwork. I am privately overwhelmed by a rush of thoughts, memories, and feelings so disparate and complex as to make even the most considered answer a trite caricature. I suppose many other anthropologists must have rehearsed a battery of suitable short answers to questions such as "How long did it take to learn the language?" and "What did you do when you first arrived?" just as I have. If even these are fundamentally unanswerable, what about "What did Indians think of you?" or "Did your children like it in the jungle?"

It must be the emotional distress generated by our inability to communicate our experiences that drives us to avoid intimate discussions of fieldwork with others. It is easier to talk with those who have also immersed themselves in a foreign culture. We are like teenagers who have a new and unique experience, and other members of our own society are forced into the role of alien adults who unwittingly widen the gulf and inspire unreasonable anger with their well-meaning curiosity. Nor are we free among most of our professional colleagues; this is because our fieldwork experiences are bound up with the raw information we bring home. The manner of professional certainty with which we have to present our material restrains and molds our account of fieldwork as it was lived through. So, yet again in writing about children in the field, we are breaking the rules: This time, they do not concern the dual organization we have built for ourselves; they are the rules of reticence that let us keep highly emotive experience intact and private.

There are all kinds of gains to be made from looking at this new subject. We will learn plenty about how adults react to fieldwork, as well as about how parents, rightly or wrongly, look at their children's difficulties and pleasures and at their own responsibilities. Perhaps it will be most useful for people thinking of taking their children on fieldwork, not so much as a source of advice, but as a demonstration of the range of thoughts and feelings and consequences accompanying such a dramatic decision.

First, I should make the most relevant point. The fieldwork trip I made with my husband, Stephen, and our children, Leo, age eight (female and nothing to do with astrology), and Tom, age five, was the second for Stephen and myself. When I look back on the original fieldwork Stephen and I did, before our children were born, I cannot imagine that we would have achieved the same ends with children. Both the kind of fieldwork we did—itself partly dictated by the nature of the society and physical conditions— and the vulnerable psyche of the first-time fieldworker would have made extra responsibilities insupportable. I am fairly sure of this, and you may judge for yourselves when you have discovered more about our circumstances in the Pirá-paraná. I am also aware that when slices of the past recede from us, the decisions and styles of behaviors of the time accumulate a kind of false necessity. We arrange our experiences in chains of cause and effect so that the host of different possibilities and uncertainties that faced us then are never as real afterward as the events that actually happened. I can tell myself that we had to do our fieldwork in a particular way, but this was never really true. There were other ways of doing fieldwork among these Indian populations, and other anthropologists have discovered their personal styles. This book is evidence of a trend toward taking children on fieldwork, and we may find that others have or will successfully incorporate their children in circumstances similar to those of our first fieldwork. If they do, I hope they will be wiser and more confident than I was when I first reached the Amazon jungle.

Reflecting on this trend, I think that it is propelled by both practical and ideological forces. Of course, they are bound together in any one case, but not always in the same proportions. The practical instance is the more straightforward. Fieldwork is an integral part of the anthropologist's chosen career, and those who have children have to make a decision about how or whether to involve their children in fieldwork. For many women and some men, this boils down to fieldwork with children or no fieldwork at all. It is hardly surprising that the many changes in the socioeconomic status and aspirations of women have increased the numbers choosing the first.

The ideological forces are more difficult to pin down, but there seem to be two principal ones, which I will take in turn.

The change in women's status may be held responsible for a kind of positive discrimination in favor of taking children to the field that arises from the partially successful abolition of the negative discrimination against fieldwork for women. Although many female anthropologists overcame it, there can be no doubt that adventurous travel of all sorts was felt unsuitable for women. A nice example comes appropriately from the Pirá-paraná River. Brian Moser, a documentary filmmaker with whom we have since collaborated closely, wrote about a two-week journey on this river in 1961. He was following up an earlier trip by making a film, but this time the party include a woman. With the touching chivalry of the young Cambridge graduate—adventurer of the day, he wrote:

> Until now we would never have admitted that a girl should be allowed to take part in an expedition, but we had to change our minds. She had been through our worst disaster and remained unscathed; we lost all our medical supplies but she remained as fit as ourselves. True, the clouds of minute black sandflies and the *nigwas* which laid their nests of eggs in our feet were a new discomfort to her. [1]

Honestly enough, he uses "admitted," thus acknowledging that altruism toward girls had been mixed with the pleasures of monopolizing the adventurer's role. Since then, we have all had the self-interested aspect of male chauvinism rammed down our throats by the women's movement. More women have undertaken the responsibilities and risks attached to fieldwork in remote places and have found that the independence, academic status, and, above all, special privilege of living close to another culture are worth the price.

In the field of basic human rights, the phrase "women and children" rolls off the tongue from habit. Revolutionary attitudes to the one "oppressed class" seem to progress, willy-nilly, to the other. Women's liberation is followed by children's liberation, and, within anthropology, no sooner was a "women's anthropology" proposed to counteract the bias of a male perspective, than a "children's anthropology" was suggested. In the same way, if we have decided that it is a good thing that women are involved in fieldwork, a sleight of thought persuades us that it is virtuous and liberated to take our children along as well.

The other, more explicit, ideological input is the romantic one. Fieldwork involves physical and psychological risks on the

debit side but physical and psychological liberty from the constraints of our own society and ordered environment on the credit
side. Disillusioned with our lot and full of conflicts about what
we want for our children, it is easy to cherish an image of them as
budding noble savages, at one with a meaningful natural world.
The positive features of this life, like most valuable experience,
are embraced by facing dangers and suffering deprivations. We
may accept this in principle, but the more we concentrate on the
romantic image of childhood in a non-Western society, the less
realistic we become about the difficulties. In our own way, we are
apt to show as much lack of imagination as those people who
annoy us with their conviction that either homesickness or snakes
will finish off our children as they step off the airplane.

Our liberated-children ideals and our noble-savage fantasies
have something in common. They both grant children an independence and ability to look after themselves that they do not
really have. If they did, it would indeed relieve us of much of the
responsibility of deciding whether to take them to strange and
foreign places, and it would also minimize their interference with
our work. There is considerable convenience value for the parent
who subscribes to these ideologies. The real facts are that children are unable to contract out of their relationships with us; they
do not know how to provide for themselves, and they have little
experience on which to base their life decisions. Of course, the
goal of childrearing is gradully to overturn these states of affairs
in whatever way we think most productive, but nevertheless they
remain as partial constraints in all relationships between parents
and preadult children. We are simply fooling ourselves if we deny
this.

Looking again at the state of childhood, it appears much like
that of the anthropologist doing fieldwork for the first time. The
anthropologist is stuck with the chosen society, economically in-
competent, and homeless, and has no experience of how to man-

age the relationships that govern the success of fieldwork. There are mitigating circumstances, such as bringing in a supply of food, getting a house built, or being able to participate in a market system; but where there is no market system, each mark of independence creates distance between the fieldworker and the raw material of social anthropology. We had virtually none of these means of independence, nor did we make much effort to obtain them. When I consider what it would have been like to take children on a first visit to the Pirá-paraná, I ask myself how two children could possibly have looked after two children of their own. How could we have given our children any reassurance and genuine sense of security when we are so insecure and ignorant ourselves?

The place we were going to take Leo and Tom to is on the equator in the northwest Amazon. We had spent nearly two and half years (1968–1971) in Colombia eight years earlier. This had been divided into stretches of three to six months in the field with short intervals in Bogotá and elsewhere. (The Pirá-paraná River is just inside Colombia; the affluent where we spent most of our time rises close to the Brazilian border. The Pirá-paraná drains southward into the Apaporis–Caquetá–Japurá branch of the Amazon, but its people have more in common with groups to the north and east, on the Vaupés–Río Negro branch. Together, all these similar people make up a complex of eastern Tukanoan speakers united by a common culture and network of alliances resulting from obligatory descent-group exogamy. The alliance system is famous in South American ethnography because the territorially based exogamous patrilineal descent groups are language-possessing units; thus, husband and wife have separate native tongues. Traditionally, these Indians live in widely dispersed longhouses, each sheltering a small, patrilineal unit. Now, most are concentrated in missionary villages or outlying hamlets. By the late 1960s, the Pirá-paraná was one of the few areas in which longhouses had not replaced by nuclear family huts.)

We spent most of our first fieldwork time in a single longhouse, accompanying our hosts on visits to other longhouses as the occasion arose. We decided that intensive, rather than extensive, coverage was best because we needed to learn an eastern Tukanoan language, and this would be easiest in intimate contact with a small number of people. There were no written sources on the language we chose (Barasana), apart from a word list collected by an early German explorer. We settled in a longhouse that had many special advantages: Two important shamans and two ritual dance leaders made up the key group of male siblings; there was a fine collection of ritual dance ornaments; and there was an adult unmarried sister who, unlike the inmarried wives, spoke Barasana. I attached myself to this hardworking, generous, capricious, and humorous lady, who was responsible for nearly everything I knew. In 1981 she died of snakebite.

In our Barasana longhouse we were closer than usual to the hallowed role of participant observer. We had no food of our own, no private living space, and nothing to do except follow our Indian hosts around, watching, helping, and learning to communicate. We had an open hearthspace near the men's door of the longhouse, just as a visiting Indian family would; we slung our hammocks here and kept our few possessions on a makeshift rack. My days were spent with the women, mainly working manioc, the staple; Stephen's were with the men, felling cultivation sites (chagras), fishing, hunting, or picking coca leaves. We ate at communal meals in which each domestic unit supplied a pot of food boiled with chili pepper and a basket of bitter manioc bread to tear off and dip in. Our diet was fish, game, boiled leaves, manioc products, insects, and wild and cultivated fruits. Game was scarcer than fish; toucans, partridgelike birds, and paca were the most common, while wild pigs and tapir were a rare treat.

Our fieldwork was broad in scope. We were as systematic as possible about collecting genealogical data and a corpus of myth, but even these subjects, which might sound ideal for "informant sessions," came to us piecemeal—snatches of conversation overheard and half understood while struggling along an overgrown trail, scraping manioc, or picking coca. These data were written serially in a notebook mixed with entries about beetle species, kinship usages, food taboos, and what we ate for breakfast. I well remember the charming but irascible eldest brother doing me the unprecedented favor of volunteering to tell me a myth. He lay in Stephen's hammock and talked on and on; his toothless mouth was stuffed with a wedge of coca powder, which muffled all he said and blew out in green puffs as he laughed heartily at his own rude jokes. I recognized names, complicated river journeys, bits of shamanic chanting, and onomatopoeia, but I had precious little idea of the story line. When he stopped, he asked me if I had understood, and I told him, dishonestly, "Not *quite* all." He roared with laughter and said it was mostly in another language anyhow.

Both Stephen and I were plagued by visions of eager Africans vying with one another to draw out twenty-generation genealogies in the Saharan sand for their honored guests. Here we were among people who would not even tell us their Indian names—we must be doing something hopelessly wrong. We often asked ourselves, ruefully, if we actually could describe any of our hosts as "informants"; at that stage, we did not understand that the professionalization of fieldwork only happens when it is over. We decided there were no informants, just some people who were less resistant to having answers coaxed out of them than others. Sometimes we thought that this was because we were gutless amateurs, but as time went on, and especially as we were able to share experiences with other young anthropologists working in neighboring groups, we became confident that the great wealth of firsthand knowledge we gained could not have been replaced by paying for Indians' time and knowledge. We did learn people's names—and much other information normally carefully guarded from white people. Paradoxically, by the time we were freely told such things, they no longer seemed to be ends in themselves. Perhaps we had grown out of the toddler stage of wanting things simply because our friends would not let go of them.

Our contributions to the subsistence economy were of symbolic value rather than a just recompense for the trouble to which we put our hosts. The question of payment, or material exchange for hospitality and information, is intimately tied to the position of anthropologists' children in the field. The ethical and emotional aspects of establishing a rewarding and equitable exchange system with South American Indians are complex and difficult enough for childless fieldworkers to struggle with, although our troubles were nothing compared to David Maybury-Lewis's with the beef-hungry Sherente.[2] However politely you ask if you can stay, explain your motives, and promise what your hosts will get in return, you are bound to be something of an uninvited guest because you have chosen the society in advance, and they have not been able to choose you. Even if it is unknowingly and unwillingly, a foreign anthropologist among Indians partakes of the treacherous authority of all administrators, missionaries, and exploiters of Indian labor who have passed through before. However earnestly you set out to define a role for yourself, in the eyes of your hosts you already have one. Where we worked, a non-Indian is either a North American Protestant missionary from the Summer Institute of Linguistics (SIL), a Colombian Roman Catholic missionary, a rubber gatherer, or a *Duturo*—a doctor in the broader sense, a collecter of anything from frogs to Indian dance steps. We were obviously *Duturos,* but unlike all previous ones, we were not constantly on the move with an entourage of boatmen and carriers, nor could we absorb and pay for an unpredictable and uncontrollable supply of food. We had to find a long-term solution, and we settled for a kind of erratic delayed exchange: In the end, those who helped and fed us most received most, and our hosts' opinions influenced our gifts to visitors from other houses. It would be less than truthful to pretend that this system ever worked to everyone's satisfaction. It did give rise to jealousies, resentment, and frustration, but it also allowed us to live closer to our hosts than any other. In the end, they became confident that, sooner or later, they would receive all our stock of gifts, and we took care to meet a good proportion of their special requests each time we returned from Bogotá. Demand was greatest for machetes, knives, cloth, fishhooks and line, cartridges for shotguns, and the wherewithal to refill empties, glass beads, matches, salt, cotton hammocks, and aluminium cooking pots. Now some twelve years later, with the cocaine trade bringing uprecedented wealth to some Indians, an ambitious man wants several sets of clothing including rubber shoes for special occasions, a new shotgun, a radio cassette, and, the ultimate, an outboard motor.

At times we knew people were resentful of our presence and had to listen to ranting elders reciting strings of lies about us to visitors from other longhouses. We would overhear them explaining that we ate all their food and wait nervously to see if this was going to be a complaint that we were mean or a compliment about our willingness to enjoy the things that most whites thought disgusting and uncivilized. It could be either, depending on the situation. Only much later did we gain enough perspective to understand the duplicity that is essential to the smooth functioning of a small, face-to-face community. In the past, marriage alliances and exchanges of ritual invitations would easily disintegrate into witchcraft accusations and feuding. Relations with strangers were inherently ambiguous; our home community could not show itself to profit too much from our presence because this would invite requests for goods from all the neighbors.

As for us, we were representatives of the wider white society that had brutally killed many members of the previous generation, destroyed the sacred goods that were the spiritual life force of Indian groups, and now, as missionaries, were trying to remodel Indian society in their own image. In spite of all this, our hosts were hospitable, generous, and patient. They are outward-going people with a strong sense of humor, yet it was often the few people with powerful and awkward personalities who took our welfare most to heart.

In my experience, when anthropologists have turned their miscellaneous experience into a neatly typed and bound volume, they look back on their fieldwork in the light of their achievements toward the end rather than dwell on the mess they made of it in the beginning. Acceptance and rejection, trust and suspicion, friendship and hostility—these are concepts too absolute to describe relations between anthropologists and the people they study, but, on the whole, our relations with Barasana had changed over the course of our fieldwork in the direction we wanted them to. This was because we learned to accept them just as much as the other way around. To do this we had to grow up a great deal. When we planned to return with our children, we felt confident that they would be well treated, and we trusted that, for us, it would be a homecoming.

sidered going without our children, but the fact that we would take them with us if we went probably made us postpone the attempt until it became a psychological necessity.

If it had been less of a struggle to arrange a research permit and grant, I think we would have worried much more about the fate of Leo and Tom. But, as all worriers know, there is nothing so soothing as throwing yourself into some practical activity. We were apprehensive about how the children would react to Indian life and to the physical difficulties and about how we would cope. I, at least, was more so than I ever openly admitted. We decided that if it became impossible to stay on in the jungle, or if the cocaine proved too alarming for us even to set out for the Pirá-paraná, we would take it in turns to stay with the children in a less threatening environment. At best, this would be the nearest frontier town, Mitú, where there was scope for working with more acculturated Indians: at worst, it would be Bogotá.

What precisely were we afraid of? First, that the children might fall ill or have an accident. The nearest medical aid would be in Mitú, reached from the Pirá-paraná by light aircraft in under an hour or by canoe and foot in over a week, passing from the headwaters of the Pirá-paraná across to the Vaupés river system. There was no way of contacting air services from the field. When we used them, we would fix the day of our return in advance and make the one- or two-day journey to the appropriate airstrip in time, then wait until the weather and other commitments allowed the flight to arrive. We abandoned the overland route after an early trial. The rivers are full of rapids and too dangerous to travel without a permanent boatman, as well as a crew of extra local helpers each time the canoe has to be hauled over a portage. The boatman, usually a mestizo or "civilized" Indian, becomes a handicap in Indian longhouses, and the journey turns into a nightmare of organization—how to send him back, how to preserve enough gasoline for the return, and so on.

During our first journey, we capsized in a rapid on the way in; and on the way back, having sent the boatman home, we returned overland by a different route. We ended by foolishly improvising a raft when the promised canoe was not at the headwaters of the river that would lead us to Mitú. On it and under it, we spent three soaking and hungry days in flooded jungle. These journeys are not only too difficult to make with young children, but would be made impossible by an invalid. We knew that, *in extremis,* we could not rely on an extravagant bribe to persuade someone to help us out of the field. If things went wrong for us, there would be no emergency communal effort on our behalf. Why should there be? There is none for Indians; even when dying they have only shamanic resources to turn to.

We were more aware of the medical risks now that our children would be with us, and took far more care in planning our small store of medicines. We had antibiotics, fungicides, aspirin, different strengths of analgesics, a minimum of bandages and sutures, and a reliable antiseptic. Antisnake-venom serum had to be ordered from Costa Rica, and conscious that we had taken it before more as a magical precaution than with any intention of using it, we visited an expert in snakebite treatment and wrote out coherent instructions.

We decided that snakebite and serious accidents were virtually the only medical worries for our children. They had the usual vaccinations, including BCG (anti-tuberculosis medicine), because they would be sharing their food and hammocks with people suffering from fulminating tuberculosis. We took malarial prophylaxis. We dismissed surgical emergencies, except those arising from accidents, as comparable to the likelihood of being killed in a car crash at home: something that could happen but that, for all practical purposes, you forget about. Later, after Stephen had left for Colombia, leaving the three of us behind because the permit was not forthcoming, Leo had acute appendicitis. As if to rub in the recklessness of refusing to contemplate this kind of emergency, I remembered the conversation I had had with a botanist at Kew Gardens the day Leo's pain started. He told me about a member of his expedition to Mount Roraima in Guyana who had prepared himself with a prophylactic appendectomy. We agreed that this was going a bit too far. Leo's illness and operation were a time of miserable anxiety for me because I kept thinking about what would have happened if we had been in the Pirá-paraná; I began to feel the enormity of the risks we were going to impose on our children. Statistics may help us decide things in a cool and rational fashion, but it is impossible to arrange emotions in a statistical model. Once disasters have happened, they have happened 100 percent. A 10 percent chance of a fatal snakebite in so many person-years means very little; instead, we get caught in a dialogue between the low probability of an unfamiliar disaster and the extent of the grief and misery should it happen.

So much for disease; there was not much we could do about accident prevention except resolve to watch the children carefully. Leo was already a strong swimmer, but we tried in vain to teach Tom. He was at the most perilous stage, having no fear of water but no desire to swim. We took life-jackets with us, but it turned out that they were used only for hilarious dressing-up sessions held by Leo and an Indian friend. The only time we were in danger on a large river, we did not have them with us.

The children would be sure to make heavy weather of physical discomforts, but we were not sure which. We had found the best solution to both heat and rain was to take off as many clothes as we decently could. We could imagine Tom doing this, but not Leo, a perpetual dresser-upper in as many layers as possible. We took a small amount of insect repellent, lightweight waterproof raincoats, and old clothes for the children. They had cotton sneakers, since leather things rot. We worried about hunger and what would happen if they refused, point-blank, to eat Indian food. In spite of the baggage problems on the single-engine airplanes, we planned some emergency supplies for especially lean times. It is surprisingly difficult to find food that is nourishing and light and likely to keep in hot, humid conditions. Prepackaged dried-meat dishes were supplemented with rice and canned sardines, and stock cubes were bought in Bogatá. We could take only enough for one or two meals a week, and much of this was offered as a communal dish to be eked out with the ubiquitous manioc bread.

Both children would miss the best part of a year at school. We took elementary math books for Leo and some reading books for Tom, mainly so that Leo would not be alone in having to do schoolwork. It was simple to pack for Colombia because holidays in France had accustomed them to traveling light. Each had a small bag of toys and favorite clothes and books. Once in Bogotá, we had to cut down possessions without alarming them by explaining that everything would get scattered, broken, eaten by termites, or removed by curious visitors. The soft-toy population had to be reduced to one teddy bear each. For Leo, there were cards; and for Tom, a model airplane and one car. Each had a few books, a thin blanket and a hammock, and a pocket knife. To help them make friends with other children, there were underwater face masks, a Frisbee, and a few candies to share on arrival. For ourselves, we added a camera, notebooks, batteries, flashlights, candles, a tape recorder, photographs of our families, and books of wildlife to entertain our hosts. Each of us had a few clothes. For the Indians, we had plenty of gifts.

Besides preparing for the children's physical needs and entertainment, we wanted to explain to them what to expect so that they would look forward to the experience without being disappointed when they arrived. This was asking the impossible. By anticipating and trying to forestall fears, it is only too easy to generate them, and so we tried to maintain an atmosphere of easy confidence. This must have made it difficult for the children to express and relieve their anxieties. I realized how inaccessible the goal of all our preparations was the day Stephen left for Colombia. I left the children playing happily for ten minutes, and when I came back home, I found them huddled together, howling in unison. Tom said Leo had explained to him that he would never see Stephen again because the director of the Colombian Institute of Anthropology would be so angry with him that he would shoot him on arrival. For her, this must have been the logical conclusion to the correspondence of the last months, and she was obviously desperate to share her terrifying idea. Unwittingly, I stirred up more trouble that night when I began to read *Treasure Island;* it had been long promised as a treat for Stephen's departure. I must have forgotton the story, and my heart sank as I scanned ahead to where Jim Hawkins's father dies.

How do you explain what Indians and jungles are like to English children? They see such a riot of color photography in books and on television. They have watched the private lives of lions and tigers, dramas under the sea, the goings-on inside beehives, even inside the pouch of a kangaroo. Besides, a bountiful vision of the Tropics is so often presented by the media as a setting for child heroes to display their skill and daring. Aware that they were liable to imagine wild animals around every corner, a lurid snake under every leaf, festoons of fruit from every bough, and themselves performing marvelous feats, we tried to do as little as possible to indulge these fantasies. Tom in particular was liable to be disappointed by drab reality because he and his best friend, Tristram, lived in a magic world of pirates, cheetahs, dolphins, and suchlike. I believe he thought it was all about to come true. Leo, in contrast, was very involved with her intense little social whirl at school and was fearful of what she would lose. Without being too specific, we tried to emphasize that they would soon be back home and that whether or not they really enjoyed it, they would be with us and would do many exciting things that most people never do. We showed them pictures of our previous field-work and left it at that.

After a long, uncertain wait, Stephen telephoned to say we would get our permit. This meant the grant from the Social Sciences Research Council would come through, and I could buy the equipment we needed and pack up the house, and we could leave. Decisions, purchases, and arrangements that might have taken months were over in hardly a week, and we arrived in Colombia exhausted. I was enormously relieved and happy to find that Stephen had foreseen this and arranged a few days on a friend's luxurious farm in sensational countryside.

After that glorious holiday, life in Colombian towns had both pleasures and difficulties for the children. We were always staying with other people, and the children suffered from being perpetual guests. Leo in particular sensed that she never had the rights and independence of a child at home, and this was exacerbated by the close watch we had to keep on them in the streets. Bogotá is a notoriously dangerous city whose monied classes protect themselves from crime by hiring household servants and paramilitary watchmen and going everywhere by car, in constant fear of kidnapping and armed robbery. Of course, the dangers are grossly exaggerated, and by exercising a kind of prudence that becomes automatic, the risks are minimalized. Even so, the loss of freedom contrasted strongly with life at home.

Being the older of the two, and by nature being finely tuned to the social world, Leo asked many questions about servants and the differences between rich and poor. She was both fascinated and troubled by the extraordinary sight of children her own age, dressed in rags, descending on the garbage cans as we put them out, eating the rotting scraps, packing up paper and discarded rubbish into bags and bundles, and fleeing within seconds. These were aspects of sophisticated city life she was not prepared for.

Later, on our way into the Pirá-paraná, we stopped in Villavicencio, at the foot of the Andes, and found ourselves somewhere to stay. To preserve our supply of cash, since checks would be of no use from now on, we chose a room in a cheap boardinghouse frequented by *Llaneros* on their nights in town. For Leo, the bare concrete room from which we heard all the night's dramas and made visits to filthy communal showers, became a glamorous ideal of hotel life. During the first of our two stretches in the Indian longhouse, she must have asked a hundred times whether we could stop off at Residencias Selectas. Another psychological roost for both children in Villavicencio was the home and zoological research station of our old friend Fred Medem. He had otters, snakes, alligators, and tortoises, but best of all was a young sloth that clung to his leg and could be fed on scarlet hibiscus flowers. Fred gave each child a tortoise to take as a pet to the jungle.

The day came when we left Mitú in a single-engine missionary plane for the headwaters of the river on which we were to live. We had been lucky enough to meet Indian friends in Mitú who knew that our host community still lived in the same place, downstream from the airstrip. The sight of the forest, with its isolated Indian settlements surrounded by cutouts of paler green *chagras* and miniature green paths, was both exciting and moving. I thought how their lives had been unfolding so far from our own and how we were seeing a society from the outside that we would soon be caught up in. Shining ribbons and mottled patches of green were about to become rivers flanked by overhanging trees measured by paddle strokes, and minutes were about to stretch into days.

We landed. The plane left, and we took our things to the longhouse nearby. The airstrip had been cleared for the SIL couple studying Bará (the language of the Barasana's principal *affines*). They were away in North America and their house was shut, but they had lived half a mile from the large Bará longhouse for many short stretches over the past fifteen years, and so the people were accustomed to white people coming and going. They knew us from the past and received us with courtesy, offering manioc bread and caramelized manioc juice with hot pepper to dip it in. After the children had obediently but suspiciously had a minute amount, we exchanged news of the intervening eight years, slung our hammocks, and showed the children the house. Suddenly Leo asked, dismayed, "But what will we do all the time we are here?" She wanted to get out her books and drawing things at once. At this point, we were stuck by the enormity of the change. How could they have imagined that life could be so different? Although we had contemplated this in England, we now realized in an immediate and rather frightening way that they would be bored and lonely. We would be their source of amusement and a human channel through which everything they said and did would have to pass. Yet we already had wasted months of our fieldwork time in bureaucratic negotiations and were anxious to make the most of every day. We saw that the children would be able to touch nothing, go nowhere, ask nothing, eat nothing, and drink nothing without our explanations, intervention, cooperation, and diplomacy. We also realized that if Leo went on using drawing paper as she did in the first half hour, we would have enough for about one day.

Everything around us belonged to someone else, and, unlike nearly every other house they had ever been in, this one did not seem to have anything set aside for children. Even the wide-open interior was illusory because elaborate rules, depending on age, sex, and residential status, as well as the time of day and formality of the occasion, govern how the space must be used. The children could not learn all this from anyone but us, and they constantly insisted on reasons. We demanded more conformity from them than was probably necessary because we were aware that it was partly our own habitual adherence to the social rules that made it easy for Indian communities to relax and accommodate us. Leo and Tom asked why women did not sit with men. Why did women and children eat after men? It wasn't fair. Why all this fuss about which gourd to drink from? Why did Indians think it would make us ill to do things that had never made us ill? We had an obligation to answer their questions, and we wanted to explain their new world to them as fully as possible, but we also had a long-standing and profound commitment to the Indian way of life that we could not possibly explain to our children.

That first day, I had a taste of how having the children there would change our customary daily life with Indians. When the headman's wife invited me to accompany her to her *chagra,* I took the children along. After a matter of minutes of stumbling over stumps and crossing bogs on slippery logs, surrounded by clouds of flies and sweat bees, they had had enough. We turned back, the children weeping and complaining and I full of foreboding and selfish disappointment.

Tom was five years old the next day. We set out by canoe for the house where we were to live. We were extremely relieved to find there was a large enough canoe and two young men willing to come with us, particularly after the disastrous walk the day before. It was at least a six-hour trail overland, and I remember being close to tears myself when Stephen and I first walked it with impossibly heavy rucksacks, our Indian guide keeping a relentless pace over slippery logs and fallen trees. Although Tom did not mind very much about how we were spending his birthday, Leo monitored it gloomily because she would be eight in four days' time, and she minded with a vengeance. She had been prepared by us for a delayed birthday; but for a few days, missing the wonderful culmination of the Cambridge year certainly added insult to each injury that came her way.

As we set off she began to pester everyone to look for a sloth like Fred Medem's and asked every five minutes if we thought we would find one. When we did, at last, see animals, they were black monkeys, but her excitement turned to bitter tears. Later, she wrote about the journey in her diary:

> On the way to the house where we were going to stay in all the time (we went in a canoe) we saw lots of pretty orchids and lots of very pretty flowers. And then we saw two black monkeys and the Indians shot at them. I thought it was very unfair and then it began to pour with rain, my skirt got wet right through in about five minutes. Then we had to stop and stay in a little house on the way because Mummy had seen some of her friends and the canoe was full of water

We arrived at the Barasana longhouse the next day. Here, where they were not used to white arrivals and had heard no warning outboard motor, they were astounded to see us with two children. A missionary had assured them that he had heard Stephen had been shot in a frontier town, and no one expected to see us again. The man who first greeted us confessed later that he thought it must be our ghosts.

The longhouse was rebuilt, but we settled in the equivalent corner to the one we had before. We identified the people we had known before and learned of all the changes. It was dismaying to find that nearly all the children of school age were away at the small Catholic mission on the Pirá-Paraná itself, where a boarding school had been started. This meant the children would spend much of the time with only very young Indian children in the longhouse.

Soon enough, we learned to appreciate how easygoing and understanding Indians were toward our children. Many of the incidents we thought we should make polite excuses about, such as their dislike of some foods, upsetting of food taboos, bouts of angry or tearful behavior, were laughed off by Indian parents as typical of the way children always behave. Indians have a well-developed concept of homesickness in keeping with the rule of exogamy, for girls must experience severe homesickness when they marry into a far-off community where another language is spoken. Many of our children's difficulties in adjustment were sympathetically attributed to "homesickness." The communal living arrangement also made longhouse inhabitants highly sensitive to the conflicting claims of the community as a whole and the separate nuclear families within it. During a communal meal, I would often be slipped a little gourd of food so that the children could eat at their own pace, and I came to understand how important the redistribution of little portions of food is—something that I had not been able to appreciate in my former role as a young, childless adult.

Gradually, a daily timetable was established, and the children absorbed the rhythm of longhouse life. Theoretically, they washed in the river at dawn, but in practice they bent this puritanical Indian rule and often substituted a hasty hand-and-face wash from a gourd outside the house. They then joined in the communal breakfast of bread and hot dips. When he got the measure of longhouse life, Tom, who always wakes more easily than his sister, became an early-morning opportunist. He would sneak into the screened-off family compartments and sit by each fire in turn. By the time official breakfast was served, he had sometimes had several unofficial ones. Breakfast is followed by a pleasant, informal time, after which women leave for their *chagras* and men either go out or stay behind to make baskets or repair the house. I abandoned the idea of going to the *chagras* every day with the women, and we decided that at least one of us should stay in or near the longhouse with the children each day.

Leo wrote in her diary and did a bit of math each morning, and Tom read some of his book aloud and copied some words or did very simple sums. Indians were fascinated by this schoolroom regime and approved of our teaching the children to be efficient at the kind of work we did ourselves. At first, they had called this our "paper dance," but they accepted that it was what we did for a living. The children's work was done surrounded by any Indian children who were at home, and often by adults too. It mainly consisted of interruptions, and they wriggled out of it at the first possible opportunity.

When they escaped to play, it was often to the river. Tom did not swim, but he flopped around splashing people; the real enchantment of the river, however, were the hosts of butterflies to be found there. We made a net, and he spent hours chasing butterflies. He had a private taxonomy of all the different colors and patterns, and was thrilled each time he got a new one. Leo liked to swim and to wash her little bundle of clothes. Indians, who swim an underwater dog paddle, found her proficient breaststroke a source of wonder. If other children were around, they would play together in the river, make houses out of odds and ends, look for fruit on the trees around the house, or dress up in Leo's clothes. Tom's most vivid memory of his Indian friends is of seeing one of them pull the head off a small chicken. The kinds of games he played with Indians did not require words, but Leo found herself frustrated by communication difficulties because her games were the sort that needed setting up with rules or an imaginative context spelled out. I was often called on to explain complicated aspects of English children's culture that no Indian child could be expected to grasp and sometimes to sort out jealous misunderstandings. By the end of our second stretch in the longhouse, after between four and five months of hearing Barasana, Leo could make herself understood quite well at a simple level and even attempted ambitious exchanges, such as telling Indian children the stories of Tom's reading books, changing the names of the animals, and sprinkling her versions with jungle spirits. Tom's approach was more direct. He was delighted with the sounds of Barasana, particularly with the dramatic exclamations, and would repeat them to himself and everyone else without minding at all what they meant.

Toward midday, the women would return with their baskets of manioc roots and sit with their boards wedged against the houseposts to grate them up. Leo demanded to try this the very first day and became such an expert over the next few months that Indian women would make me offers to exchange daughters. At first, the quartz chips set in the grating boards gashed her hands, but, by the end, she even managed to finish off professionally, gathering the remnants into a cone-shaped bundle and grating away to nothing. Afterward, she liked to stand with the women around their tripod stand and pound up the mash in a basketry sieve.

Sometimes we went for walks with the children or took them on short food-gathering expeditions with Indians. They found it more pleasant to come with us to pick coca leaves in the late afternoon than to sit in *chagras* in the midday sun. It is an advantage to miss the sand flies, which plague the longhouse from 3:30 onward. Tom learned to put up with them, but Leo, who is a great deal more fastidious, would be driven wild by them and retire under her blanket with both sets of clothes on at once.

Just before dusk is perhaps the best time in a longhouse. Men return from the day's expeditions, others prepare coca, meals are served, and in-between times women make manioc bread on their huge ceramic hotplates. Boiled manioc juice from the day's harvest is served in the center of the house, and children fill their own little gourds. Those who are not occupied often sit out on the sandy plaza as darkness falls, and the children dare each other to stay outside longer, shrieking warnings about jaguars, spirits, and snakes.

Sometimes before dark, we reserved a special time for our children during which we would lie in our hammocks around the family fire and play word games, read stories, and talk. Often they asked to be told myths. Leo liked to be read to from *The Sword in the Stone,* E. E. Nesbit books, and other long "chapter books," as she called them. Tom was fixed on a character named Captain Pugwash and a book about nocturnal animals that we came to know by heart. He nearly always insisted on the same pages about luminous creatures, particularly after we had found a click beetle with two large, green headlights. Sometimes, when there had not been much to eat, we cooked a little of our rice. This family intimacy was invariably interrupted—by Indians guessing aloud what we were saying and wanting explanations of all the pictures, by Tom poking things in the fire, or by men asking Stephen to take a turn at coca pounding. We tried to preserve candles and batteries by gathering early; besides, our giant altar candles were a fatal attraction for Tom and Leo, who seized on all the wax drips, shortening the candles' precious lives.

Hammocks were popular with both children, but the microclimate of our family corner was a perpetual source of dispute. Leo, who insisted on creature comforts, liked the fire burning as she went to sleep and her blanket tucked around her just so. Tom always said the fire was too hot and stuffy. I solved the blanket problem by sewing them into sleeping bags, but Leo never slept as well as Tom. He threw his blanket overboard and went out like a light, peeing happily through his hammock during the night but hotly denying it the next day.

My predictions about which foods the children would like were wrong in the beginning. We were disappointed that they did not immediately appreciate fresh farina (toasted manioc grains, somewhat like sour-tasting breakfast cereal) and fresh manioc bread, sugarcane, and miriti fruits, but an Indian diet has its own logic of taste, so they soon came to like most of the things that Indians themselves prize. The same thing had happened to us before. One of the principal efforts we contributed was to get them to eat without dropping things on the dirt floor. Tom lost lots of his food this way and was often told off by Indians for careering around the house raising dust near baskets of manioc mash.

Manioc bread is obligatory; at all meals it is dipped into the dishes of boiled food spiced with chili. Fish was gutted and boiled with scales, bones, and head still on. Game was gutted, and the fur or feather stubs singed off before being roughly jointed and boiled. When food was plentiful, meat, fish, or ants, termites, caterpillars, and beetle larvae would be preserved by smoking, to be boiled later. The children loved anything smoked, but Leo objected to the more usual mush of fishbones and scales eked out with manioc fiber, served when food was scarcer.

The Indians have lots of kinds of food but they never mix them. They have meat, fish, fruit, caterpillars and frogs. Some of them I don't like but most of them I do like. The things I don't like are things like caterpillars because I think you shouldn't eat that kind of food and frogs I haven't tried but I don't think I would like them. Lots of things depend on if they are fresh. I only like the fresh things. Like often when they get fish, they put pounded up manioc to make it go round. . . . I like meat best.

The wet season was more prolonged than usual that year; the house was being reroofed, which occupied the men for much of the time, and two of them went through exacerbations of their chronic tuberculosis, so we were often hungry. Food was frequently the subject of Leo's daily diary entry, reprinted here just as she wrote it:

Yesterday I and Tom and a girl called Betty went to get some manioc leaves in the manioc garden. It was very hot and I did most of it. What I did was I always took a stalk in the middle of the tree and I picked the smallest leaves and put them in a basket. We did it for half an hour and then we thought it was a lot so we went home and gave it to Mummy. But Mummy said it would make a tiny bit. So I said "Tom lets go and get some more!" Tom said "No, its much too hot." But I said "Tom, we are very hungry" and so in the end he came. After, I grated them up then I went and got some water and Betty came too and gave me the spooks.

One day I asked her to write what she would eat if she could choose, and her real preferences were revealed:

For breakfast I would like some white bread and peanut butter and clover honey and pure apple juice in my own mug. For lunch I would like shepherds pie with lots of crispy

potatoes and 3 drops of HP sauce. Then for pudding I would
like water ice and chocolate milk shake. For tea I would like
a swiss roll and a chocolate cake and some cocoa. After, some
ham and bread.

This was a far cry from boiled caterpillars, but the children did
adapt, and, at the time, they thought a small portion of soggy
rice, cooked in a chicken-stock cube to add the allure of mono-
sodium glutamate, was a delicious treat to compensate for a hungry day. They learned to enjoy most of the insect foods too. We
worried that they did not get enough to eat sometimes and would
visit old house sites to dig up the tiny sweet potatoes that no one
else thought worth bothering about. Both children were skinny
each of the times we left for Bogotá, and we were relieved that we
had arranged to take them for only two months at a stretch.

Our ruthless banning of toys turned out to be justified. The
children seemed to realize that their toys would have been out of
place and did not miss them unduly. The teddy bears were a
source of comfort and were given waterborne rides in pots and
gourds when rainstorms turned the plaza into rivulets, but by the
time Tom's was carried off by a miserable starving dog, he was
able to cope with its loss. He was happier chasing things than he
would have been with toys and cars; he was given a child-size
blowpipe with which he hunted lizards. He spent hours trying to
make fires, and the one real outburst of anger he caused was when
an Indian got alarmed that he might burn the house down. Children's fire games have sometimes led to this. Indians showed the

children how to make things from dried palm leaves and gave them children's carrying baskets and the little dye rollers used for body painting.

Both collected bits and pieces that caught their fancy, and the first flush of disapproval over shooting beautiful creatures was softened as their magpie instincts took over. Leo's moral qualms went by the board when macaws, green parrots, and toucans were brought in for the pot; she vied with Tom for feathers and beaks.

Tom made valiant efforts to learn to fish, making his own hopelessly inadequate little rod and baiting it with grasshoppers, which he caught himself. After a patient wait, standing in a canoe at the port, he was convinced of the difficulty. Experience also taught him that animals are rarely seen. He had been obsessed with great cats in England and had imagined himself gamboling in the forest with jaguars; at first he was disappointed, as we had guessed he might be. Over time, however, reality became exciting for both of them. They saw caterpillars like decorated Christmas trees, large snakes, trees ablaze with flocks of macaws, armadillos, and other exotic things. Tom always had his friend Tristram in mind, and made stores of mementos to show him when he got home. For Leo, even the things she had dreaded most became exciting:

> On the way back we had great fun: as well as seeing ants and caterpillars we saw two poisonous snakes. One was a coral and the other was a snake called "a pile of eagle feathers." The coral was black and yellow bands and a red tail and the pile of eagle feathers was pinky-brown and black. Daddy killed the pile of eagle feathers and kept its skin and she had lots of eggs. Daddy told us how to tell when they are dangerous. 1. a very funny tail. 2. a sensitive pit. 3. a head in a heart shape. 4. 2 fangs. 5. very rough scales. 6. and any brightly colored snake is a coral.

Another time, she wrote ruefully:

> Pasico found a red tortoise. And my Mummy and Daddy
> were the first people in Colombia apart from the Indians to
> find one. He hit it with a machete not realizing that a man
> called Fred would love it. Then they took it down to the river
> to wash its meat. Daddy opened up her gut and she had
> some parasites. We looked at what she had been eating and
> she had eaten fish and fruit and shrimps.

Other expeditions sounded better to her in theory than they were
in practice—getting honey, for instance. She complained that
she did not see the bees' nest because "there were ants as big as a
strawberry and they squeak."

We had thought of pets before we left Bogotá because this
would give the children something of their own to care for. Fred
Medem had given them each a small tortoise, and tending these
became a morning ritual. Leo called hers Fred, and Tom's had
many different names. Leo made them elaborate leafy homes and
organized a complicated diet and exercising regime. Tom, in his
usual position as stubborn and absent-minded assistant, was detailed to watch them during their run and to carry bits of fish gut
that his sister did not like touching. Panic and recriminations
followed when the basket was ready, and he had lost them. After
many such losings and findings, a vicious species of soldier ant
invaded the basket, and the tortoises met a tragic end. We resolved to find new pets, if possible more satisfying ones, for the
children had often sadly reflected that they did not think their
tortoises loved them much.

We could not persuade anyone to lend us a small parrot, and
our friends convinced us that a macaw would be too vicious and
eat too many vegetables. Tom tried giant grasshoppers, but
howled bitterly one day when he found the Indians' pet toucan
eating his largest one on top of the roof. One family had a baby

monkey for a while, and Leo adored it. "He makes funny noises with a round mouth when he is happy and he hisses when he is cross. And he puts out his hand and snatches everything that goes by." For the last month, we did have the perfect pet as Leo noted:

> A few days ago about a week ago we got a baby marmoset. He is black all over with a white upper lip. At first we kept him in two baskets pushed together and at night Daddy slept with him. After, Daddy put an old T-shirt of Mummy's in one basket, turned it upside down and tied a string round his neck and put him in. A bit later he lived in my hair and now he sleeps with me at night and sits on my head all day. He eats caimos, bananas, pawpaw, avocado, sugarcane, pineapple, horseflies, custard apple, cockroaches.

Later, he jumped into the fire and had to have his paws bathed and bandaged daily, occupying hours of our time. Leo's entry headed "When our poor monkey got burned in the fire" ended bravely, "It hurts him a lot but he won't die." To our amazement, he didn't die, and when we left we took him to Mitú and then Villavicencio, clinging to one or other blond head all the way, and presented him to Fred. The children were heartbroken to lose him, but he would never have survived the cold and altitude of Bogotá.

From the beginning, both children regarded Indians as much like anyone else; they became especially fond of some and warier of others. They were content to be left in the longhouse without us for an hour or two at a stretch, and when we traveled, would happily go in different canoes from us. Tom even informed us one day that he had arranged to go downstream, a day's journey, to stay with another family of visitors. He told us that he would come back when people happened to pass upstream and assured us he would be quite safe. The mere thought of this filled us with panic and, needless to say, he was not allowed to go.

Indian beliefs and ritual rules were above Tom's head; he was only involved inasmuch as they curtailed his amusements. Leo was very much more observant and curious about them—and more critical. Like Evans-Pritchard, who found the Azande system of witchcraft and magic as good as any other for ordering daily life, we had become quite used to functioning within the Barasana ritual system. Although we did not believe in the elaborate set of mystical sanctions that constrained our daily lives, we did subscribe to the value of the behavior they related to. It was hard to explain this to Leo, and her dogged questioning revealed us to be base hypocrites at times. She was always careful to maintain a conceptual divide between what Indians thought would happen and what she thought would happen. She did not think they were foolish, but she did think they were wrong. Colombia provided her with her first real encounter with religious life, and it puzzled her.

> There was a dance and it was on all night because the Indians think the world will stop if they don't. First it was some flutes and trumpets made from a special kind of palm tree bark. Me and Tom and Mummy weren't allowed to see them because the Indians think you would die. When we were allowed to come in, the proper dance was ready. It was very pretty and I liked their white and yellow and red head-dresses. They danced with bamboo canes round four posts.

Tom was irked by social conventions of all kinds. He liked to lead a life unencumbered by things just as much as by rules. Both children discarded their shoes because they found themselves hampered by them on slippery paths, but Tom discarded all his other clothes as well. When he saw children in G-strings, he demanded one, but after a while he had to be persuaded to put even this on. Indians called him an "uncivilized animal"; most of the time they teased him kindly, but when we visited other houses, they insisted he observe the minimal modesty.

We were well aware that having children with us gave our relations with our Indian friends warmth and mutual understanding. Before, we had been hardly grown up even in our own society, yet had been trying to share the concerns of adults. Returning also consolidated our place in their community history. We saw *chagras* Stephen had helped to fell and I had helped plant, now abandoned and visited only for a few straggling plants of fish-poison body paint or hallucinogens. We knew just which children were born the same season as Leo and were able to see the children of our former visit returning with bundles of fish or baskets of manioc, part of adult life.

From a practical point of view, the children did absorb a great deal of our time and emotional resources. The social and economic division between men, on the one hand, and women and children, on the other, meant that I spent rather more time caring for them than Stephen did. Both of us achieved a great deal of work, but it would be unrealistic to pretend that the children did not prevent us from doing much more. I am also convinced that it would be an intolerable strain for a single parent to manage in these circumstances. Not only did we need our double comple-

ment of emotional resources, but it also required two people to
help the children on the long walks between longhouses and for
one of us to allow the other to go on Indian expeditions that the
children would be unable to keep up with. In many ways, this
mixture of joint and alternate child care was not so different from
the one we had evolved at home. We did not consider taking
anyone to help us care for Leo and Tom in the field; only someone
who spoke both English and Barasana could have done it anyway,
and there was no such person.

Looking back, this stretch of fieldwork with the children was a
success, a valuable and enjoyable experience for all of us. It was
an enormous pleasure for us to have integrated the two great
experiences of our adult lives: life with Indians and life with
children. As it turned out, nothing very frightening happened to
us. If it had, we would have been unable to forgive ourselves for
imposing our goals on our children. The things we had learned
and the importance our return to the Pirá-paraná played in our
lives would have seemed bitter and worthless. Chance is not to be
played with lightly, and we knew we were taking risks. We were
lucky: Tom's worst accident was to cut his foot badly with a
machete; Leo's was to drink poisonous unboiled manioc juice,
which she thought was banana soup. The Indians assured us she
would be sick and dizzy for a day and night, and she did have to
be carried for much of the journey we made the next day, but she
got better that night. Our medical care for our children was confined to daily sessions digging burrowing fleas out of their feet.

Some aspects of our fieldwork were an emotional and physical
ordeal for our children, but both were proud of their stay and

pleased they had done it. By the end, Leo was longing to be back with her friends in England, but Tom wanted to stay in the Pirá-paraná. She embraced her life at home wholeheartedly, but he took several months to settle down. His head was full of parrots and monkeys and lighting fires and chasing giant insects; he found school monotonous and often asked, pathetically, if he could go back. The homecoming had its compensations, however. He was envied and admired by his friends, one of whom was overheard to say, "Tom Hugh-Jones is the untidiest boy in our class, but he is allowed to be because he was in the jungle."

Notes

1. Brian Moser and Donald Tayler, *The Cocaine Eaters* (New York: Taplinger Press, 1967), p. 194.
2. David Maybury-Lewis, *The Savage and the Innocent: Life with the Primitive Tribes of Brazil* (Cleveland, Ohio: World, 1965).

MIMI NICHTER AND
MARK NICHTER

3   A Tale of Simeon: Reflections on Raising a Child While Conducting Fieldwork in Rural South India

Conception

During our first two years as co-researchers in rural South India, hardly a day went by without someone asking us how many children we had. To our reply, "None," the next question would invariably be, "How many years have you been married?" Our reply of three years would be followed by silence and a pitying look at Mimi. In time we came to understand the meaning of the look and the silence: It was possible that Mimi was a barren woman. Three years was pushing the reasonable limit for conception. Mark's virility was not questioned; childlessness is attributed to women. Mimi's explanation that she was practicing birth control was looked at as a paltry excuse. What woman, in her right mind, would get married and not have at least one child? What mother-in-law would allow such a thing? Occasionally, women would whisper *bunja* to each other behind Mimi's back. *Bunja* is a term that likens a woman to a seed that has been thrown to the field but has not sprouted. If *bunja*, a woman is not invited to auspicious occasions such as weddings because she is considered unlucky.

Not having children was particularly problematic because of the nature of the research we were carrying out—focusing on lay health ideology and medical culture. Ironically, it was often easier for Mark, as an apprentice of *ayurveda*, the classical Indian system of medicine, than for Mimi to ask questions relating to children, children's illnesses, and delivery. Such questions were met with a somewhat skeptical and joking look by many informants, who said that Mimi needed to have the experience herself in order to understand their responses.

What made matters worse was that in an Indian village, a woman's fertility and menstrual pattern is something others are very much aware of because of restrictions that separate women during menstruation. During the second year of our research, we were living in a joint family while studying *ayurvedic* medicine. At that time, Mimi did not menstruate, which was considered serious both within folk health ideology and the *ayurvedic* medical system. After some months of concealing this condition, it was recognized by one of our patron *ayurvedic* practitioners, *vaidya*, who became insulted that we would spend so much time studying *ayurveda* and yet would not undertake appropriate treatment. He was ready to break off relations at a critical point five months before we were to leave the field. Understanding the cultural importance of the illness, Mimi decided to seek treatment. Although we had experimented with *ayurvedic* medicines for many of our health problems, this presented somewhat of a dilemma: Not only did Mimi not consider it an illness to have stopped menstruating but, given our living conditions, she considered it somewhat of a blessing. After two months of treatment, Mimi's menstrual cycle was normalized, and after three months of treatment, the *vaidya*'s wife half jokingly asked Mimi if she had the desire for sour foods, a sign of pregnancy.

Preparations for leaving the field after two years of research were particularly hectic, since it was the festival season for village gods and a time of local possession-cult activities. During the many possession rituals we attended, we were invariably given blessings by the deities to return to India with a son in the near future. As fate would have it, the month we returned to Scotland, Mimi had the desire for sour. The news of her unplanned (by us) pregnancy was met in India with claims of credit from both *ayurvedic vaidya* and devotees of the deities who had extended their blessings to us. These claims extended to our child a sense of belonging when we returned to the field twenty-three months later—a sense that remains to this day.

Returning to the Field

When Simeon was almost two, we were afforded a second opportunity to conduct anthropological research in South India. Our research focus continued to be folk health ideology and the health behavior of the rural poor, but this time particular emphasis was placed on illness relating to malnutrition among children as a group at risk. Fieldwork was to be carried out in two regions, one in which we had already worked, the other a region with which we had only slight familiarity. Our first concern about returning to the field was privacy; we had had little privacy during our earlier period of fieldwork and felt that, as a fledgling family unit, we would require considerably more personal space. Our second concern was that Simeon would become a spectacle, an object of curiosity to be passed about from person to person. We knew that Simeon did not like to be picked up by strangers; even at age eighteen months he was willful and did not like to be constrained. Moreover, by being passed around to a large number of people, Simeon would be exposed to illness to a greater degree than we. We recalled the commonality of scabies among children in households where children were handled by one another. Although we discussed these potential problems before returning to the field, once we arrived in India, these concerns were offset by more immediate problems, such as finding a house and someone to assist us in caring for Simeon.

Our first difficulty was finding a house for rent in our rural field sites. During our previous fieldwork, we had spent most of our time living with families. This had afforded us a fairly routine life style but little privacy. Locating and setting up our own household was far more difficult than we first imagined. There was little choice of available dwellings, and in both field areas we had to settle for houses that needed considerable repair. Upkeep of a village household presented an onslaught of daily chores required to meet basic necessities: securing sufficient water (ten to fifteen jugs a day) from the well for cooking, bathing, and the washing of pots; collecting firewood for cooking; obtaining perishable provisions; removing stones from the rice; tending the hearth; taking the clothes to the river for washing on the rocks; and so on. This was time-consuming, and we set out to find someone to help us keep house as well as help care for Simeon. This also proved more difficult than we had first imagined.

We hoped to find someone who would live with us more as a friend and assistant than as a servant. We recognized that this person would play an active part in establishing our identity in the community, particularly in the region where we had not previously lived. By necessity, the person would need to be of a caste that was somewhat middle range in the ritual hierarchy. A person of too high a caste would intimidate others from entering our house. Conversely, if the person were of too low a caste, our high-caste friends would be reluctant to enter our home. We were also aware that whoever worked for us would affect our communication network. Many people would come to our employee to find out what kind of people we were, what our purpose was, what we ate, whether we lent money, whether we bandaged wounds.

It was difficult to find someone willing to take on the responsibility of watching a child as active as Simeon. We wanted whoever watched Simeon to respect his individual freedom and his independent spirit—behavior that frightened most village women, who thought that it made the child liable to a variety of troubles ranging from spirit attack and the evil eye to physical danger. Moreover, few villagers did not already have other commitments in the specific season in which we arrived. Additionally, there was little precedent for watching someone else's child. Child care was a chore done within the family; watching a child was the responsibility of older girls or the grandmother when a mother was busy in the fields.

Economically, although we could afford to pay handsomely for child care, we were caught in a bind. We had chosen to live within the parameters of village economy. To pay someone an exorbitant amount of money, by village standards, would influence the way in which people interacted with us. We could only offer a sum deemed appropriate by villagers, at least in terms of direct benefits (indirect benefits were another matter). We knew from our previous field experience that we would be judged by the community partly on the basis of how we managed our household—including the people we picked to work for us and our relationships with them.

Experiences with Child Care

In the first field site, we hired the mother of one of our research assistants, who was very poor and had recently lost a child. Under our employ, Kuchila, a proud and sensitive woman, experienced much emotional distress concerning the responsibility that went along with both care of the house and child care. While anxious to please us, it was often difficult for her to permit Simeon to act with the freedom we allowed him. For example, Simeon would want to wander outside the house and explore the channel that ran along the paddy field. An Indian mother would not allow a child to do this until the age of six or seven. During his escapades, if Simeon fell or got a cut, others in the village would criticize Kuchila for failing to watch him properly. We came to understand that Kuchila's duty may have been to abide by our wishes, but her morality was dictated by her culture. Unknowingly, we were asking her to place duty above morality, and this often constituted a conflict.

After six months in that field area, we returned to the region in which we had previously lived. We imagined that setting up a new household would be relatively easy because of our familiarity with the area. But a new set of difficulties faced us. People in the area assumed we could manage on our own, and so we were left relatively alone in terms of helping hands. For help with housework and child care, we decided to hire a young boy, with the notion that we could train him. Timappa was fourteen, but because he was small in stature, he appeared much younger. Although he had not had much formal education, he was intelligent and eager to learn. He entered into a sibling-type relationship with Simeon, and the two boys became good friends.

Life Style

In the field, our life style was mediated by Hindu culture as well as by our own health ideology. For the most part, our diet followed the prevailing system of folk dietetics. As vegetarians, we had been following a fairly Asian diet even in the West, so this was not difficult for us. Primarily, we cooked our own food, which was similar to that of the local population. Simeon was a good eater and enjoyed local dishes, although we did not pressure him to eat foods he did not like.

There were few points of cultural conflict pertaining to our feeding of Simeon. In the village, a young child is fed from his mother's hand until he becomes aggressive enough to fend for himself. In keeping with our cultural dictates of fostering a child's independence, we had encouraged Simeon to feed himself from an early age. Women would often scold Mimi when they saw her not feeding him by hand, particularly if Simeon was just looking at his food but not eating it. Sometimes the scolding would be quite sharp, and on occasion, Mimi would come back with a rebuttal focusing attention on Simeon's size and ability to eat. This would silence her critics temporarily but not convince them about our kind of social learning. Simeon's size and behavior was rather deemed to accord with his constitution, *prakrti*.

Another point of criticism made by villagers concerned Simeon's left-handedness. With its associations with defilement, villagers strongly discouraged Simeon from eating with his left hand, and Simeon just as adamantly kept on using it. This was taken in part as a reflection of his constitution and in part a reflection of Mimi's mothering.

A common assumption in the village was that when a child cried, it indicated hunger or an overactivity of worms. To us, this seemed a simplistic understanding of a child's desires, and we made an attempt to ask Simeon what his problems were. Villagers found this attempted cognitive exchange humorous, if not odd, for a young child was not thought to have judgment or reasoning ability, *buddhi*. Children were thought to gain *buddhi* at about the age of four when they became aware of kin terms and noted differences in social distance between relationships. This difference in the perception of intelligence manifested itself in a number of ways, the most notable of which was punishment. According to our perspective, when children understand right from wrong, they become responsible for their actions and liable to punishment when wrong actions are repeated. Although not disciplinarians by nature, we were not opposed to an occasional spanking when Simeon's antics became dangerous. Villagers believed that spanking a child younger than four was not only inappropriate but dangerous, for fear was associated with spirit attack and illness. Paradoxically, however, village children would be warned against roaming by being instilled with a different kind of fear: "Don't go there, there's a spirit there. A ghost will get you if you go there."

Simeon's wanderings from the periphery of the household *were* sometimes dangerous, for the world outside was full of open wells and the occasional wandering water buffalo. Our way of dealing with Simeon was to be firm. While a slap on the backside was not used as a first resort, it was nonetheless employed as a fifth resort. This was met by overt displeasure by villagers, who, depending on their familiarity with us, would take us aside for a lecture on child care.

One incident that is particularly memorable involved Simeon's crawling through a barrier of thorn bushes placed around an unused well. Seeing the danger, Mark ran to the well and dragged him back. Simeon started to scream, "I want go." Mark replied, "Okay, if you want go, then let's go"; he took him to the well and held him over it for a good look. News of the event traveled quickly. Villagers who heard the story were aghast and told us that fear experienced by a child around an open well made the child vulnerable to *ganderva* spirits. Preventive action was deemed necessary. Having studied local cosmology, we did what was culturally expected; we secured a protective talisman for Simeon from a local exorcist. Two months later, when Simeon fell ill with a respiratory illness, some villagers attributed this to the spirit of the *ganderva* that inhabited the well. On occasion, when the well incident was recalled, Mark would note that Simeon no longer approached wells. Villagers attributed this to the power of the protective device around Simeon's neck, not to Mark's childrearing methods.

Child Development

Many of the differences between our treatment of Simeon and villagers' treatment of their children revolved around beliefs about child development. We were anxious to teach Simeon as much as we could, and we encouraged him to find out about new things—to be active, to explore. We taught him words for things outside (e.g., the stars, the names of herbs), while village parents mainly concentrated on teaching words for things inside first: most important, kinship terms.

Our inquiries into developmental markers, for example, at what age a child was expected to walk or talk, were considered odd and were continually answered with a polite "When they

walk, they walk. When they talk, they talk." Rapid development, while desirable from a Western perspective, was a source of
worry and concern for villagers. For one thing, a child who was
quick to develop would be susceptible to the evil eye, which
might result in boils on the child's skin or stammering. The
latter condition might occur as a result of someone remarking,
"Oh, how well he speaks."

Another concept that affected notions of child development was
ayashu, or fixed life span. If children develop too quickly—by
acting with maturity greater than their years—families suspect
that their life span will be short. This concept was rarely discussed
overtly; in fact, we did not discover it for many months, until a
young child died.

A third notion that mediated ideas of development was *prakrti,*
constitution. If a child was lethargic from malnutrition, parents
would often assume it was the child's constitution to be "that
way." Many villagers had never seen a child as active as Simeon,
and it was generally assumed that this was a result of his inher-
ited constitution. Even Simeon's curiosity was interpreted as constitutional; after all, weren't his father and mother always asking
questions and constantly moving here and there? Through Simeon, we came to appreciate a valuable lesson in the importance of
constitutional rationale within local cosmology—a lesson that
influenced our work on health communication and conceptual
negotiation. [1]

Treatment of Simeon

Villagers had few notions of the child as an individual with a
will of his or her own. Instead, they viewed a child as a source of
entertainment. Thus, often when Simeon was busy at play, some-

one would come over to him and pick him up. At first when he protested, people would think it funny. Eventually he developed an effective technique for ending this behavior: He learned that a sharp pinch to the nipple would invariably lead a woman to put him down promptly.

Adults subjected Simeon to constant teasing, offering him something to play with and then, moments later, asking for it back, citing a kinship term: "I'm your mother's brother, *mava*, can't I have that now?" Simeon's responses to the teasing game were subject to different interpretations, depending on who the teaser was. At first we expected that if Simeon gave the object back immediately, he would be praised for his willingness to share with close relatives. Although this was true some of the time, on other occasions, when he did not relinquish the object, he was praised for being clever. We came to understand that teasing a child and then observing the response was a way villagers could evaluate a child's character and personality. Despite the fact that neither we nor Simeon liked this practice, teasing was a major form of social interaction, and we could do nothing to prevent it.

Not uncommonly, older, non-Brahman women would walk up to Simeon, pull on his penis, pretend to eat it, and say, "Um, a chili pepper, it's so good to eat." Mark could not help but chuckle about a fairly obvious Freudian interpretation to this phenomenon. More important to note here is the difference between the interactions that Brahmans and non-Brahmans had with Simeon. In contrast to the penis pulling of non-Brahman women, our Brahman friends from our first fieldwork experience were embarrassed by Simeon's nudity. Simeon did not like wearing clothes. While few of the non-Brahman three year olds whom we lived near wore clothes, in a Brahman household, women would scold Simeon, saying, "Shame, shame," if he walked around without shorts. Once, when Simeon was running around half naked with a stick in hand, Mark made the mistake of saying to a fictive mother-in-law that he looked like a wandering ascetic, *sanyasi*. Mark received a good scolding. We later learned that a *sanyasi*, as world renouncer, was not looked on favorably in Brahman households. Furthermore, one should never compare a child to a *sanyasi* or encourage a child to be like a *sanyasi*—to do so would be the antithesis of the child's socialization into the family unit.

Impact of Simeon's Presence

Simeon's presence in the field contributed to our fieldwork in four ways:

- First, it was easier for villagers to relate to us as a family unit. People were interested to see how we interacted with our child and were more conscious of our needs in relation to Simeon. Having a child gave people a familiar subject to talk to us about—an area where they had much expertise. This enhanced rapport and, to some degree, increased trust. Not only were we visiting another country, but we were also raising our child in that culture.

- Second, Simeon's presence gave our investigation of lay health concerns and health behavior a new dimension and meaning. Our questions about health, particularly children's health and pregnancy, were now perceived as relevant, and people would go out of their way to explain health culture to us. In fact, much of our best data came from illness narratives that friends and neighbors related to us as a means of providing important technical information on child care, as well as subtle information on responsibilities in child caretaking. The data collected on children's and women's health during our second field trip were far richer than those from the first; not only was the knowledge broader, it was also deeper. Believing that, as parents, we understood more, people told us more. People did not simply relate abstract stories; instead, they reminded us of appropriate and inappropriate behavior. Villagers warned us of inappropriate behavior, such as taking Simeon out on a full-moon night without a protective covering over his head—a local preventive health measure to ward off the cooling effects of the full moon.

Part of our research concerned health communication, particularly in regard to children. Discussions with villagers about Simeon's health, and why he was bigger than other children his age when he lived on a similar diet, gave us considerable insight into the kind of health education strategies that would be acceptable and unacceptable. We came to understand how many differences in development and health status are rationalized in respect to constitution and how much of the advice applicable to one child was not considered to be relevant for another because of notions of differential habituation. For example, what was good for Simeon was not, at first, considered good for other children because he was viewed as coming from a cold climate and being a wheat eater, not a rice eater as were the people there.

■   A third way Simeon's presence affected our fieldwork was in teaching us how culturally bound and judgmental we were. Simeon was like a mirror reflecting our own socialization and biases.

■   Last, but not least, Simeon was a delightful source of amusement, who made our fieldwork far more human by adding humor to every interview we conducted with him present. In fact, we took Simeon on a great many of our interviews because strangers seemed to trust us more with a child. Many people had heard of us via indigenous communication networks, and we had requests to visit people's houses with Simeon. Beyond language, Simeon's antics and curiosity were a source of enjoyment to the villagers in a place where children provided one of the few constant sources of entertainment.

Going to Delhi

After leaving India, we were asked to become health consultants for an international development agency for a few months. Many people are far more worried about living in rural areas of developing countries than in cities, where one can ostensibly isolate oneself to a greater degree and control one's environment. Our experience contradicted this. Perhaps the greatest irony of our field trip with Simeon was that his health was far better in the countryside, where we took water out of a familiar well and had a more systematic way of life.

Upon returning to India initially, our experience in Delhi, living in Defence Colony (an enclave for the Indian upper middle class intermixed with embassy families), gave us a false sense of security. We had running water, most amenities were at our fingertips, and Simeon could be kept visibly cleaner without much difficulty. Because our work schedule was very demanding, we hired a full-time housekeeper, an *aiya*, who spent a majority of her time with Simeon in our house or the houses of her friends. Our days were long at work, and the time we spent with Simeon was considerably reduced—a fact that saddened us after having been a close-knit family who spent most of the waking day together. Having spent much time in the village with people who had some mild ailment or another, it took a number of weeks before we became concerned about our *aiya*'s health. Because she had come highly recommended to us and had previously worked for an embassy family, we had not gone out of our way to have her examined by a doctor. Once, however, we spent an entire day with Simeon and the *aiya*, who by this time had become a friend. During a discussion of health and our work with *ayurveda*, the woman started telling us about her health problems. While relating her history, the possibility of the woman's having tuberculosis occurred to Mark, and he arranged for her to see a doctor. The woman was found to have an active case of tuberculosis, and when Simeon was retested, it was found that he had a positive reaction to a skin test. The doctors recommended that he be given a one-year dosage of INH, an antituberculosis drug. Although a positive test is not uncommon or a cause for great alarm, we shared feelings of guilt for having put our work in front of our parenting and for becoming lax in respect to our own health routine, which we had followed more diligently in the village.

Returning to America

Even before arriving in the States, we began to notice differences in attitudes toward children. In the early hours of our flight, when the plane was filled with South Asians, people lavished attention on Simeon. Stops in Europe brought on new passengers, and we began to hear "Shh" and to observe looks of annoyance at the "inconvenience" of being near a child. Simeon began to notice this attitude in his first month back, and it perplexed him. The kinship socialization he had learned in South India was extended to those adults who treated him kindly and displayed interest in him.

Another difficulty that caused Simeon problems in the United States was his language, which was a chop-suey combination of Kannaḍa, Tuḷu, Hindi, and English. What is more, different languages were used to express different feelings and intentions. Few could understand him, and adults in particular showed annoyance that although he looked like an American child, he could not speak English. We became aware of the intolerance of Americans toward people who cannot communicate well in English.

Simeon's first three months back were a cross between humor and paradox as he tried to negotiate a new culture. One image that remains in our mind is his instructing another child not to touch a Strawberry Shortcake doll but to collect flowers and place them in front of the doll as if it were a deity!

Perhaps the most amazing thing about children is their adaptability. Within six months, Simeon—with the assistance of his grandmother, who is an elementary school teacher—was speaking English and was well versed in the "Sesame Street" world. Unfortunately, with his increased ability to speak English came a decrease in his ability to speak other languages.

In terms of the lasting effect of the experience on him, the most striking behavior that seems to remain is that Simeon has retained a great curiosity about people who have different customs and speak different languages. He has little fear of meeting and interacting with new kinds of people—a trait that has proved adaptive for a six year old attending a local school in Hawaii. Mark has found "games" an apt referential framework for discussing culture with Simeon. Each culture, like each game, has a different set of rules and manner of playing, different positions, and so forth.

Now, at age six, Simeon can relate to India only in terms of the photographs he sees. From time to time, he receives letters from India and has grown curious about knowing more about the country. We are planning a field trip to Sri Lanka and India this coming year. This plan accords with our interests, as well as our desire to reexpose Simeon to a different culture at an age when his consciousness is rapidly expanding, as indicated by the questions he asks about the world. We sincerely hope he can acquire a retroflex *r* and that he will be able to overcome the intimidation many American children feel about learning new languages. On this trip, we look forward to reading the journal Simeon has begun to keep, as a way in which to share his impressions and gain a glimpse of how a child experiences the world around him.

Epilogue: Paradoxes

In 1983, we were given the opportunity to carry out fieldwork in Sri Lanka in conjunction with a health education and behavorial science training program Mark was to help develop. Simeon was just turning seven and was about to go into the second grade. He had spent the last year going to a local school in Hawaii and experiencing the freedom that comes when a child takes the training wheels off his first bike. His curiosity was blossoming, and we were engaged in the difficult art of simple explanation. A sign that hung on our refrigerator read: *"Because" is not an explanation; try again!*

We were to leave for Sri Lanka in July, but civil disturbances broke out and our trip was postponed until October. Having already sublet our house and having no short-term employment prospects, we decided to travel through Indonesia, a country that had long interested us as a possible site for future work. Much of the next four months was spent traveling through Sumatra by local transporation from Banoda Atjeh to Padang. Travel through Sumatra was grueling. Simeon held up remarkably well through a string of ten- to sixteen-hour, smoke-filled, claustrophobic bus rides, a five-day adventure on a small tramp steamer, and long hikes between settlements. He was very excited about travel, drawing the line only when it came to eating Padang food, excessively chilied even for our Indian taste buds. Simeon joined us in our effort to learn Bahasa Indonesian and elementary phrases from local languages. He was rewarded for his attempts at speaking by smiles, and it became a game to look into his pocket-size dictionary, find a word, try it out, and see what response it would evoke. Often the people Simeon chose to befriend became our best informants and guides. We came naturally to trust those who would spend quality time with Simeon, as opposed to those who would simply amuse themselves at his expense.

A great breakthrough for Simeon during the trip was discovering the utility of math by paying for things. Simeon was impressed by the denominations of Indonesian currency—of having to exchange thousands of rupiahs for a bus ticket or hundreds for vegetables. The concept of money having relative value provided questions for more than one long bus ride. Adding up bills and figuring change gave him his first sense of real responsibility. For local merchants, totaling and paying bills provided the makings of a great educational game to which they could relate. With a wink or a nod to us, they would try to trick Simeon by giving him a little more or a little less change. Simeon even befriended a pickpocket in Padang who spent hours demonstrating his craft to him, to the bemusement of his foodstall friends. Simeon took the lessons very seriously and became an apt spotter of mischief at his eye-pocket level.

Simeon spent a majority of his time with adults and adolescent boys during the trip. He gravitated toward children whenever given the chance, but it was older people who demanded most of his attention. We became anxious to get to Sri Lanka and settle down so that Simeon could make some friends his own age. Our image was that of Simeon wandering from house to house, as he had in India, joining groups of older boys as they searched for fruits. Reality was to prove otherwise.

The Sri Lanka we came to was much different from that experienced five years earlier on a six-week visit to the island. Streams of Japanese private minibuses crowded roads where only government buses had plied, Gulf money was conspicuous, islandwide television had been introduced, tourism had expanded, and an edge of ethnic tension was in the air. Mark's direct involvement in the health education training program was not to begin until January. To immerse ourselves in Sinhala culture as quickly as possible, we settled in a village recommended to us by a local oracle. Who better to ask for advice about housing, in the absence of a rural real estate agent?

We came to occupy the house of a retired schoolteacher in a village thirty miles inland from Colombo. The landlady and her meek husband were actively involved in community service groups, seemed very security conscious, and were intent on teaching us the principles of Buddhism. The landlady was a client of the oracle, who was helping her cope with her twenty-five-year-old, unemployed son. The young man stayed at home in preference to seeking a job beneath his status, that of a graduate in a country where white-collar unemployment is high. Just down the hill, but on the same property, lived the landlady's married daughter, also a teacher, her two-year-old child, and two orphan servant girls who were sisters. One girl was nine and the other eleven. On our arrival, the landlady moved into her daughter's house, while her husband and son moved into a nearby vacant building that had previously housed a cooperative society. We paid a reasonable rental, which was badly needed for house repairs. A perfect setup, we thought. A spacious old house, two acres of rubber trees, a good well, teachers to help us with Sinhala, a twenty-five-year-old "boy" with a picture of Bruce Lee on the wall to guard the house while we were away, kids nearby for Simeon to play with, and an opportunity to learn about the dynamics of community action groups. But we praised the oracle's divination powers a little too soon.

Our problems began when Simeon attempted to play with the two servant girls when they came to the house to do chores. We had offered our host family free access to the rooms in the house we were not occupying and hoped to develop a close personal relationship with them. Although the landlady was very cordial to us, she scolded the servant girls for not doing their work when she found them playing with Simeon. We discovered that they had been instructed not to play with Simeon whether or not they had work. The girls were servants, we were told, and playing would lead to bad habits. Their life was one of work. Simeon discovered that the girls had not been taught to read or add. He questioned us about whether it was right to keep children from playing, whether it was right for the girls to be kept ignorant in a household where there were two teachers? Couldn't we teach them? Having read about the Buddha in a popular comic-book series, Simeon questioned whether this kind of behavior was what the Buddha, the big teacher, would have wanted from his followers? Why couldn't we just tell the landlords, who were always talking about Buddhism, that they were making a mistake?

We indirectly approached the landlady about the fact that the girls did not attend school. The landlady took the attitude that she and her daughter were doing a great social service by taking in the orphans. The children, she stated, did not want to learn reading and adding. Anyway, they were cared for and would always have a home. We understood this to mean that so long as the girls were kept illiterate, they could be socialized to be dependent and not entertain foolish dreams about going to the city or the Middle East to work as domestic servants when they became older. An exodus of servants to the Middle East had made servants hard to come by in Sri Lanka at this time, and we imagined that the family's "social service" served their own needs. We discussed the girls' situation with Simeon, pointing out to him that, on the one hand, the landlady had saved the girls from becoming street beggars, and on the other hand, the girls would later become slaves to their illiteracy and seclusion from the world. It was their being prevented from learning, more than their shabby dress and sleeping on gunnysack, that disturbed Simeon. We were curious to see how he would respond to the girls' situation over time and in accord with his own moral reasoning.

Simeon decided that the adults were wrong and that children needed to play. He introduced a game of hide-and-seek, began learning Sinhala phrases to whisper to the girls, and began sneaking them pieces of candy. One day, when the younger girl looked sad and Simeon was at a loss for a Sinhala phrase to express his sympathy, he kissed her. Shocked, the girl ran to her house and told her sister. The landlady was informed and soon came running, irate. Had we no control over our son? Did we not realize that such an act could spoil these poor innocent girls, who were under her protection? We could not understand the woman's rage at a seven year old for an innocent kiss. Even by indigenous standards, her reaction seemed excessive. Later, we learned from the oracle that the landlady's son had been involved in a scandal that centered on a love affair with a girl from a neighboring household. This incident had almost resulted in the boy's leaving home and the family's reputation being spoiled. The oracle had saved the day by divining that the boy's unusual behavior resulted from sorcery arranged by the girl's family, who wanted him as a son-in-law. After weighing the ramifications of his actions and realizing that he stood to lose his inheritance, the boy consented to an exorcism.

The landlady feared loose talk about her family to the extent of becoming paranoid about the smallest incident. We only wished we had heard the story of the love affair before allowing a friend to bring an eighteen-year-old girl to the house to help us with the housework. Needless to say, the landlady was beside herself and complained about the girl's moral character from the minute she arrived. It took us three weeks to put all the pieces of the puzzle together. The girl was returned to her home, and we secured the services of an old woman, who became our cook, and a twelve-year-old girl from the village, who helped the woman lift objects and care for Simeon. One condition of the new girl's stay was that she learn to read, write, and add.

The kiss was the end of Simeon's contact with the two servant girls, who now remained in the landlady's daughter's house most of the time. Simeon began to get interested in the two houses on the other side of the rubber trees as a potential source of friends. His wanderings to these houses were cut short by our landlady, who scolded our old servant for letting him go near such bad people. Although our landlady and her neighbors greeted one another cordially in public, they had only minimal contact. Our landlady, who was an officer in several community self-help groups, feared sorcery attacks from her neighbors to the extent of locking her well at night with an iron plate.

Research revealed that animosities between the neighbors involved unpaid loans, boundary disputes, status jealousies, and zero-sum psychology. A retired rural development officer, who became our research assistant, explained that rapid social change had intensified the politics of status. At this time of increasing social mobility and power brokerage, an impression management game was in play. People were spending scarce resources on status items to appear better off than they actually were. As our informant put it, "Nowadays you don't know whether smoke coming out of the neighbor's kitchen means they are cooking something to eat or just trying to lead you to believe they are." In Sri Lanka, kindness and compassion, Buddhist virtues, command respect and give one status, whereas selfishness, equated with cruelty, causes a loss in status. The game thus became one of acting kind in public—through such acts as feeding priests, visiting the sick, and attending funerals—attempting to convince others that you were more prosperous than you really were. In spite of being sociable in public, you did not develop close private relationships with those you were trying to impress. To do so might encourage them to ask you for a loan. To refuse the request would cause you to lose status by appearing selfish, whereas to agree to a loan might place your own family in jeopardy or reduce their capacity to maximize capital for future gain. The best policy was to maintain an acceptable degree of social distance from the neighbors.

Children of the rural middle class engaged in this game were being socialized to fit the politics of status management. A child would be encouraged not to become overly friendly with a neighboring household. The language used to discourage children from friendships with the neighbors was very judgmental; people were characterized as good/bad, kind/cruel, and educated/uneducated—the latter referring more to being cultured than literate. This was language we had cautioned Simeon against while we were in Hawaii, where he had to contend with ethnic stereotypes. Simeon had been socialized to see different sides of people and consider their circumstances. He had been told that there were no bad boys or lazy people, but boys who did bad things and people who acted lazy because they had no proper motivation to do otherwise. People could change, if change was supported. Simeon wanted to know why our landlords, who were teachers, thought the children in the next house were bad? Even if their parents were bad, that did not necessarily mean the children were bad, or did it? In his own way, Simeon applied his social learning perspective in a context where he heard people categorized as if their characters were predetermined. Naturally curious, it was only a matter of time before Simeon actually met the kids in the next houses; he concluded that they were nice and that only an adult who did not understand children would think they were bad.

As soon as the landlady discovered Simeon's attempts to make friends in the neighboring houses, we were asked to intervene. If we were to remain in the house, then we had to comply with the request. We decided to do so, but also to search for a new house. We explained to Simeon in no uncertain terms that complying with the landlady's request went against our own principles and values.

Soon after, we moved away from the village, closer to Colombo. We placed Simeon in an international day school and moved into a group-living situation with Mark's health education students. Simeon was offered much love and attention by the students, but we sighed when our new landlord described the neighbors as bad people and asked Simeon not to play with their children.

Mark's mother, whom Simeon referred to as Ajji Bea, came to Sri Lanka in the later weeks of our stay. It was her first trip to Asia. She traveled with Simeon for three weeks and described her most memorable experience on her return. The experience involved beggars.

Simeon had a number of encounters with beggars in different social contexts. We had discussed that the act of giving was as much for the giver as the receiver because it made one feel good to share with those in need. Simeon learned that giving a coin and a smile to someone in need can be beautiful but that being accosted for money can be ugly and dehumanizing. We held to no firm rule in our treatment of beggars. Simeon always carried a few coins and felt at liberty to give, should he choose to do so. Having been overwhelmed by beggar children before, however, Simeon recognized that there was a dynamic to giving that demanded a consideration of the proper amount to give and who was watching.

Ajji Bea's story illustrated Simeon's perceptions. While staying in a village on the southwest coast that had recently opened to tourism, Simeon and his grandmother were approached by a few beggars. Over Simeon's protest, Ajji Bea gave them too large a sum by local standards and soon was overwhelmed by beggars, who accosted her whenever they showed their faces on the beach. She continued to pay these "poor souls," thinking they would be grateful and leave her alone. Nothing Simeon said could dissuade her, and she wondered about his "callousness." Finally, Simeon came up with a plan: Ajji Bea, who is allergic to fleas, kept her distance from the local dogs. Much against his grandmother's wishes, Simeon began feeding scraps of bread to a few dogs, re-marking on how hungry they looked. Soon, dogs started con-gregating around the hotel and fighting for the scraps of bread. Simeon threw the dogs a big piece of bread, which drove them into a frenzy. This resulted in a dogfight, and a few dogs were bitten and limped away. Simeon remarked that, sometimes, doing what seems right only makes for more trouble. Life was tricky like that, he said. His grandmother relied more on his judgment for the remainder of the trip.

What did we learn during this field trip? During our travels, we discovered that children can be very good judges of character. Rather than being overprotective, we tried to allow Simeon the chance to use his intuition about people, within reasonable lim-its. In the village, Simeon helped us gain insights into the pol-itics of child socialization. Moreover, our sensitivity to the issue of human rights was heightened. Paradoxes long recognized on a more intellectual plane were seen through our interaction with a child with open eyes and heart. The child's questions sharpened our research and induced reflexivity.

Note

1. M. Nichter and M. Nichter, *An Anthropological Approach to Nutrition Education* (Newton, Mass.: Education Develop-ment Center, International Nutrition Communication Ser-vice, 1981).

4 "Daddy's Little Wedges": On Being a Child in France

In 1950–1951 when my father had a sabbatical, we went to live in Roussillon, a village in southeastern France. I turned five that year. My brother David turned three.

I remember very little of the year in Roussillon: a pig being butchered down the street, some kids I played with, losing my first tooth, my father trying to light a fire on bone-chilling mornings when the *mistral* blew, a few details of life at school. I got my French nickname, Johnny, one day when the teacher told someone by that name to pay attention; I looked around to see who Johnny was, and found everyone looking at me. At some level I must remember more, since I still have dreams set in Roussillon.

I'm told that I quickly learned to understand French, but for a long time I would not speak it. Finally, my father took me to task about this. I assured him I would start speaking French when I had learned one more word. The word learned, I began speaking correct and fluent French, with a heavy Provençal accent. I forgot my French as soon as we returned to the States, however. I forgot more slowly the script I had learned to write in Roussillon, but I was forbidden to use it at the Haverford Friends' School. Script was not taught until the fourth grade, and the teachers said it would not be fair to the other children if I was so far ahead of them.

My father taught French at Haverford College. We lived on the Haverford campus, from whose generous confines David and I never ventured alone. Our family spent the summer months at my mother's parents' cottage, in the woods overlooking Lake Michigan. We had gone to France because my father wanted to find out at firsthand about modern French country life—the basic culture in which the language is embedded. He also wanted to help Americans understand the French, and to that end he wrote a book about Roussillon, *Village in the Vaucluse.* There's a picture of me in the book. David's picture is on the cover of the later, paperback editions.

We went back to France in 1957–1958, when my father had another sabbatical. I was eleven and had just graduated from the sixth grade. He now wanted to study a contrasting sort of village, devout in religion and right-of-center in politics (Roussillon had voted Communist). I knew this. I did not know about the strain the year in Roussillon had put on my parents' otherwise happy marriage, which I now see influenced the way we came to France again. I also see, having become an anthropologist myself, that there is a fundamental difference between living abroad as a child and understanding a strange culture as an adult. My case may not be wholly typical. For one thing, my father was not an anthropologist, so he (and we) did not think of our experience as "doing fieldwork" but simply as "living in France for a year."

Moreover, this was not the central episode of my father's career, which had already included three or four trips to France. Thus the French were not an unknown quantity to us, at least vicariously through him, and in general he was a reliable and sympathetic guide to their ways.

Still, I imagine two things about my own experience are generally true. First, a child's initial sense of *dépaysement* is worse than an adult's, since it is unbuffered by such intellectual constructs as "another culture" and by such exercises as keeping a journal. I find that my most vivid and elaborate memories of France in 1957–1958 are concentrated in the first few months and reflect great bewilderment and dismay. But things are easier for a child when the initial shock is past. Without really understanding them, I internalized French ways rapidly and thoroughly, learning French culture without learning much about it.

Second, a family is inevitably drawn in on itself when it first ventures abroad. Suddenly without playmates and lacking a long view of the time to come, you find your parents and siblings dominating your world. This disconcerting period may pass fairly quickly, as you learn a new language easily and are immediately enmeshed in village life through playmates and classmates. It did for David, anyway. For various reasons, however, including my wanting to put as much distance as possible between him and me, our family's stay in France in 1957–1958 reinforced an already strong solitary streak in my personality. Families and cultures differ, but I suspect that whether a child is gregarious or solitary, his (or her) family ties are loosened during a foray into the field.

We came to France in easy stages in 1957—easy from an adult's point of view. I now realize that we did so largely for my mother's sake, since her first introduction to France had been extremely trying.

In 1950 she had never been to France before. She knew very little French, and for the first two weeks we stayed in a "miserable" old-fashioned *pension* in an out-of-the-way part of Neuilly, while my father commuted into Paris to make contacts and decide on a general field site. When we finally moved to Roussillon, to a house that, as my mother put it, "was no great shakes, though it had its points," she was able to help with some of his work—copying census data, for example. Nevertheless, like many an anthropological spouse, if only she had known it, she often felt desperately trapped at home with two small children, marooned in an alien world. As I see it, things were made more difficult for her because, being the product of a settled middle-class Midwestern childhood, she ventures diffidently into strange territory on her own. She is an adventuresome hostess but a reluctant guest—and Roussillon offered small scope for her talent.

My father already knew France, in a sense. Certainly he knew French, and although he had some trouble understanding the Roussillon dialect, he could always make himself understood. His assimilation into village life was easier than my mother's— indeed, easier than most anthropologists'. Moreover, he is (as he always describes himself) from southern Indiana, the son of a Methodist minister. Moving from one small-town parsonage to another was a regular feature of his childhood. Unperturbed by living in makeshift quarters, he has the knack of making friends quickly wherever he finds himself. I believe he saw Roussillon as somewhere that, through his own sympathetic immersion in it, could be made directly comprehensible to the folks back home. Immediately deeply absorbed in village life for professional reasons as well, he spent as much time as possible away from the house. A permanent result was a good book. A temporary result, reinforced by my own mother's attitude, was a certain estrangement between them.

Apparently they decided—rightly, on the whole—that things would go better the second time around. We sailed from New York in midsummer. My mother, David, and I disembarked at Plymouth. We were met by some old friends of my parents, who drove us to their house in Oxfordshire. My father went ahead to Paris to talk with colleagues and decide which region of France we should live in. In England we did some sightseeing, but mostly we stayed home and took country walks in the short breaks between the inexplicably elaborate rituals of meals and elevenses and tea. I read *The Lord of the Rings* for the first of a dozen times that year. I was very unhappy. I often lost my temper anyway, and now my distress took the form of flying into particularly passionate rages at, for example, the complicated preparations taking a walk or a drive seemed to require. I must have been a trial to live with. Besides, I was on the verge of an American adolescence and therefore deeply mistrusted all grown-ups (as well as David, of course).

In a few weeks, after my father had done his preliminary research and settled on southwestern Anjou, we joined him and went to live for a month or so in a lovely hotel near Saumur, on a bluff overlooking the Loire. From there we drove around visiting villages and looking at houses we might rent. My mother had the final say over where we would live. I seem to remember places in terms of books and food, and although I forget what I was reading then, I can still almost taste the hotel restaurant's *sole meunière,* to which we often treated ourselves. In the woods behind the hotel David and I busied ourselves building a little "house" with walls of piled-up stones. Our parents declared it too dangerous to enter, but we disobeyed them. In England David and I had also built a little house, which we thatched with grass cuttings from the lawn.

A real house was hard to find. Some lacked such basic amenities as running water; others were like one I remember in, I think, Le-Pin-en-Mauges, a village my father thought promising—dark, cramped, and clammy. Toward the end of the summer, my parents settled on Chanzeaux, where for the time being we would have to live in half of a double house. It had a primitive kitchen downstairs. Upstairs there was a little room for my father's study, a big room with a fireplace that served as both a living room and our parents' bedroom, and a bedroom for David and me. The water was unsafe, so David and I were enjoined not to swallow when we brushed our teeth. Drinking water was kept in a big earthenware amphora, disinfected with a bit of bleach, which gave it an odd taste of laundry-day. In a courtyard behind the house there was a privy, which some men with a tank-truck came and emptied so we could use it. In a few weeks we expanded into the whole house, whose other half had a flush toilet out back. Downstairs there were a better kitchen, a dining room with a little, blue-green, ceramic Franklin stove, and a room we never used. There were two more bedrooms upstairs.

Our house was near the center of the village proper, or *bourg,* on a corner at one end of the Place de l'Église. (The *bourg* had about three hundred inhabitants; the rest of the *commune*'s eleven hundred inhabitants lived in scattered hamlets and farms round about.) Around our end of the *place* were a few houses, a grocery, a bakery, the more popular of Chanzeaux's two cafés, a nearly defunct wooden-shoemaker's, and a mechanic's shop. The far end of the *place* was dominated by the church—an immense, hideous structure of greenish and grayish stone, dating from the late nineteenth century. Next to it stood a much older bell tower in which a party of Chanzéens had been martyred by the "godless" forces of the Republic during the Vendée counterrevolution. The *mairie* stood next to the bell tower and then the street led up a long slope lined with houses to the Catholic boys' school, out into open country, and to villages that remained beyond my ken.

We moved in on a Saturday in mid-September. I remember perching with studied nonchalance on the bottom half of the Dutch door between our kitchen and the street, eating an orange while I covertly eyed a gaggle of village children who were more openly eyeing me. When my mother said to come to dinner, I got down with (I hoped) dignified reluctance. On Sunday, we were awakened early by the babble of voices outside our windows as men passed from early Mass to the café. Practically the whole population of the *commune* attended Mass every week. On Tuesday, school began.

Chanzeaux had a state school and two Catholic ones. The state school had only about a dozen pupils, mostly children of the very poorest Chanzéens. One of the Catholic schools was for girls and the youngest children; it was taught by nuns. David and I went to the Catholic boys' school, the École St. Joseph. (Since we are not Catholic, my father had gotten special permission for us to attend it from the bishop of Angers.) It had two rooms—one for *les petits,* taught by a woman I knew only as Mademoiselle, the other for *les grands,* taught by a stocky, strict, but kindly man named Monsieur Bédouin. He and his wife lived in a house forming one long side of a schoolyard of clayey packed gravel; the other long side was formed by the school itself, and the short sides by privies at one end and a shed at the other. You came into the schoolyard through the shed, by a door next to the house. M. Bédouin had a big desk on a platform at the front of the classroom, flanked by two blackboards. A crucifix hung on the wall behind his desk. He seldom sat up front, but walked up and down the aisle between our desks, giving a dictation or looking over our shoulders at our work. We sat four or five to a desk, arranged by age. The youngest of *les grands,* about eight years old, sat at the back to M. Bédouin's left; the oldest, about fourteen years old, sat at the front to his right. In winter the room was heated, after a fashion, by a smoky, black, coal-burning, pot-bellied stove.

David and I discovered all this sooner than we had expected, since my father had assumed that the term would begin on October 1, as in other French schools. He, and we, thought we would have time to make friends and learn some French before school began. Instead, on Tuesday morning we found ourselves near the church, formed into ranks with the village children, not wearing smocks like theirs and not carrying little satchels filled with scholarly impedimenta, neither of us knowing a word of French—except in the morning I had presciently gotten my father to teach me how to say "I don't understand," which for some reason I garbled as *"Je comprends ne pas."* We were marched in two files up the street, and, again formed in files, into the classroom. The boys knelt on their benches. David shot me a panicky glance—what do we do now? Guessing what they were up to, I shook my head slightly. Then and thereafter we stood or sat while the other boys said the prayers that punctuated the day: an Our Father, an Apostles' Creed, a decade of Hail Marys, or an Act of Contrition. (If a boy came to school late, he knelt alone and muttered an Act of Contrition.) Prayers began the day and ended it, and preceded and followed lunch (when we all went home) and the ten-minute recess each morning and afternoon. There were many strange customs and strict rules: no opening your desk without permission; hands on top of your desk at all times. Arithmetic problems were written on the blackboard, and the whole class chanted out the solutions together. At lunchtime we were marched back down the hill and dismissed with a double clap.

It was all pretty scary. Howling, David and I refused to go back in the afternoon. Our parents were sympathetic and said we did not have to, but when the time came, we went back anyway. (The march up to school was a feature of the first day only; but every day we were marched down to the base of the hill to be dismissed.) At recess we quickly came to grief. We were used to playing on grass, so we kept skinning our knees badly until we learned not to fall down. David had to come home early that first afternoon, and my parents took him off to have a tetanus booster shot. (There was no doctor in Chanzeaux, but several in neighboring villages.) A day or two later, I also hurt myself. M. Bédouin searched around in a little red bilingual dictionary of mine and asked haltingly, "You have evil?" In the dictionary I saw that "evil" meant *mal,* which might also mean "hurt," so, bravely and in order to avoid a shot, I shook my head.

As the initial shock wore off, I came to like the École St. Joseph better than the Friends' School. The rules were clearer, for one thing. In Haverford, if you misbehaved by getting too rowdy in class (Just how rowdy was that? It was hard to say) you would be warned that you were being unfair to the other kids. If you persisted, you would be sent to sit outside the principal's office, to feel guilty but secretly unrepentant. You were supposed to do well in class; but you were also supposed to be sympathetic to those who did less well and unresentful of those who did better. In Chanzeaux there was no rowdiness—unless M. Bédouin left the room, of course; and then if you chose to talk or pass notes or even leave your seat, you did not have to fear a classmate's betrayal later. Punishments for minor offenses were swift, measured, and often physical: M. Bédouin might pull your hair or your ear, or make you stand in the corner, face to the wall, arms folded. (He treated David and me leniently, and our hair was too short to get a grip on; but we got our ears pulled often enough.)

Boys might do their lessons well or poorly, but each was expected
to do his best. You could have your ear pulled for a page of
careless penmanship as well as for misbehaving. What an American educator would call "creativity" was not encouraged; you
learned your lessons by rote from the boldface passages in the
textbooks. Sometimes M. Bédouin would comment on the
lessons. He informed us that most of the Angevin canals, whose
names we had to memorize, were no longer in use, and that the
Freemasons (who, I suspected privately, did not really figure as
large in the Revolution as our history book suggested) celebrate
Black Mass. But we were not required to know such incidental
information. So long as you were well behaved and did your
lessons conscientiously, your life and your thoughts were your
own.

Everyone in the *classe des grands* was given the same lessons
every year, which by dint of repetition the older boys knew better
than the younger ones. We studied arithmetic, *calcul mental*
(doing arithmetic in your head), French history and geography,
Angevin history and geography, French (grammar, spelling,
etc.), penmanship, and catechism. Penmanship was one of my
weakest subjects. I never did master the scratchy pens you dipped
in a well of purple ink on your desk. But just as he realized that
an eight year old would not know his history as well as a twelve
year old, M. Bédouin tolerated my *mauvaise écriture* as long as I
was obviously doing my best. Still, I had to recopy many pages,
and of course on compositions and dictations I was marked down
for bad penmanship, as well as for mistakes in spelling and grammar. David and I were excused from catechism, and I got into the
habit of spending the lesson time drawing cartoons of life at
school. The characters were all dogs, with a bespectacled teacher-
dog modeled on Howland Owl in *Pogo*.

At first, David and I were seated with the youngest of *les grands*.
My ambition was to be seated with the boys my own age. This took

several months, and of course required learning French—which, whatever the grown-ups said, did not magically "come back" from the year in Roussillon. I worked hard at it and took the grammar lessons seriously. (Assiduous reading of *Tintin* comic books helped a lot too.) David, being a gregarious soul like my father, at once began speaking something that gradually approximated French more and more closely. As in Roussillon, however, I said as little as possible for weeks, wanting to speak correctly if I spoke at all. I could divine the meaning of most words, but had to ask my father about hard ones like *fruit-de-vos-entrailles-est-béni* ("blessed is the fruit of thy womb"). By the end of the year, our French was fluent and accentless, but sometimes awkward. I never did get the hang of saying *s'en servir de* instead of *utiliser,* and the correct usage of *dont* still eludes me. David has forgotten a good deal of his French. I remember most of mine, probably because I was just old enough to retain in an adult way a language I was just young enough to learn in a childish one. This must be one of the few advantages of puberty.

Outside of school, David had many playmates—including a little hellion by the name of Louis Guicheteau, whose ear (to no one's surprise) M. Bédouin pulled so hard one day that it began to come off. I had few playmates, not so much because of my different temperament as because few children had been born in Chanzeaux in my birth year, 1945. This demographic fact neither surprised nor disturbed me; at the Friends' School, too, my class was always small, and the only child my age on campus had left three years before, when his father went to teach at Chicago. Besides, the handful of Chanzeaux boys my age or a bit older were farm children, who hurried home to do chores as soon as school got out. On the other hand, I now realize that there was something very American and small-familyish about my disdain for the company of "David's friends"—*bourg* boys a year or two younger than myself. Later in the year, when David was enrolled in one newly founded parish boys' club and I in the other, there was also something American about our (failed) attempt to engender rivalry between them, conceiving of them in terms of the competitive, semiconspiratorial playground "gangs" we knew at home.

Sometimes after school or on Thursdays (when we had the day off; there was school on Saturdays) I went to a friend's house to play a board game called "Jeu d'Attaque"; and after a baptism, I always joined the village children to scramble for the almond candies and small change that the baptismal party threw out as it left the church (to our parents' horror—the street was none too clean what with the horses and cows that passed that way; but it never seemed to do us any harm). But mostly I went on long walks—along the rutted tracks beside the river; up past the conical remains of windmills into open fields on the high ground above the river; through remnants of the hedge country on whose borders Chanzeaux stands, where bits of pasturage were jumbled between brooding hedgerows of bramble and oak; and as far afield as the outskirts of wine country to the east. As often as he could, my father joined me these walks, which are among his fondest memories of Chanzeaux, as they are of mine. I enjoyed his company, and the projects we set for ourselves. We traced each brook to its source, but we never did finish walking all the borders of the *commune*. I was always afraid, however, that he would ask David or my mother to come along, so I used to set out immediately after school—*tant pis* if he wasn't home.

At Thanksgiving, we all went to visit the big American army base at Chinon. We stayed off-base at the house of a colonel with whom my father had arranged to do some shopping at the PX. At an officers' mess we ate turkey and mashed potatoes and had fresh milk to drink, and I suppose we must have seemed as exotic to the soldiers as they did to us. The colonel had three children a bit older than David and I, a girl and twin boys. They spoke no

French, although they were "learning it in school." They told us how, once, the girl had bravely bought a loaf of bread at a local bakery. David and I were not impressed; every morning one of us would run across the street for a breakfast *baguette*. Even the milk tasted strange, since we had grown used to wine or water with meals. My mother only narrowly avoided collapsing in laughter when the colonel's wife proudly showed her how she had coped with strange plumbing by planting ivy in the *bidet*.

In the fall, a former student of my father's came to visit—and stayed all year. George was a painter. His car (a Morris, I think) was crammed with all sorts of wonderful things, including a tape recorder and his Skye terrier named Bonny. The tape recorder was important only in the long run, for George sometimes played a tape of hit tunes—Elvis, Chuck Berry, "Rock Around the Clock." When I got back to Haverford, this introduction to pop music offered one of the few, precarious links between my cocooned life on campus and the brash and boastful culture of my peers at the day prep school I started going to, where the talk was all of such mysterious things as parties, dates, "rumbles," and pranks involving cars. Bonny was important right away. I had always wanted a dog, and now she came along on my walks after school every day. For a grown-up, George proved remarkably trustworthy and companionable, perhaps because he was rather boyish himself. Since we were both early risers, we usually ate breakfast together before the rest of the family got up. He made the coffee, and I did my homework.

Probably without knowing it, George helped me over the worst trauma of the year. My parents had asked him to coach me in seventh-grade mathematics, using an American textbook so that I would not be behind when I entered the eighth grade back home. One day, just after Christmas, he and I were having a lesson in the dining room when one of my parents called for me to come upstairs, please. I found them all in the living room, in front of the fireplace, crying. David was sitting in my father's lap. A letter had just come from my mother's sister, saying that my grandfather had died a few days before Christmas. His and my grandmother's cottage in Michigan was, after Haverford, the chief focus of our existence. I had last seen him waving good-bye from the pier in New York. I too burst into tears. Then, in a sudden resolve to be tough, I stopped the tears and stumbled out and down the stairs to the dining room. Sensing something was badly wrong, but without asking what it was, George put me back to work at the day's math lesson.

Another episode was probably more traumatic for my parents than for me, though I was at the center of it. In mid-February I got a stomachache, with vomiting and a slight fever. I stayed home from school, of course, but otherwise no one (least of all me) made any fuss. I had these stomachaches two or three times a year. They usually lasted a couple of days. This one persisted and got worse, however, and the doctor came. Then, one night when the pain got awful, he drove my mother and me to a private hospital in Angers, the nearest city. My appendix had to come out right away—it was on the point of rupturing. At the hospital they did not even bother to take off my pajama top (a red turtleneck of which I was particularly fond), which surprised me; and I was amused that the only thing they did before wheeling me into the operating room was to give me a suppository: How French, I thought. When I came to, desperately thirsty, I recalled with effort that I was in France, and with relief that "*eau*" was so much easier to say than "water."

My case had dangerous complications, so I spent three weeks in the hospital. Most of the time, I was fed intravenously, and a tube ran through my nose down into my stomach. My pajama top got pretty grubby, and my mother said why not cut it off. But the nurses said no—it was such a nice shirt, and besides, it kept my neck warm. My parents were a lot more worried than I knew, but except for the pain and hunger (I couldn't eat for ten days), it was not a bad time for me. After all, we were in provincial France, where the rituals of hospitalization are less elaborate and severe than in the States. My mother, who was good company and a good nurse, stayed in the room until all danger was past; the nurses, who were nuns, were devoted; and one day when I was nearly well, the surgeon came in from the operating room to show me the appendix he had just removed from a Chanzeaux schoolmate of mine. (I had asked him to do this.) Later, I learned from my father (who had it from David) that at school the daily prayers had been offered to *"notre petit camarade Johnny."* I was touched, but privately thought it unlikely that this had speeded my recovery. When I was in the hospital, I read *Village in the Vaucluse.* I liked the way my father followed Roussillonais through the stages of their lives, from infancy to old age; and I wondered what it would have been like to grow up there—doing military service and (maybe) marrying the little girl I had been secretly in love with. But I found his Roussillon a large, complicated and curiously timeless place, where I made no difference worth speaking of; my own small Roussillon lay in the past, like kindergarten.

At Easter, my grandmother came to visit. We took a trip with her through southern France and into Italy, spending three or four days in Roussillon. Everyone told me how I had grown, and asked if I remembered them. I did not, though the sights and smells were familiar. My grandmother flew home from Switzerland. Anxious to be "home" in Chanzeaux ourselves, we drove back across the Massif Central in a single day.

In Siena, David and I had bought fancy marbles beautifully wrapped in colored paper. Marbles were all the rage at school just then, but unfortunately these proved impossible to play with. The paper came off, revealing a drab clay core. The Chanzeaux boys played marbles for keeps, using painted clay marbles and a heavy shooter called a *bidou.* At first David and I played poorly, but he soon improved to the point where, he remembers, M. Bédouin reprimanded him one day for letting his swollen pocket of marbles rattle in class. I lost more often than I won, and was aware that, as a "rich American," my seemingly inexhaustible supply of marbles to lose made me a marginally tolerated competitor, swelling my playmates' winnings without enhancing my own prestige.

Toward the end of the year, the boys my age took an examination for a Catholic primary school certificate. The examinations were held in a nearby town and lasted all day. I had been given permission to take them too, if I was willing to be tested in catechism as well as the other subjects. I studied hard and memorized the catechism, but at the end of the day my name was not read out with those of the successful candidates. It was small comfort that (as my father learned later) I had done well in every subject except arithmetic, and the examiners figured, rightly, that my weakness there had nothing to do with being tested in strange subjects in a strange language. In a sense, however, it was a relief to be graded by such fixed standards. At school one time, I subtracted seven from twelve and got what looked to M. Bédouin like an eight. I meekly accepted his remonstrance and a poor grade, aware that in America I would have protested that I had really written a sloppy five.

Having passed (or failed) this examination, most of my friends left school for good. And now that the year was winding down, M. Bédouin no longer kept us at our lessons all day, but broke off early to read *Tintins* aloud to us with great relish. He did a masterful, almost self-parodying Capitaine Haddock.

We left Chanzeaux in late June. Our year there proved to be the first and, in a way, the least upsetting of a series of dislocations, since (except for my grandfather's death) I imagined that I would be returning to pretty much the same world I had left. We spent the rest of the summer in Michigan, as usual. In the fall, I entered a new school where, being American after all, I lacked the foreigner's privilege of not being expected to know how to behave among my peers. The next year we moved to Cambridge, when my father took a job at Harvard. Here was another strange world. The Harvard campus, such as it was, was nearly lost in the city. David and I had never crossed a city street on our own before, and now each morning we had to dash across a highway on the way to school. We lived in three houses in four years, and then I went away to college on the West Coast.

Just to round off the story: I majored in English in college, but since anthropologists seemed to be cooler people who did more interesting work than literary critics, I decided to go to graduate school in anthropology. I did my dissertation fieldwork in the Faroe Islands, and have since done another stint on Dominica, in the West Indies. As an undergraduate, I had spent a summer working on a Chanzeaux farm, doing fieldwork as well as working in the fields. Thus I contributed to the book some of my father's students put together, *Chanzeaux: A Village in Anjou.* Otherwise, my experiences as an ethnographer's child are rather indirectly related to my becoming an ethnographer myself. Nevertheless, the year in Chanzeaux did reinforce my taste for keeping an onlooker's reserve while doing whatever other people do.

I have been asked, "What advice would you give parents contemplating bringing children into the field?" Several things come to mind, based on my experiences in Chanzeaux as well as on my own (although childless) fieldwork in Scandinavia and the West Indies.

First, I would not want to be out of reach of a hospital if I still had my appendix.

Second, about my mother, and mothers and women generally, since child care usually falls to their lot. My mother had a better year in Chanzeaux than in Roussillon. David and I were old enough to be in school or out on our own most of the time, and we were past the age of childhood diseases. Our house was not much better, but she had learned that "only a year" is a long time, so she immediately made it as comfortable as possible. On the other hand, she made few close friends in Chanzeaux, partly because (like me) she was reluctant to speak French but (unlike me) was not forced to increase her command of it through long, daily exercise. She went marketing every day at the various shops around the *bourg*, but perhaps her closest connection with village life was through Michèle Bellard, a cheerful, wonderfully sharp-witted young woman from a nearby farm, who came in every morning to help cook, clean house, and do the wash. George was a fine cook, too, and my mother often had his company and help. (Cooking is another of my mother's talents.) Nevertheless, she often felt lonely and beleaguered in Chanzeaux. This was partly the result of her reluctance to let an alien society absorb her; but it also stemmed from my father's more observant than participatory style of doing fieldwork, and from a certain rigidity in Chanzeaux's culture.

When my wife, Gail, and I began our fieldwork on Dominica, she declined offers of "a girl to help" and, awkwardly at first, since this was not the way white people were supposed to behave, joined the village women doing their wash by the shore, fetching water, "going to garden," marketing in the next village, and attending Mass. Letting other women instruct you in child care, as they do in gardening or doing the wash, must be bitterly offensive, but it may be worth following their lead as far as your conscience allows. (Cultures differ, of course. Dominican children tend to be hateful; but Faroese children are much nicer than American ones.) In fact, partly because she has children, a woman's assimilation may be easier than a man's. Much of "women's work," including child care, has a certain universality about it, whereas "men's work" tends to be more specialized, requiring a more elaborate apprenticeship. Certainly the village women accepted Gail more or less as one of themselves much more quickly than the village men accepted me. She went to garden long before I managed to go fishing. Yet, depending on the culture, "a man's work" may also draw a woman into local society. Early on in my fieldwork in the Faroes, I helped my neighbor build his house, along with his father and mother's brother. Partly by helping his mother to prepare a meal for us, my wife got to know her, and soon she began going next door to knit with her. Visiting and knitting together are important social activities for Faroese women, and by engaging in them my wife both overcame her inital fear of trying out her halting Faroese (mine was scarcely better) and developed a relationship approximating one of kinship. Our households exchanged labors and favors that, if we had had children, would have included helping to look after them. I wonder what would have happened in Chanzeaux if, for example, my father had spent a few days actually working at a threshing bee or helping with the *vendange*. Would my mother have joined the other wives at their share of the work? As it was, the activities he did take part in seldom involved the rest of us.

Still, it might have been extremely difficult to penetrate *bourg* society in this way. In the Faroes, casual visiting from house to house is a vital institution, families are close but not exclusive, and in "our village" over half the married women came from elsewhere. Thus the way was clear for a strange woman's assimilation into local society. The same is true of Dominica, although for very different reasons. There, people gather casually out-of-doors, and the nuclear family is a notably flimsy institution. In

Chanzeaux, however, women did not gather casually at home or in public, although they met briefly in the shops. Families kept their distance—except after Mass on Sunday, when farm families dined with relatives in the *bourg*. Naturally, we had no relatives in the countryside. Moreover, the village's most important institution was the church. Being non-Catholics, we therefore felt ourselves barred from many activities. It was only by special permission of the bishop that David and I attended the Catholic school. I wonder, then, if my mother, even assuming that she wanted to, could have joined groups like the parish theatrical club for married women. As it was, Chanzeaux's Catholicism and strong family life left us taking part piecemeal in village activities, and, ironically, weakened our own family as an institution.

Third, this brings up the matter of David's and my role as adjuncts to our father's ethnographic enterprise. I was well aware of our general usefulness. I dubbed us "Daddy's little wedges," realizing that we were earnests of his good intentions, and gave him a natural entrée into village life. He avoided exploiting us directly, however, either by pushing us into activities we did not want to take part in or by questioning us systematically about what we were learning about village life. In a way, this was wise. I should certainly have resented being treated like an informant. Still, I would have liked to take a more active part in my father's research, whose aims I understood fairly well. I remember being disappointed that he was only sporadically interested in my observations of life at school, for example. Now I understand why: They were peripheral to his own concerns, very small parts of the larger picture he had of Chanzeaux. Nevertheless, I imagine that in general—and depending on his (or her) children's ages and temperaments—an ethnographer would be well advised to pursue their interests seriously, not only because they may lead in unexpectedly valuable directions, but also because to do so may reinforce children's self-consciousness and hence their ability to cope with their strange new world.

Better than David, I also understood the problems of my father's research, particularly the fact that his assimilation, as well as ours, was a matter of delicate balances—of going to the Catholic school, for example, but not joining our classmates in prayer. One day, David took it into his head to stand at an upstairs window and shower handfuls of cap-gun caps on an eager little crowd of village children. Realizing what was up, I immediately joined the children, although I wanted no caps. Seeing all the children, my father began taking pictures, but then he realized why they were there. He stopped David's game, and reprimanded him. David says this was the first time he really understood how important it was for us to avoid the stereotype of "rich Americans." Of course, by local standards we were rich; but it occurs to me now that a deeper ambiguity lies embedded in this little episode, akin to my mother's lack of involvement in village life through my father. We all assumed we were just "living in France for a year," while my father alone studied the village. This freed us to involve ourselves severally as much as we wanted in village life. It might have strained us all to act more concertedly, but as a family we would probably have benefited from feeling that his project was all of ours—that we were all trying to understand the place, not merely live there.

I am not blaming my father. Family tension is built into doing fieldwork because of a crucial difference between an ethnographer's task and his family's experiences. (I say "his" more or less arbitrarily.) The ethnographer sets out to sample a wide range of local life. Establishing himself as a semi-outsider, he is judged by standards partly of his own contrivance; he maintains a critical distance by keeping a journal; and by necessity his understanding is often rather passive, based more on observation, reflection, and informants' statements than on active involvement in local activities. His wife and (especially) his children may understand local life less fully, but they must take a more active part in it, actually going shopping, doing homework, playing marbles, or whatever. Their daily routines and the standards by which they are judged are narrower, more rigidly set by local norms. They may not have the time, training, or inclination to keep a journal, although letters home or, in my case, cartooning, may serve a similar function. In short, the ethnographer's culture shock may be milder than his family's. Clearly he should understand this.

However, it is not so clear what balance should be struck between the requirements of doing one's fieldwork, and the conflicting emotional needs of one's family. Doing fieldwork demands an almost obsessive absorption in local life. As an ethnographer, I know few worse feelings than returning to the village after a few days away, and finding that it has all gone strange again. But the ethnographer's wife may need more vacations and distractions than he can afford, especially if, like my mother, she finds herself in a state of chronic culture shock, having to fit her routines to local patterns without being able to fit fully into local life. My mother particularly craved contact with fellow mothers from her own culture. She remembers how wonderful it was to read in a copy of one of Gesell's books on childhood that she had ordered from the American Library in Paris, that David and I were no more "impossible" than most American children our age.

Children's own needs are different. A child's inital shock at having to learn a new culture may be greater than an adult's, but it passes more quickly. Children may therefore need fewer distractions than their mother does—in fact, they may be upset by them.

Finally, my own experience suggests that the really disturbing thing for a child is being between cultures for very long. There is a family story about David in 1950. We had gone to Paris at Christmas, where we stayed at the Hôtel Lutétia. As we were driving back to Roussillon, David began crying, "I want to go home!" Where was home—Haverford? No. Michigan? No. Roussillon? No. Well, where did he mean? Wailing, he answered, "The Hôtel Lutétia!"

If I were taking children to the field, I should try to make as brief as possible the time between leaving one home and settling in a new one, between one school and another, one set of friends and the next. Yet, no matter how easily this transition is made, a family going into the field is bound to be drawn in on itself, so it may regain an importance it had been losing for a child. I think this is one reason I reacted so queerly to my grandfather's death: It came at a time when I had to depend particularly heavily on a family from which I was trying to disentangle myself, keeping ties with its individual members while beginning to reject it as a whole. My problems in this and other respects were of course partly a matter of my own awkward age and temperament; but I imagine it is generally true that an adolescent is more vulnerable in the field than a younger child, when a family he (or she) is growing away from looms suddenly out from the mists of childhood. More generally, I suspect that, not yet being so set in their ways, children of any age adapt to a new culture more easily than an adult can. Their immediate problems are with their parents, and only secondarily with the foreign culture through their parents' own more tortuous adaptation to it.

Postscript

I sampled another point of view in the early summer of 1985 when I took my nineteen-month-old daughter, Sarah, to the Faroe Islands for two and a half weeks. Gail could not come. We stayed in the village I first studied in 1971–1972, with a family I had lived with several times since. Our hosts, Kristian and Sólvá Nielsen, were eager to see their "American grandchild." I wanted to show Sarah off and do some quick research on the rapidly developing village fishery.

Our trip was interesting, I think, because it fell just short of being "in the field."

American friends and relations seemed impressed that I was so casually taking Sarah to such a remote place. (The Faroes, an internally self-governing, culturally distinct dependency of Denmark, lie roughly half-way between Norway and Iceland, some 300 kilometers west northwest of the Shetlands.) Gail and I did not think it so extraordinary. She had also stayed with the Nielsens, and the Faroes are less alien to me than, say, New Jersey, where Sarah's grandparents live. We would be staying with people who are exceptionally hospitable, even by Faroese standards, and Sólvá is a far more experienced parent than Gail or I will ever be. (The Nielsens have eight children, four of whom still lived at home.) Moreover, we knew that Sarah herself welcomes interruptions of her usual routine, is used to being looked after by people besides Gail and me, and has always enjoyed traveling and meeting new people. Indeed, as a traveler Sarah surpassed my most sanguine expectations. Except for a sodden episode on the final flight back to Boston, when I had run out of dry diapers, we enjoyed each other's company.

Obviously, a child's basic temperament is no less crucial than an adult's in going to the field. You have a taste for new scenes, or you don't—and even anthropologist adults vary greatly in this respect! Sarah's sensible, accommodating nature made our trip a success, the more so as she was not burdened by anxieties of my own about our destination.

Actually being in the field, however, is not the same thing as going there. It involves, I believe, a double accommodation to alien ways—a more intuitive, emotional apprehension that precedes and motivates a more intellectual one. It is difficult to sort out how and when these processes come into play for an older person. I have often suspected that the first two or three weeks are critical, for it is then that one's mental processes seem most out of phase with each other and, indeed, with reality. Ever since we moved to Chanzeaux in 1957, for example, I have noticed that it takes two or three weeks for my dreams to catch up with where I actually am. In the following weeks, increasingly detailed insights find conscious articulation, gradually forming a set of coherent propositions. But a small child is relatively free of the intellectual contrivances by which an adult thus makes sense of a new world. Sarah's reaction to two weeks' life with the Nielsens, then, may suggest something about the quality and timing of a person's intuitive accommodation to a strange culture.

I say this in hindsight. At the time, I had other preoccupations.

First, mindful of what I had written about my own childhood experiences in France, I was worried about the delay between leaving one home and settling in a new one. As well as the flights from Boston to New York to Copenhagen to the Faroes, and back again, our trip involved overnight stopovers in Copenhagen and, in the Faroes, going by car and ferry from the airport to the village, three islands away. On the way over, Sarah took the changes of scene in stride—even the final ferry ride, which Atli Nielsen described, with seafaring understatement, as "a bit raw." On the way back, she was uneasy. I had discovered, however, that she liked knowing where we were going. Reciting our itinerary became a favorite game. Sarah would fill in names of people, means of transportation, and notable features of our waypoints, and announce them happily as we met them: the boat, sleeping, *another* bus, the *big* plane, and finally "Mommy!"

Then there was the matter of language. Sarah, who had an active vocabulary of perhaps a hundred and fifty words, was clearly beginning to use language to organize her experience. However, seeing how brief our stay would be, I should not have worried that she would be upset by an alien linguistic environment. She seemed unconcerned by the strange talk, and her most pressing needs were perfectly understandable without language. Moreover, the Nielsens' teenage daughter, Randarsól, had learned a good deal of English from school and pop music, while Sólvá soon picked up Sarah's brand of English. The resulting *lingua franca* proved surprisingly flexible. After a few days in the village, I sailed over alone to Tórshavn, the capital, to do a day's library research. Sólvá, who was still nervous about communicating with an English-speaking child, armed herself with a tattered bilingual phrasebook dating from 1940. It was a comfort, she said, just to have the book at hand, despite the limited utility of such phrases as "I have forgotten a penholder." The crisis came when Sarah asked for me, and it passed when Sólvá answered, "Dada dook-dook-dook-dook bish." "Dook-dook-dook-dook" represented the sound of a boat's diesels. Sarah seemed satisfied to learn than I had gone fishing.

Sarah immediately took to some things about life with the Nielsens. She liked the food, which included such esoterica as fulmar eggs and aged mutton; she loved the novel custom of being tucked into a baby carriage while Sólvá or Randarsól ran errands or visited friends and relations around the village; and the high point of the day was bottle-feeding a lamb in the yard. Other things she merely tolerated, like having her diapers changed standing up. And she clung to some homegrown habits. She did not allow even Randarsól, her favorite, to put her to bed at night. More generally, Sarah never fully adjusted to the five hours' time difference between Boston and the Faroes. She was often sleepy, wakeful, or hungry at awkward times. This problem, which may have been exacerbated by the almost perpetual summer daylight in these latitudes, would naturally have resolved itself over time.

Other, more intractable problems seemed on the verge of emerging. First, there was the issue of childrearing norms. In about 1800, a resident Danish clergyman wrote, in words that still hold true, despite his disparaging tone:

> The system of child-rearing which [the Faroese] have adopted for their children is none of the best; for as the parents entertain too blind an affection for them, they are allowed too much of their will; and it is astonishing that the children, notwithstanding their neglected education, should grow up, become ingenious, active, and well-bred.[1]

Combined with the Nielsens' hospitality, grandparental affection, and, at first, a certain gingerliness in dealing with a foreign child, "the system of child-rearing" produced a notably indulgent atmosphere for Sarah. Her tendency to claim things ("Mine!") went unchecked, for example, creating occasional tension between her and the Nielsens' youngest child, who was obviously ambivalent about finding someone younger in residence. An indulgent parent myself, I felt unable to say no as often or as sharply as I would have done at home, or to let Sarah cry briefly if she awakened in the night. Only tiny infants are let cry in the Faroes and then only for a very short time; and instead of facing verbal prohibitions, Faroese children usually find their attention distracted or a forbidden object quietly put out of reach.

The incipient problem here was not so much that American and Faroese norms differ, but that, however admirble the outcome of Faroese childrearing practices is by American standards, it is achieved only over a number of years, by inculcating countervailing norms of emotional reserve, generosity, and cooperativeness among friends, and, particularly for girls, responsibility in looking after younger siblings and cousins. I do not know how Sarah would have reacted to *only* a year's experience as a guest child or as an only child in the Faroes. She already seemed to sense a discordance between American and Faroese indulgence. She was happy with me, or with Sólvá or Randarsól; but she got out of sorts at times of transition between us and when, as at mealtimes, she faced divided authority and expectations.

A second incipient problem was more mine than Sarah's. I had never really realized how time-consuming fieldwork is. Since Sarah was happy to be left with her "Faroese grandmother" for several hours at a stretch, I was free to interview people or spend the day in Tórshavn. However, I did not have time to write up my notes properly, or, perhaps more important, to wander about hoping for a productive conversation with someone—the sort of errancy that makes fieldwork immediately tedious and ultimately profitable. This made little difference during a short, repeat expedition with limited aims, when I did not want or need to participate fully in local activities. But in different circumstances, other arrangements would have been necessary.

Discovering these would doubtless have been a useful ethnographic exercise, probably leading to an unwelcome but nearly universal feature of doing fieldwork: having to change one's research topic in midstream. Being able to leave Sarah with Sólvá mitigated my oddity as a single, male parent; for, as I already knew, Faroese fathers have few responsibilities for child care or other domestic tasks. (When Sarah and I took walks together, it seemed nearly as singular in village eyes as my still-remembered habit of going out with Randarsól eleven years before.) I now realized that the pattern Sarah had fallen into with Sólvá is becoming more common in the village. Grandmothers are increasingly responsible for child care as the fishery has developed and more mothers can, or must, work in the processing plant. This is a development of some cultural consequence, in part because working mothers must sacrifice some of a woman's traditionally central, prestigious status as mistress of the home. If our stay had been longer, I would have forsaken the dock and the fishing fleet to follow Sarah into the no-less-changing realm of domestic arrangements.

Finally, there is what I think of as the "three-week-syndrome." Robert Redfield comments, in a passage worth quoting at length, that

> the first impressions of any human community are often clear and—at the moment—convincing. The time to write a book about the national character of a people other than one's own is in the first weeks of the first acquaintance with them. Never again does one have so vivid and compelling an impression of them.
>
> If one does not write that book it may be because a certain amount of scientific training and sense of responsibility prevent one. And one knows that . . . one's first impressions give way to understanding based upon a deeper knowledge of particular fact. After knowing the whole as one thing, intuitively, one begins to know particular things, critically, and, it seems, less surely. . . . The intuitive apprehension of wholes does not cease; but now it is limited and controlled by particular knowledge subjected to testing and proof.[2]

In my own experience, the turning point comes in about three weeks, when "there" seems to become "here"—when one seems to reach an intuitive acceptance of a whole way of life that none-theless remains incomprehensible in detail. What Redfield fails to add, of course, is that the continuing process of detailed investigation, note taking, and testing one's intuitions is, for the field-worker, not only a scientific necessity but also a way of working out the emotional problems of immersion in an alien culture. Moreover, this way is closed to children too young to keep a journal, write letters home, or, as I did in Chanzeaux, draw car-toons or take long, solitary walks.

Near the end of our stay, Sarah did an interesting thing. For two weeks, she showed little or no concern about the world we had left behind. During our last few days in the village, however, a favorite occupation became sitting quietly with me and going over some pictures I had brought along. She would tell what they showed—"Mommy," "the car," "the house," her playmates—and listen attentively as I spun vignettes of daily life in Massachusetts. Was she trying not to forget the shape of old routines as she began to sense the shape of new ones? I suspect so, for her interest in our return itinerary also arose during these last few days, suggesting that she was measuring the distance between two worlds. We left, I think, just before the three-week syndome took effect. Dealing with it may be among one's most serious responsibilities as a parent in the field.

Having stopped just short of being in the field, Sarah and I reverted to being mere travelers, homeward bound. Wandering Copenhagen's busy streets on our last night abroad, we sampled the tourist's pleasure of being neither here nor there, without the routines that regulate the existence of children and adults alike. She soon forgot almost everything about the Faroes except "the boat." A year later, she still remembered Copenhagen, however. Episodes of transition apparently stick most vividly in her mind, as they also do in mine in recalling Chanzeaux and (despite volumes of assiduous notes) my other experiences in the field.

Notes

1. Jørgen Landt, *A Description of the Feroe Islands . . . translated from the Danish* (London: Hurst, Rees, and Orne, 1810), p. 388.

2. Robert Redfield, "The Little Community," in *The Little Community/Peasant Society and Culture* (Chicago: Chicago University Press, 1960), p. 18.

MORTON KLASS AND
SHEILA SOLOMON KLASS

5 Birthing in the Bush: Participant Observation in Trinidad

In the beginning of July 1957, we arrived on the island of Trinidad, then part of the British West Indies. We were a childless married couple. When we departed, at the end of June 1958, we were a family: Our eldest daughter had been born in April 1958 while we were living in an East Indian village, conducting fieldwork among descendants of immigrants from India.

One of us (Morton Klass) is a professional anthropologist. The data collected, with Sheila's assistance, contributed to his doctoral dissertation, to numerous scholarly articles, and to a book based on the dissertation: *East Indians in Trinidad: A Study of Cultural Persistence.* [1] Sheila Solomon Klass is a professional writer. In the field, she assisted her husband, but she also wrote a novel, *Come Back on Monday,* [2] and kept a writer's journal—in addition, of course, to having a baby. Her observations and experiences in Trinidad were ultimately published as a memoir: *Everyone in This House Makes Babies*.[3]

This essay, then, reflects the views and notes of the two of us. It includes extracts from our published works and reflections from our separate journals and notes, and from our joint and separate memories.

To provide a degree of anonymic protection for the people among whom we lived, the name of the village was changed in our published works, and to avoid any possible confusion between an anthropological community study and literary memoir, we each chose a different fictitious name for the village: *Amity* in the writings of Morton, and *Arcady* in Sheila's memoir. Herewith are examples of our different perspectives and writing styles:

> Almost from the first, my attention was directed toward the village I have called "Amity." This village was by no means a unique phenomenon, but it provided a relatively rare—and for my purposes ideal—opportunity to study all aspects of rural East Indian life within the physical bounds of one community. Everything to be observed in Amity could be observed elsewhere, in other East Indian villages, but in one case the people of the particular village had no ricefields to cultivate and in another they had no temple, and so on. In Amity, there was a full round of life.[4]

> Arcady is a pocket in a vast apron of sugar cane. Once we left the houses of the market town of Chaguanas behind us, the road had ribboned for miles between featureless, ten-foot high rows of Trinidad's ubiquitous crop. Now palm trees are as romantic as they're painted, the brilliant red flowers of the *immortelle* tree are glorious, and cocoa in the pod is unexpectedly fragrant, but sugar cane, I insist, is nothing but overgrown crab grass. It surrounds the village on the three sides (with the swamp on the fourth), and it surrounds the lives of the villagers on all sides. It is the source of all

their tragedy as well. I grew to hate and fear those waving, rustling green leaves and stalks.[5]

The house in which we lived for our entire stay was of wood with a galvanized iron roof. Like most East Indian houses at the time, it was raised, on concrete pillars, some six feet off the ground. It consisted essentially of two large rooms (living quarters) and one smaller one serving as the kitchen, with an external drainboard on the window as its sole convenience. Windows were open and unprotected by screens, although there were external shutters to protect against heavy rains and possibly against burglars. The one set of stairs led up to an open, though roofed, verandah.

The house was set in the rear of the schoolyard, providing an excellent view of the center of the village, although very little privacy for us. Our toilet facilities consisted of an outhouse in the schoolyard, a short distance from our house. It was labeled GIRLS in foot-high white letters painted on its outer wall, but, happily, it was no longer used by the school. Its wooden door, an amenity belonging to the previous tenant, had been carried off by him as part of the furniture. An hour after our arrival, for one dollar, we became owners of a custom-made latrine door. Humble as that latrine undoubtedly was, it figures in this narrative.

Potable water was piped from the main line to a point directly under our house. Unfortunately, pressure was generally low, and so we, like our neighbors, had to fill our water barrels during the evening hours when there was a flow to tap. Electricity had preceded us to the village by only a few years but was now available for lighting and even for a radio. We had a car (an ancient Austin) parked under our house, but the nearest telephone was in the nearest town, some four miles away.

We were both approaching thirty years of age when we went into the field; we had been married for some four years and very much wanted children, but with Morton in graduate school and Sheila working, parenting had not seemed advisable. We both liked Trinidad and almost immediately felt at home on the island and in the village. There were certainly lacks and discomforts, but graduate students in the United States are hardly accustomed to luxury; in Trinidad, Sheila was at leisure for the first time, and we could even afford the services of a young woman to help us with housework.

We began to think seriously of having a child. A consultation with a competent Trinidad doctor (who was also a good friend) reassured us about Sheila's health and about the general feasibility of our plan. By September, we knew that Sheila was indeed pregnant.

It was, of course, some months before Sheila's interesting condition became apparent to the villagers. For people who customarily married in their mid-teens and who not uncommonly were grandparents in their early thirties, we could only be viewed as a childless and comparatively elderly couple. The title of Sheila's book reflects the awe expressed by our neighbors at our achievement and the common belief that it was attributable solely to some miraculous quality of the house in which we resided.

Nevertheless, pregnancy was a common enough event in the village. Women who were pregnant casually loosened the waists of their dresses month by month, until at the end of the pregnancy the dresses were completely unhooked and unzipped at the waist.

Sheila searched Port-of-Spain shops for some simple, American-style maternity clothes. She found the prices prohibitive and the styles—involving silk, lace, embroidery, ruching—inappropriate for cold-water washing. So she took an old blouse pattern, bought some pretty cotton printed cloth, and set out to make herself some loose, yoked, sleeveless tops. After the blouses, she planned to make several solid-color cotton wraparound skirts.

CHAPTER 1: Justine and Steve with friends (above); Justine working at the post office (below); Justine and Steve with the town butcher in Jamaica (previous page).

CHAPTER 2: Tom in the Amazon.

CHAPTER 3: Simeon joined in numerous local activities in rural South India. In the facing near picture he is "dancing chō-chō, the dance of the Halakke Gowdas during Holi. He used to go to all the rehearsals, and was delighted when one day they dressed him up and asked him to dance with them."

CHAPTER 4: Jonathan and David during morning prayers at school: "I look disgruntled because my father seemed so worried about the click of the camera"; "scrambling for the candies and small change thrown to children after a baptism." Taken in Chanzeaux, France, 1957–58 by Laurence Wylie.

CHAPTER 5: Sheila Klass (below) holding her Trinidad-born baby, Perri, at the local weekly service at the Hindu Temple to Shiva; men and women sit on separate sides.

CHAPTER 6: Baby J.P. and Jackie, each with friends in Jamaica.

CHAPTER 7: Lisa and Luke, the two eldest, outside their first house in Escobines, Spain; "Lisa stands in studied disregard of the girls who—attracted by the novelty of our family—often assembled in the portal of the house across the street. In Sunday best they improvised this chorus line for us. While Luke is frankly dazzled by them, they succeeded only on subsequent visits in drawing Lisa into the vitality of their street life."

CHAPTER 9: Sarah, Nathanael, and a next-door neighbor in Brazil; Nathanael "surrounded"; Nate at grave of Chicken George (counterclockwise from left). Photos by Jennifer Hughes.

CHAPTER 10: "Josina and her pal Mohammed, the son of our friend Hassan Bodani, in Khartoum, Sudan." Photo courtesy of Bruce Gilbert, Rhode Island College.

Her sewing the blouses by hand intrigued and amused the village women. Hand sewing, they felt strongly, was only for those too poor to afford machine-made clothing; handwork did not make respectable clothing. The conversation was repeated so often that Sheila finally succumbed to having her skirts sewn by a local seamstress on her machine. This pleased our neighbors greatly.

A number of the women came by to caution Sheila about things to avoid during pregnancy: She must not sit or lie down during an eclipse, or the baby would be born bowlegged; she must not use knife, scissors, or other sharp implements, or the baby might be injured; she must not recline in a hammock, or it would be difficult for the baby to emerge; she must not go out evenings with her head uncovered, or she would feel the ill effects of the "falling" dew.

There were many positive suggestions as well. She was given a gift of cow's colostrum (first milk), which would make her own milk rich, and pounds of okra, which women swore by as beneficial in pregnancy. Daily doses of castor oil were advocated by some, as was squatting (although *never* in front of a door). "Sleep with your husband as much as you can," a forthright village woman advised. "It opens the passages and makes the birth easier." She finished off with a bit of extra encouragement: "Don't be afraid. You no go die."[6]

Although Sheila was teased once, if gently, on the occasion of a woman's ribald party that customarily follows the birth of a baby ("Who put that in your belly?"), no comment was made to Morton about his wife's condition by any of the men before the child was born. We were aware of our neighbors' interest, but for the most part they expressed it circuitously, as in efforts to predict the sex of the unborn child. Most of the predictions were made by women, but at least one man (to our knowledge) took a stab at it. The telltale signals varied from prognosticator to prognosticator, but the overwhelming majority were convinced it would be a boy. Sheila's reaction:

> Here were a poor, depressed people who needed sons to work on the land, sons to care for them in their old age, sons to bring daughters-in-law into the house to do the work. When they had daughters, they had to raise them carefully, guard their chastity, marry them off in expensive weddings—and then the girls went to their grooms' villages to live and were not any help to their aging parents. Our neighbors valued boy children, and, since they were fond of us, they wished us the greater joy of a son.[7]

As the foregoing indicates, particular kinds of data were being released to us—certain insights were being arrived at by us—primarily because Sheila was pregnant. That is, had we remained childless, we would have learned less, or would have gathered the data with much more difficulty. We are not referring simply to advice on diet or on avoidances for pregnant women; the data in Morton's book on midwifery were offered freely to Sheila *because* she was pregnant: Midwifery "is considered an 'unclean' occupation. . . . A woman can learn the techniques of the profession only *after* she has had a baby herself. Before that, she is considered too 'stupid.' "[8]

Sheila, as a mother-to-be, was deemed no longer "stupid." She found the midwife (fictitiously referred to as "Mistress Ramlogan") informative and loquacious:

> Mistress Ramlogan proceeded to describe her apprenticeship in midwifery. It began with the study of anatomy with—and on—her mother-in-law. This lady had stripped off her clothes and, pointing to the "veins" in her arms and legs, had demonstrated how they ran into the body, their connecting places and weak spots. Through this laboratory method, her students had learned how to "place veins back" by rubbing.

> For example, when a pregnant woman falls and "twists" a
> vein out of place (has pain), Mistress Ramlogan readjusts that
> vein by massage. She also "rubs" strained backs, arms and
> ankles.
>   She worked as her mother-in-law's assistant until the older
> woman died, then she inherited the practice.[9]

Why did she learn the practice from her mother-in-law and not
from her own mother? Because, as the midwife explained, "She
cannot teach her own daughters the trade *before* they are married,
and once they are married they live too far away.[10]

This practice of mother-in-law to daughter-in-law inheritance
Morton labeled *socrulineal* inheritance, a variety little studied in
the anthropological literature.[11] One is suddenly tempted to inquire: Is there so little reference to the phenomenon because it is
indeed so rare, or does the paucity of anthropological comment
reflect the fact that there have not been many pregnant fieldworkers?

In any event, Sheila was pregnant. She was also fortunate in
that her pregnancy was comparatively easy and fairly uneventful.
Most fortunately, we had the counsel, when it was needed, of a
particularly competent doctor—one, for example, who resolutely
refused to prescribe thalidomide for his pregnant patients, despite all the encomiums of the pharmaceutical companies. As he
told us years later, he had no reason at the time to be suspicious;
he simply could not bring himself to try new substances on pregnant women.

At first, Sheila considered having the baby in the village with
the aid of the midwife, but she flinched at some of the latter's
practices. No matter how difficult the birth, for example, the
midwife never sent for the doctor unless the baby was dead.

> "What do you do if a woman is in very great pain during
> labor?" I asked. "Do you give her something?"

> "I buy two aspirins and give it to her," Mistress Ramlogan
> replied without hesitation. The wonders of anesthesia were
> not unknown to her.
> "Good-bye," I said, "and thank you."[12]

We were lucky, too, in finding a clean and well-appointed
nursing home in the town of Tunapuna, not too far away. It was
run by an East Indian husband and wife, both doctors, and although it lacked the cachet of some of the urban, "upper-class"
establishments, Sheila was delighted from the first visit with the
staff, the ambience, and the procedures. This nursing home consisted of a group of dispersed white cottages hidden among the
poinsettia, orange-red flamboyants, and lush fruit trees: mangoes, sapodillas, fig bananas, and rosy cashew fruits. The doctors'
family lived in the slightly larger house; the other buildings were
the examination–receiving cottage, the labor rooms and patients'
quarters, and the offices. There were accommodations for a max-
imum of fifteen patients.

According to our best estimate, the baby was due around the
end of April. We hoped, somewhat playfully, that the arrival
would coincide with that of the new West Indian Federation—
April 26—but that day came and went without precipitating
any newcomers into our family. Just as well, perhaps, since the
Federation had a very short life indeed before it broke up and its
components became such independent states as Trinidad and To-
bago, Jamaica, and Barbados.

In any case, our offspring waited until late in the day on April
29:

> It was five o'clock. I dressed myself in the loose blouse and
> the new green wrap-around skirt I had sewed for the journeys
> to and from [the] Nursing Home. I added my toothbrush to
> the long packed suitcase and snapped it shut. While I was
> working, I became aware of loud clatter outside. I peered

out. Our porch was crowded with married women! Whether clairvoyance or some occult signal system was responsible, I never learned. All I do know is that fifteen minutes after I realized that labor had begun, the whole village knew. Our closest female neighbors were already comfortably ensconced on our gallery. Small groups of women were assembling on the road near the standpipe and the school. I felt rather like the dilatory grand marshall of a parade. [13]

Sheila's first assumption was that the women had arrived just to keep her company until Morton arrived with transportation to the nursing home. She soon discovered that simple companionship was by no means all they had in mind. They were there to protect her—as they would any woman about to have her first baby—from her ignorance of the pitfalls that might lie in her path. For example, when Sheila experienced a sudden urgent need to visit the outhouse,

I rose, excused myself and started down the steps. Mrs. Bhim was on her feet instantly.
"Where are you going, gel?"
"I'll be right back."
"No." She held my arm. "Don't worry with that. Use a 'tensil. Hear me! Use a 'tensil."
"Please, Mistress Bhim, wait for me on the gallery. Sit down and wait. I'll be right back."
"No. Are you studying to have a baby in there? Use a 'tensil. [14]

Under the watchful eyes of the women, Sheila was kept safe until Morton arrived with the car. The trip to the nursing home was uneventful, and Sheila was fortunate once again: Despite her age, the birth was swift and relatively easy. In the opinion of the attending obstetricians, dilation was satisfactory, and no episiotomy was necessary; and so none was performed. Two years later, giving birth in an American hospital where episiotomies were routinely performed on every mother, Sheila remembered the Tunapuna nursing home with great wistfulness.

There was indeed a relaxed quality—a human quality—to the nursing home that may simply be beyond the capacity of a large American hospital. We were lucky, for example, because at the time of Sheila's arrival there happened to be comparatively few women in residence. Despite all the efforts of the doctors to predict times of birth and therefore space the arrival of their patients, there were inevitably days when they were deluged with women giving birth; on other days, like the one on which we arrived, the place was half empty. The staff urged Morton to spend the night in one of the empty rooms, adjacent to that of Sheila, and so the three of us spent our first evening together: Sheila in bed, Morton sitting by her side, and our daughter sleeping in a basket at the foot of the bed, with only a tiny drop of vermix in her ear to remind us of her recent arrival. And in the morning, Morton, like Sheila, was awakened in his bed by the arrival of a most noninstitutional breakfast.

After breakfast, Morton returned to the village in a taxi driven by one of the village men. The driver inquired as to Sheila's health and then as to the sex of the baby. When told that it was a girl, he was silent for a moment, then seemed to change the subject. He began to discuss his own children, and, as Morton noted in his field journal: "He told me he was surprised to find he liked his little girl best of his two children (she was more 'true').

We had known, of course, of the preference of the East Indian villagers for sons, and one may assume that we would have learned of this even if Sheila had never been pregnant. There were, however, subtleties of insight on the matter that did come with the birth of our daughter. Many of our village friends, like the taxi driver just cited, tried to comfort us for what they perceived as our disappointment. One old lady said to Morton,

"Thank God, thank God—what is it, a boy?" When he told her the baby was a girl, she said, "Well, we must thank God for whatever He gives us!" Nevertheless, many men offered, as their form of comfort, the interesting view that while sons were an economic necessity for a family, daughters were a pleasure to a *father*.

In a few days, Sheila returned to the village with the baby, and with the bill for the childbirth and all attendant costs: $60 (U.S.). We sent the bill on to Blue Cross for reimbursement.

Many of Sheila's women friends came to visit her, bringing gifts for the baby, particularly amulets for protection against the *maljeu*—the Creole word used by East Indians, as well as West Indians, for the "evil eye." Again, our understanding was deepened, as for example when we discovered the reason why one old woman, with whom Sheila had been especially friendly, never came to visit her in those first days following the birth. Morton met the woman one morning in the street, and she inquired after Sheila and the baby. He suggested that she come and visit. The woman hesitated, then pointed out that it might not be advisable. She herself was barren, and people believed that, whatever the conscious feelings of childless women, their deep grief and envy could be dangerous to newborn infants, and, particularly, could convey the dreaded *maljeu*. A passage in Morton's book reflects insights and information gathered in this conversation, as well as at other times:

> East Indian magic tends to be protective and remedial rather
> than malevolent. Although it is believed that there are
> Indians capable of performing "bad" magic intentionally,
> most misfortunes are ascribed to error rather than to intent.
> Thus, there is a prevailing fear of the "maljeu," or evil
> eye . . . but it is rarely said that the "maljeu" is given
> intentionally. The "maljeu" can be given by overly effusive
> compliments to a child by a person who means no harm.

> Children are considered to be particularly susceptible to the "maljeu," and are required to wear a protective string about the waist. Certain people are considered particularly capable of giving a "maljeu," whether they wish to or not. Barren women are not permitted to view newborn children for fear that their grief and envy at not having children of their own will injure the infant. [15]

The village women's perception of Sheila as a mature adult began with their awareness of her pregnancy. After the actual birth, the changes that occurred in her relationships with the women were therefore subtle rather than dramatic. In Morton's case, however, there were sharp changes in the behavior of certain men, particularly older men, immediately attendant on the birth of the child. One older man, for example, who had always been polite but reserved, greeted Morton a few days after the birth in a startlingly relaxed and familiar way. After a pleasant conversation, Morton expressed his enjoyment of the meeting, indicating his regret that they had never had a long and intimate conversation before. The older man smiled and explained that he viewed Morton as a "family man" now, someone like himself.

Another, younger, man inquired how it "felt" to be a new father, then began to reminisce about the birth of his own first child. He volunteered the information (for the first time) that he had actually been carrying on an affair with another woman while his wife was pregnant but that the sight of his first child changed all that. He realized then, he said, that he was a father as well as a husband and that he had responsibilities that he must not avoid. He said that he never saw the other woman again.

It should not be assumed that the arrival of the baby went off with fairytale ease. We were fortunate in many respects, but there were indeed problems. One of the most serious was that Sheila found that she was not able to nurse the baby, as she had planned, and that it would be necessary to introduce the baby to a bottle and to prepared formulas. This was frightening because we were very aware that in the Trinidad countryside the mortality rate for bottle-fed babies was far greater than it was for those who were breastfed.

Our doctor undertook to calm our fears. He assured us that we would have no problem if we followed his instructions meticulously. He showed us how he wanted the bottles and nipples sterilized, how the formula was to be prepared, and how all was to be assembled and stored. He imposed two strict rules: First, only one of us was to assume full responsibility for the entire procedure so that there could be no possibility of confusion about who had done, or was to do, what. Since Sheila was busy enough with the baby, Morton took on this task. Second, he insisted that if, at any point in the proceedings, uncertainty developed—Had Morton taken his eye off the bottle? Could a fly have settled, even momentarily, on an unwatched nipple?—then the entire process was to be aborted and begun anew.

The procedures were followed religiously, and the baby thrived, but Morton became poignantly aware of the reasons why East Indian women had such difficulty in following the same instructions, with such terrible consequences. To destroy a batch of formula and start anew was for us an inconvenience, a waste of time. Reboiling bottles and nipples could also be an inconvenience, but again only a minor one. For a poor East Indian woman, however— the wife of an impoverished cane laborer, for example—the cost in formula and fuel was a serious matter. Yet such a woman had many more distractions. There were other children demanding attention, there was food on the stove, and so on. Furthermore, her understanding of the dangers, despite all warnings, was inevitably limited. How much damage could one tiny fly do? she might ask herself, rubbing the nipple with her finger before putting it in the baby's mouth. Was it really necessary to throw out expensive formula and set a pot of water to boiling? The problem is not so much that the village woman may be ignorant, and it is certainly not that she lacks affection for her child; the problem derives from circumstances that conspire to make successful bottle feeding almost an impossibility.

So we had the good fortune to return home with a healthy child, much to the astonishment of the doctor in New York who examined her on our arrival home. Would we do it again? The opportunity, fortunately or unfortunately, never arose. We did go back into the field a few years later, this time to India, with two small children, and we had other experiences to contend with, including the bite of a rabid dog. But that is clearly another story!

Notes

1. Morton Klass, *East Indians in Trinidad: A Study of Cultural Persistence* (New York: Columbia University Press, 1961).
2. Sheila Solomon Klass, *Come Back on Monday* (New York: Abelard-Schuman, 1960).
3. Sheila Solomon Klass, *Everyone in This House Makes Babies* (New York: Doubleday, 1964).
4. M. Klass, *East Indians in Trinidad,* pp. xx–xxi.
5. S. Klass, *Everyone in This House,* p. 11.
6. Ibid., pp. 114–118.
7. Ibid., p. 113.
8. M. Klass, *East Indians in Trinidad,* p. 136.
9. S. Klass, *Everyone in This House,* p. 106.
10. M. Klass, *East Indians in Trinidad,* p. 136.

11. Ibid.

12. S. Klass, *Everyone in This House,* p. 111.

13. Ibid., p. 149.

14. Ibid., p. 150.

15. M. Klass, *East Indians in Trinidad,* pp. 181–182.

MELANIE DREHER

6   Three Children in Rural Jamaica

In June 1978 I left my husband in a comfortable Connecticut suburb and set off with three young children to conduct fieldwork in rural Jamaica. Jackie was seven at the time, Colby four, and J.P. only nine months.

We have one of those "his–hers–ours" families. Jackie is my husband's daughter from a first marriage, Colby is mine, and J.P. is a joint effort. I had been awarded a postdoctoral research fellowship by the National Institute on Drug Abuse to study childhood cannabis use in rural Jamaica. This project was the outgrowth of a study I had conducted five years earlier that examined the relationship between cannabis use and the performance of work among agriculturalists. During that research I found, serendipitously, that many parents gave their children cannabis, or *ganja,* in the form of tea or medicinal tonics in order to make them stronger, brighter, and healthier. The goal of this research was to describe the values and behaviors that surround the use of cannabis by children and test some of the folk beliefs commonly associated with this practice.

We had been to Jamaica as a family in January of that year while I carried out the pilot phase of the research. The baby, of course, was too young to remember, but Jackie and Colby had had a wonderful time, spending long days on tourist beaches with their father and their aunt (his sister, who had come along to help with the baby). This trip would be different. They would be confined largely to the village, which was several miles from a beach, and while the tropical weather had come as a relief from the January snows of Hartford, the heat in July and August, particularly in this area of Jamaica, was unrelenting. They would have to fit in with Jamaican children, which required a sensitivity to the Jamaican patois—certainly not a new language but a dialect not, at first, easily understood. Finally, their father would not be there except for a week toward the end of the trip, and they would be in the care of a Jamaican nanny whom we had not yet met.

I had given them little preparation for what it would be like. I did insist that they leave all their toys home and bring only things that could be shared with other children. There was considerable weeping and wailing and gnashing of teeth, and they were incredulous that Fisher-Price was not a part of daily life in all corners of the world. I remained resolute, however, and they eventually gave up their pleas.

In some respects, I too was poorly prepared for what lay ahead of us. I love an adventure, was not sure what to expect, and therefore decided that I would start worrying when I got there, which is exactly what I did. The magnitude of the task ahead of me first became apparent when we arrived at Norman Manley Airport in Kingston, and I had to figure out the logistics of getting through Customs, picking up the rented car, and getting our belongings out to the loading area. This was not a trivial matter; in addition to the usual accouterments of fieldwork—clothing, camera, typewriter—I now had a Snuggli carrier, umbrella stroller, portacrib, Ring-Ding walker, and a vast supply of diapers, Pampers, bottles, and nipples. I hated to leave three little children sitting on a curb in a strange airport, but transporting kids and things all over the airport seemed equally unthinkable. After a hasty appraisal of their mental and physical status, I decided to let Jackie and Colby stay with the luggage at the pickup area, while J.P. and I (now making a conscious effort to remain calm) went to get the car. Miraculously, the whole procedure took only five minutes. I picked up the car, loaded the kids and baggage into it, and we were on our way.

It was at that critical moment in the airport that I suddenly realized that I was all alone with three small children in another culture. I felt depressed and worried. My husband, Joe, had always taken an active role in raising our children, and now, when I needed him most, he was not there. Although I prided myself on being independent, self-sufficient, how would I be able to make all these decisions by myself? I suppressed the urge to ask myself, "What ON EARTH have I done?" and settled for an incipient migraine instead. The two-hour ride to Dover (a fictitious name) was hot and dusty, and the traffic and driving conditions seemed much worse than I remembered. The children's spirit of adventure also was quickly replaced by more basic needs, such as hunger, thirst, fatigue, and the need to go to the bathroom or have a diaper changed.

Dover is a large, densely populated community comprising several smaller neighborhoods, located on the parameters of a sugar estate. It was not a new field site for me, being one of the settings where I had conducted my dissertation research several years earlier. I had made arrangements to stay for the first few days with some old friends, Ron and Merle Dixon. I had known

Ron since 1972 when he was in senior management in the sugar estate I studied. We became friends when we discovered that we had the same birthday, and have remained friends ever since. Warm and gracious hosts, they had taken time off work to be home for our arrival. Jackie and Colby readily accepted Merle's offer of a cold drink but shyly and rather humorlessly backed off from Ron's affectionate teasing, preferring, instead, to sit on the floor and stare at the television. Embarrassed, I tried to coax them a little, while making some feeble attempts to explain to Ron about the marathon day we had had so far.

In the meantime, Merle Dixon, who is a fabulous cook, prepared a delicious dinner replete with Jamaican specialties. J.P. giggled and drooled and sampled everything. Jackie and Colby refused to eat and asked to be excused so that they could go to bed—an extraordinary request for my children. Actually, I was relieved. I had wanted to impress Merle and Ron with how sophisticated, polite, and charming my children could be. Instead, they neglected to say please and thank you, complained about the food, and unceremoniously rejected any attempts to cheer them up. I had never seen them quite so awful and found it painfully disconcerting.

By this time, I had a searing headache and gladly agreed to Ron's suggestion that I too go to bed early. We set up the baby's crib and he fell asleep at once. I *tried* to sleep, but was now consumed with thoughts of all the things I had to do in the next few days, not least of which was finding a place to live. The *good* news was that the Dixons had lined up a friend of theirs from Kingston to be our housekeeper. Best of all, she had been a maid at a northern coastal resort and had worked regularly with American families. Although I had hoped for someone from the area, who could facilitate the children's introduction to the community, in retrospect, Minna was a blessing. As a stranger to Dover, her commitment was totally to me and the children, and she carefully monitored everyone and everything entering and leaving the house.

The next morning was more of the same. Ackee and salt fish were set before Jackie and Colby, who had never seen anything more exotic than a poached egg for breakfast. With an agonizing mixture of consternation and compassion, I watched them pick at the ackee and swallow, with difficulty, a fried ripe plantain. Later, they confided that they had thought that the ackee was a scrambled egg and simply were not prepared for the admittedly unusual taste of Jamaica's national dish. Frankly, my eagerness to procure a house for us was not the only reason that I was happy to leave the children behind that morning.

Relying on old friends, I found a house within a matter of a few hours. Coincidentally, and happily, it was next door to the one in which I had lived five years earlier; familiar neighbors would ease the adjustment process and provide a smoother entry for me and the children. The house was located in a government "scheme," or development, called Top House, constructed with the intention of providing housing for low- to moderate-income families, which were, in fact, sold to supporters of the incumbent party for investment. The owner of the house was not occupying it; after a bad experience with previous tenants, the owner had decided not to rent the house again and had moved out all the furniture. After a good deal of persuasion, which included paying about four times the normal rent and transporting all the furniture back and forth, she agreed to let us have the house for the summer. It consisted of a living room, two bedrooms, a kitchen, and a bath, the entire square footage of which was less than my living room at home. But it had running water and electricity. I negotiated a refrigerator from a neighbor who had two—one for her personal use and one for her apparently thriving "suck-suck" (the Jamaican version of a popsicle) business. She agreed to rent the refrigerator to me for the amount she ordinarily would have earned selling suck-suck over a two-month period. This convinced me that if I wanted to send my kids to college, I should start selling suck-suck. Looking back, I am sure that we would have managed without a refrigerator, but at the time I was concerned about having fresh milk on hand and the complications of preserving meat, which could be procured only once a week.

I was exhilarated by accomplishing all this in one morning and by the warm reception and generously offered assistance from my old friends at Top House. When I got back to the Dixons, Minna had arrived and was sitting at the table with Jackie and Colby and J.P. while they drank milk and ate bread and butter with jam. It was love at first sight. She was gentle, patient, and had a wonderful sense of humor. During the morning, she had enlisted Jackie's help in feeding and dressing J.P., making her feel enormously important. She had also taken Colby to the back shed to see the Dixon dog's new puppies. I breathed a sigh of relief; the worst seemed to be over.

That evening, we had a much more pleasant dinner. Colby was full of stories about the puppies and thrilled when Ron said he could have one of them to raise while he was in Jamaica. Jackie had taken over the care of the Dixons' two-year-old daughter and was basking in all the compliments about her babysitting abilities. Again, however, they both picked at their food and asked to be excused from the table before the rest of us had finished. Jackie, in particular, complained that her stomach hurt and continued the modified hunger strike that she had initiated the evening before. I tried not to show a great deal of concern; stomachaches were Jackie's usual reaction to stress, and I was confident that eventually she would get hungry and eat.

The next day, we left the Dixon household and became the newest residents of Top House. The size of the house did not seem to bother Jackie or Colby, and they were delighted to see that Dover was teeming with children. Minna and I quickly set about sweeping up the house and cleaning the windows and toilets and sinks until we nearly succumbed to the fumes of disinfectant. We were assisted in our efforts by Bonnie Brown, a cane cutter who had showed up at my door years before, asking if he could have $10. I told him I would give him the money if he would plant some flowers for me. He agreed, and when I came home the next night, he had planted some beautiful flowers, but only on the right-hand side of the house. I complimented him for his work, but told him that I had also wanted some flowers on the left side of the house. When I came in the next evening, he had planted flowers on the right-hand side of the house to the left of mine! I knew then that I was dealing with a very unusual person. I never did get flowers on the left side of my house, but Bonnie came faithfully every day to cut the grass with his machete, or to wash the car. Now, it was as though the five years had never elapsed. He came every day to do whatever needed to be done. And, even more important, his presence provided a father figure for the children, whom he delighted by catching mice by their tails with his bare hands.

Our furniture included a dining-room table and three chairs, two armless "armchairs," two dressers, and two double beds. I had brought bedding and towels—old ones that I was prepared to leave behind—and we purchased some kitchen utensils and plastic dishes and cups. I felt that the two older children might feel uncomfortable sleeping with someone whom they did not know, so I shared my room with them and put the portacrib in Minna's room; if J.P. woke up at night, she could attend to him without waking the other children. Although I knew from our earlier trip in January that Minna would disapprove of J.P.'s sleeping alone in his own little bed, she never said anything about it. I assumed she had resigned herself to this feature of American childrearing until one night after we had been there about two weeks. I was the last one awake and went in to make sure that the mosquito net was secure on J.P.'s crib. When I entered the room, I found the two of them comfortably snuggled up in Minna's bed. They both seemed happy with the arrangement and remained so throughout our trip.

At first, Jackie and Colby spent a lot of their time playing with their new puppy while gradually meeting the neighborhood children. Jackie still refused to eat, however, and continued to complain about the pain in her stomach. Already slender, after five days of not eating, her cheekbones began to stand out like little points on her face. On the sixth day, I decided I had better do something, so I took her into Kingston where an old friend had made arrangements for her to see a very conservative and sensible elderly physician. I think now that my handling of the problem was complicated by the fact that I am not Jackie's real mother. I suspected that she was homesick and missed her mother and father, but was not sure what to do about it. I was less willing than I would have been with my boys to take a stand and wait until she finally stopped complaining and started eating. After carefully examining her, the doctor told me he could find nothing wrong; wisely, however, he gave us a prescription, which assured Jackie that, whatever was the matter, it was accessible to medical intervention. Now that I knew that there was nothing physically wrong, I decided to use another tactic. In a slightly tear-filled voice, I related to Jackie how difficult the past five days had been for me also—particularly without her daddy—and that I was relying on her, as the oldest, to help us get over these rough times. I am sure that, from Jackie's perspective, this was a startling admission, since I ordinarily prefer to deal with children from a position of strength. Predictably, she rose to the occasion and promised her support. While we waited for the prescription to be filled, we went to the Kingston Sheraton for lunch. I am not sure whether it was the attention of a physician or my psychological appeal or simply the familiar environment of an American hotel (or perhaps all three), but she cheerfully consumed a giant tuna-fish sandwich—her favorite food—and two chocolate milk-shakes. She was fine for the rest of the trip. She never really developed an enthusiasm for Jamaican food, but the pain disappeared with only a single dose of medicine, and her disposition improved dramatically.

Several weeks later, when I was in a Kingston shopping center buying some batteries for my tape recorder, I noticed a fancy delicatessen. I had never seen one in Jamaica before and decided to investigate. On entering, I found such delicacies as Kellogg's Corn Flakes, individually wrapped Kraft American cheese, and five cans of Star Kist tuna. I started to take all five cans and then I looked at the price: $4.50 a can. I debated for a while and then thought how much Jackie would appreciate this special treat. I bought one can. Jackie was delighted. Minna prepared it immediately and put the bowl in the refrigerator. Later, Jackie came in from playing to make herself a sandwich, but while carrying the bowl from the refrigerator to the table, it dropped out of her hands and shattered on the hard tile floor. The tuna was irretrievable in a pile of smashed glass. I could not believe it. Neither could Minna or Jackie. After a very long five seconds, we all laughed—it was the only thing we could do. That night, when I wrote to Joe, I asked him to include half a dozen cans of tuna fish on his list of things to bring to Jamaica.

During those early weeks, I wrote to my husband almost every night, not because I felt compelled to fulfill some sort of wifely duty, but because it helped me put each day in perspective. I realized that discussion and decision making regarding the children had become an almost nightly ritual in our house, and I missed it terribly.

After a week, one last "arrangement" remained to be made. As a single field worker, I found a car useful but not essential. With my children there, I felt that I had to have a car in the event of an emergency, particularly with a small baby. But it was not long before I found the car more of a liability than an asset. My informants constantly asked me to take them here or there, and I did not feel that I was in a position to refuse. After a week with a lot of driving, I knew I had to find another solution. I contacted an old friend and informant, Peter, who had a car and was not steadily employed at the time. He was willing to serve as a modified chauffeur, making himself available whenever I needed a car. I paid him a weekly rate in addition to gas, oil, and minor repairs. It was much cheaper than the car rental, and I felt good that the money was going to someone local rather than to Hertz. As I suspected, village people were much more reluctant to ask Peter for a ride, and I was able to ease out of that obligation without offending anyone. In addition, Peter provided yet another father figure in our household. Now I had finished constructing my Jamaican family: two mothers, two fathers, three children, and a dog.

After the first weeks, the yard was almost constantly filled with neighbor children. They hovered around Jackie and Colby even while they ate and eagerly ate any food that they did not want. This suited everyone, as Jackie and Colby did not have to listen to my lectures about wasting food. Their playmates were also major consumers of our mosquito repellent. My reluctance to cover my children with harsh chemicals was superseded by my reluctance to see them scratching and infecting mosquito bites, so I had brought with me ten cans of Deepwoods Off. After we were in the house for about eight or nine days, however, I noticed that all three children were starting to get bitten. When I went to get the repellent, I could not find a single can. Jackie and Colby absented themselves during this search, but at last Minna volunteered that "It finish." But how could that be? Ten huge cans of Deepwoods Off gone in less than two weeks? She explained that Jackie and Colby had enjoyed spraying so much that they had sprayed all the other children on the street as well. Every morning, after I left the house, all the neighborhood children formed two lines, and Jackie and Colby would give each a thorough spraying. "Off" became another item for Joe's list.

The children played constantly from morning to night. In marked contrast to the Jamaican working-class children, who work very hard, my children were free to romp and play all day long. I was interested to see their reactions to the responsibilities their Jamaican friends undertook, which were not merely exercises in adult life but essential endeavors to the economic and social survival of their households: child care, cultivation, carrying water, gathering wood, tending animals, and so forth. Interestingly, my children never thought of these activities as work. Chores for the Jamaican children were joys for mine. They accompanied their Jamaican companions on their twice-daily excursions to the village standpipe to fetch water and were thrilled to go to the bush to pick mangoes or tether goats or collect eggs. They loved being included in these activities, and, apparently, the Jamaican children loved including them.

They found Colby particularly amusing; indeed, the big event of the summer was Colby's wedding. Colby, at age four, had fallen in love with Janet, who was fifteen. A most unlikely pair, they were inseparable. Wherever you found one, you would find the other. This relationship was the talk of the neighborhood, and soon a wedding was arranged, complete with homemade ring and a terrycloth veil for the bride. It was a spectacular event, with the bride on her knees, Colby standing next to her to compensate for the difference in height, and the whole street in attendance. The ceremony was performed by the head of the mosquito-control team (the closest we could get to a public official), and everything "went on fine" until Colby refused to kiss the bride at the end. Despite all the encouragement from the wedding guests, Colby remained steadfast: He *would* sleep with her, since she was his wife, but the only "girl" he would kiss was his mother.

Even J.P. got in on the action. I remember arriving at the home of an informant who casually mentioned that she had just seen my baby ride by on a fish cart. Since I had left him earlier, smearing porridge on the walls of our little verandah, I thought I had better investigate. Sure enough, two sons of the fish vendor decided it would be great fun to take J.P. on a ride through the village. He sat in his diapers like a miniature Buddha, enjoying himself thoroughly and smelling like dead fish. After that, it became a major source of entertainment for local children, and they would line up for their turn to take J.P. for his daily ride.

Although we were supposed to have running water, the time was "droughty," and we had to go to the standpipe to catch water. It was definitely a problem, given all the diapers that had to be washed, but it was certainly less of a problem for us than for our neighbors. We had managed to secure five plastic buckets used for storing pigs' tails—*"Yech!"* said Jackie, *"Yech!"* said Colby—which Bonnie carefully washed and then filled with water. On particularly hot days during our siege of no water, Peter drove Minna, the three children, and me to a mineral spring about ten miles away, where we bathed properly. Colby and Jackie loved these excursions and still remember them as a favorite part of their Jamaican experience. On the way back, we would stop at the standpipe and fill our pigs'-tail buckets for the next day. It was inconvenient, but our time there was too short for such activities to cease being another game and become just a tedious chore.

I never really worried much about the children's safety. I warned them not to pet dogs and showed them what a scorpion looked like. Also, they were highly visible in the community, and everyone knew and protected them. Having started my career as a nurse, I felt reasonably competent to take care of any minor illnesses or emergencies that might occur. A small hospital a few miles away provided the next level of care, and I made it my business to cultivate a personal relationship with the local private physician. Actually, it turned out that *I* was the only casualty requiring a visit to the hospital. While walking back home from an interview one dark night, I was bitten on my ankle by one of those snarling, emaciated Jamaican dogs I had warned my children about. At the sight of blood oozing into my shoes, Peter and Bonnie lifted me into the car (although I was perfectly capable of walking) and beat the dog with a vengeance. This was followed by a hair-raising ride to the hospital emergency room, with Peter swerving purposefully in an attempt to sacrifice any dog that was unlucky enough to be on the road that night. At the hospital, I received a tetanus injection that hurt much more than the dog bite. Jackie and Colby were profoundly silent during this experience. They were concerned, as was I, not so much about the damage done to my ankle but with the realization that they were extraordinarily dependent on me in this faraway place. Acting on the theory that the contingencies least provided for are those most likely to occur, I went around to all my friends, leaving numbers where they could reach Joe in the event of an emergency.

Now, I often shudder when I think of the things that *could* have occurred. For example, one of the beliefs shared by some parents is that *ganja* tea prevents or alleviates mosquito-borne fevers, which are endemic in certain areas of the island. To evaluate this assumption properly, I expressly selected Dover, which was surrounded by thousands of acres of mangrove, a breeding ground for every known variety of mosquito in Jamaica. It never occurred to me that *my* children would get sick, and, from my perspective, they never did. Interestingly, however, while preparing to write this paper, I found a letter (which I reprint verbatim) that Jackie had written to her grandmother, and it presents a very different perception of the children's health status.

Daer

 grama Attridge and family. how have you been, hope
thing's are o.k. I am o.k.. at first I was realy sick but now
I'm fine, I realy enjoy it here. after I got sick I got a sun
blister on my lip. that was realy bad too. It killied like
anything i just got over it to day, but I'm fine now don't
worry. have you been o.k. hope you weren't sick I'm getting
realy long hair. now that I'm all better, J.P.'s, sick. before
J.P. was sick colby had had a belly ake. for two in a half day's
but he's fine now. but J.P.'s still sick both me and J.P. had
too take medicen. it made me better, but J.P. is still sick.
 I'm going too say good bye now Love and Kisses Jackie
        xo

As my husband's arrival became imminent, we all grew more
and more excited. Finally, the day came, and we waited at the
airport with our noses pressed against the glass of the Customs
room for what seemed like an eternity. Joe fit right in, as I knew
he would. Our experience with some northern Maine clammers a
few summers back had demonstrated to me that he was capable of
meeting people at every level of society, making them feel comfortable and feeling comfortable with them. The local men were
as anxious for his arrival as we were. They had concluded long
before that, as a woman, my brains were too weak to handle the
effects of *ganja,* but they were eager to share the "weed" with my
husband. Recognizing that this was part of his initiation, he accepted an invitation to the "yard" of P.K., the largest *ganja* deal-
er in Dover. Colby begged to go along to be with the "big men,"
and fortunately, Joe consented. The rest is all a secondhand account, but according to Joe, they rolled him an enormous *ganja*
cigar and lit it for him. After inhaling about three times, he
noticed that everyone's mouths began to assume massive proportions, and his own mouth became extraordinarily dry. He also
found that he had a great deal of difficulty saying anything that

could be construed as intelligent or even relevant. Evidently, the other men were sensitive to his predicament, and P.K. suggested that he might like something to drink. Joe agreed and was soon presented with half a tumbler of 180-proof white rum. After two gulps, which he later compared to swallowing a flaming saber, he considered that if he did not leave then, he might be there for several years. His homing instincts superseded his need to establish his manhood, and he faintly remembers suggesting that he get Colby back home before dark (it was then about 2:00 in the afternoon, and we were no more than a ten-minute walk away). He attempted to rise, but was overcome by the force of gravity. Finally, with Colby's assistance, Joe freed himself from the log on which he was seated and began the odyssey home. When I returned that evening, I found Joe in bed and knew immediately what had happened. Bonnie and I sobered him up with some sweet lemonade. Whatever opinion the local men had about Joe's ability to consume *ganja* or rum, they kept it to themselves and evaluated him on other terms. Even though he failed the test, they always included him in fishing expeditions, domino games, cricket matches, and other "things masculine" in Jamaica.

The last two weeks of our stay, the social workers and teachers put on a summer crafts program in a neighboring community. One of the teachers asked me if Jackie and Colby would like to attend, and I thought it would be a nice, unpressured opportunity for them to see what school is like in another culture. At first they seemed to enjoy it, but on the third or fourth day I noticed that Colby was less than enthusiastic about going back. Probing this apparent reluctance, Jackie told me that the day before the teacher had severely scolded Colby for dropping a rubber band under his chair and then asking for another because he could not reach it. I explained that, in Jamaica, rubber bands are not in endless supply as they are in the United States; in fact, I felt that the teacher's response to what was an inadvertent act by a four year old was excessive. After some deliberation, I decided not to send them back again. They were delighted. I wanted them to have the exposure, but I also wanted them to enjoy their experience in Jamaica. The incident had called into question some of my basic values about childrearing, and I made the decision to stick with my own culture.

Jackie spent much of her remaining days in Jamaica collecting addresses and making faithful promises to write. Colby spent his time teaching his dog tricks and imploring me to let him take the pup home. "Brownie" was definitely the best-fed and best-treated dog on the street. He was fat and coddled, but, unfortunately, he could not hold his own with other Jamaican dogs. He was constantly being rescued, by Colby or Jackie or a neighbor, from the hungry dogs that tried to take his food.

On the morning we left, everyone gathered around the car. Minna began to cry, which, for some perverse reason, amused the other well-wishers no end. Consequently, our departure was more cheerful than it otherwise might of been—except, of course, for Minna. The children's emotions were mixed: happy to return to their friends and familiar surroundings, but sad to leave their new home away from home. With few exceptions, they have very fond memories of Jamaica. They never got used to some of the cuisine, but loved the array of fruits—gennep, mango, pineapple, star apples, and an endless supply of ripe bananas. They ate a lot of soup and a lot of rice and gravy, and judging by the size of the bill I received the day before we took our leave, were sustained to a large extent by suck-suck.

While children are seldom mentioned in the literature on fieldwork, several veteran fieldworkers had assured me that the children would be helpful in collecting data on their own age groups, and given the subject matter of my research, I expected this would be the case. But while they did, indeed, provide both useful information and access to other children, I am not sure they contributed anything that I could not have gleaned myself, and probably more expeditiously. In fact, I suspect it took me twice the time to accomplish half the work that I would have normally accomplished. Their presence did, however, provide me with enormous insight about the way in which I carried out and combined my roles as mother, wife, and anthropologist, and certainly about the fieldwork process itself. In her class on field techniques, Margaret Mead often compared cross-cultural fieldwork to psychoanalysis in which one's personal values and customary behavior are held up for scrutiny and evaluation. Bringing one's family into the field subjects that family to the same scrutiny in a way not otherwise possible.

Comparing my children with Jamaican children was particularly revealing. Jamaican children are polite. They are quiet in the company of adults, do as they are told, speak when spoken to, say good morning and good evening on entering a room, eat all the food on their plates, are too mannerly to ask for more, and are properly flogged when they are disobedient. In comparison, my children appeared hopelessly spoiled. They complained about the food, scrapped among themselves, and occasionally interrupted my conversations for the most trivial reasons, such as the whereabouts of their crayons.

If people thought they were rude, however, their tolerance for my verbal, assertive children seemed boundless; particularly for Colby, whom the suck-suck lady claimed would "turn lawyer when him seven." The only activity for which they admitted frank disgust was Colby's propensity for catching toads. Although this is well within the cultural expectations of small children in New England, it is not in Jamaica, where it is viewed as the most contemptible of activities. In that arena, Colby stretched their indulgence beyond its capabilities. Although I admired the behavior of Jamaican children, I could not get myself to discipline in the Jamaican style. Our neighbor, Mother Lewis, entertains everyone

on the street by her thrice-weekly beatings of her grandniece
Gracie. On one occasion, a man walking by, hearing Gracie bawl
during a beating, called to Mrs. Lewis to "save him a piece of the
liver." This incident then became part of local culture, to be
repeated by anyone at subsequent floggings. Colby and Jackie
responded to this kind of corporal punishment as though they were
observing life on another planet. They never, for a moment,
thought that I would do that to them, and they were right. I am
sure that some of my behavior seemed incomprehensible to my
informants; for example, making the children sit on the bed until
they apologized or were ready to behave. Jamaican children would
have considered this a privilege rather than a punishment.

The morning before we left, Mother Lewis called me over to
her house to tell me that Colby's puppy was dead, killed by the
other dogs during the night. I was both stunned and saddened,
but decided not to tell Colby. I asked Peter to take the children
for a last trip to the beach so that Bonnie could bury the puppy in
their absence. Although he was disappointed that the puppy was
not there when we left, Colby never suspected his demise, and to
this day I have never told him. Although I do not have a particular liking for dogs, I was profoundly affected by this incident.
Without Colby and Jackie there to protect it, that puppy never
really had a chance in what was literally a dog-eat-dog world.
You have to be tough to endure in certain kinds of environments,
and he had never been forced to acquire the behavior needed to
survive. I could not help but allegorize. I wondered if I was
overprotecting my children. Was I too soft with them? Was I
doing them a disservice by not making them stick it out in school
or by not giving them the kinds of adult responsibilities that
Jamaican children have? Will they be tough enough to survive in
the real world?

Another discovery that I made during the trip has to do with
my fieldwork style. I had never realized what a one-way process

fieldwork had been for me and, I suspect, for many single re-searchers. I tend to be a very private person, carefully segregating my professional from my personal life. I had, of course, shared personal information about my family and culture, but only that which, as I later understood, was designed to elicit information from my informants. They never saw me in my own social con-text—with family and friends or at the workplace—and while they could gather something about life in my culture, they did not really get a fair exchange of cultural information. A revealing incident occurred in the Jamaican village where, as a single wom-an, I did my first fieldwork. Although I privately had what, by most standards, would be considered an active social life, I was concerned about creating any gossip about myself that could possi-bly compromise the fieldwork process. Therefore, I cautiously remained as socially neutral as possible, specifically engaging in no relationships with members of the opposite sex that could be construed as anything but platonic. Interestingly, this had just the opposite effect on my informants; all the men in the village thought I was weird, and the women thought I must be having a love affair with their husbands. Otherwise, why would I be so secretive about my personal life? When I discovered this, I quickly coopted the extension officer from the local tobacco company, who seemed like the most reasonable candidate for the task, and asked him if he would occasionally stop by for a visit or escort me to the beach or a dance. He happily agreed, and everyone breathed a sigh of relief: I was "normal."

Now, surrounded by my children, it was impossible to set aside my other roles or to be culturally neutral. They were too young to alter their behavior for the purposes of research. Like it or not, my children are archetypical middle-class American chil-dren—representative of our child-centered culture that Margaret Mead so aptly described. They wear Nike sneakers, jeans with names on them, and shirts with alligators on them. They believe

in Santa Claus, raise their own chickens, and know how to oper-
ate computers; and the only reason they do not watch television
much is because we cannot get any reception where we live. They
love baseball, football, Jay Geils, Pac Man, pizza, and
McDonald's. They hate taking baths, brushing their teeth, putting away their clothes, and getting ready for Sunday school.
Jackie's burning ambition was to be a hairdresser, for which she
practiced by combing her own hair almost continuously. Colby
summarily rejected my attempt to explain the facts of life with
"That's the most ridiculous thing I've ever heard," and J.P. was
consumed with theological inquiries, such as, "Who is stronger,
God or Superman?"

When all is said and done, they are real culture carriers. They
responded humanly, without deliberation and without conceal-
ment. In so doing, they exposed me in my other roles, as wife
and mother, and in all my cultural trappings. Not being able to
control the flow of information as I had in the past took some
getting used to, although now I see it as a much more democratic
approach to our craft.

Finally, it became abundantly clear to me from this experience
that one of the features that distinguishes fieldwork from other
kinds of sociological research methods is its pervasiveness. It is a
twenty-four-hour, seven-day-a-week job. I had never thought
much about this until my husband innocently asked, "Are you
finished work now?" or "What time will you finish work today?"
These seemingly innocuous questions produced a corporeal reaction. How do you explain fieldwork to nonanthropologist husband and children? That it is ongoing, never complete? That
concepts of time off and time on are irrelevant? That work is
integrated with every aspect of your daily routine, including
mealtimes and recreation? That the only time the work stops is
when you physically remove yourself from the fieldwork situation? This total immersion is what I love about fieldwork, but it

is also what made it so difficult bringing children to the field, for they, also, are a total experience. Like fieldwork, they never really leave your consciousness, and despite the competence of helpers, your children are definitely a presence and require a constant vigilance. So there I was, with two twenty-five-hour-a-day jobs. For women like me, when it comes to my own performance, I am not a compromising person. I wanted to be a great mother and a great fieldworker.

The physical care of the children was not demanding. I do not think I changed ten diapers the whole summer. For the most part, Minna did everything domestic—marketing, preparation of meals, laundry, housecleaning—and she was assisted in these tasks by Bonnie, who was always on hand to run to the shop or play with the baby while Minna was cooking. The commitment of time came in making certain that everyone was happy and comfortable, inspecting Colby's lizards, watching Jackie skip rope to one hundred, taking J.P. on his little walks after supper. The responsibility of parental attention and encouragement ordinarily shared with Joe now became entirely mine, and *that* was time-consuming. I tried to combine the two roles by including the children in various village events, such as cricket games, festivals, concerts. Nevertheless, it was difficult, at best, to record events and simultaneously supervise their behavior, answer their questions, explain what was going on, reject their requests for more ice cream, ensure their safety, and so on.

Would I do it again? I *did* do it again, but not right away. The impact of that first experience convinced me to go to the field alone for the second phase of research the following summer. I missed them terribly, but the freedom to work unencumbered was uplifting, and I collected more data in six weeks than I had in the two and a half months in Dover. On a more recent fieldwork trip, however, I took Colby, age nine, and J.P., who was five. Colby had such wonderful memories of our first excursion that he was visably disappointed that it was different this time. Although we lived in a beautiful house with a swimming pool, located where the nights are deliciously cool, he complained that he liked our first house better and that he had had more fun there. A visit to Dover one day, however, left him astonished that we could have lived in such a tiny house and endured the intense heat and mosquitoes. He expressed his feelings clearly in a letter he wrote to his uncle after the first week, "We live in a nice house but the food is disgusting and the people around here are dumb . . . also it's very boring." J.P., on the other hand, was now old enough to appreciate Jamaica for the first time. He had countless playmates, and the more outrageous his behavior, the more everyone was amused. For fieldwork purposes, I think the younger they are, the easier. As they get older, they miss their friends and bicycles and movies and baseball games.

As far as advice to parents who are contemplating bringing their children to the field, first and foremost, secure plenty of reliable help. But do not think for a moment that anyone is indispensable. If a housekeeper or babysitter does not work out, or cannot hit it off with your children, the helper will make life more difficult rather than easier. Somehow, you will survive without that person and work out a better solution. Second, whatever you can arrange in advance with regard to house, car, housekeeper, and the like, *do*. You can be assured that 50 percent of the arrangements will fall through anyway, but at least you will have the other 50 percent.

Third, and most important, anticipate that your children may go through their own form of culture shock, which may be expressed in a variety of forms: uncharacteristic behavior, depression, somatic complaints. I recommend, if possible, a more gradual introduction to the culture—some advance preparation, of course, but also perhaps a night or two in a comfortable hotel instead of heading directly from airport to field site, as I did. We all would have been in a better frame of mind after a night at the Sheraton, and would have avoided much of the tension and awkwardness that came from both fatigue and a sense of displacement. Also, it does not hurt to bring some familiar foods for the transition period. On the last trip, I took a huge jar of chunky peanut butter, strawberry jam, and (if the truth be known) a container of marshmallow fluff. Disgusting stuff, but it helped. These were also foods that the children could offer to their new Jamaican acquaintances and, again, promote more of a cultural exchange instead of a one-way flow of cultural information. Finally, relax and enjoy the children, and learn from their responses and the responses of your informants to them. Do not expect your children to put their own culture on hold, as you might do. They will be living the culture that you are only studying.

7   Our Ulleri Child

The night was clear, and I could see the shining surface of the water as it poured from the leaf spout into the spring pool. I cupped my hand in front of my chin and bent over to catch some of it. The climb was worth a drink that did not have to be boiled first. "Sweet water," the Musuri villagers called it. I dabbed my mouth with the end of my cotton sari and turned to sit on a large, flat stone the women used for washing clothes.

The brilliance of the stars gave depth to the darkness. The high ghostly Himalayas framed the nearer, more familiar hills. All I could hear in the distance was the barking of village dogs and the steady, far-off drumbeat of Mudoo, the local medicine man. Tiny fires dotted the black bowl of the valley. One of those fires was close and comforting. Mudoo's wife would be sitting by the hearth with her children, perhaps smoking, waiting for her husband to return from his strenuous efforts to cure the sick buffalo. My eyes were drawn to a reassuring, starry presence.

"Orion *Sahib,*" I called aloud. "If our two little girls are watching you from their dormitory window, tell them it is time to go to bed. Their mother says so."

This was my most precious hour. I could leave the hut full of villagers visiting my husband and disappear into the night, knowing no one would dare to follow me. In Nepal the spirits that roam about after sundown are thought to be unfriendly, and no one wishes to cross their paths.

My mind wandered, as it often did, to little Ben. I remembered seeing him squat on his short husky legs, watching a pair of beetles struggle to push their round nest of dung across a trail to safety. I felt at once a sad kinship with dung beetles that reached the trail's edge, only to see their cradle kicked by a careless traveler and all their eggs trampled underfoot.

My tears returned. In the darkness I did not have to hold them back. Suddenly the stars and the fire in Mudoo's hearth blurred and ran together, and I allowed the memories of another village to return.

It was almost two years before that we had left our home in the United States for Nepal. We had come with such confidence. My husband, an anthropologist at the University of California at Los Angeles, and I accepted the demands of his career with equal enthusiasm. We both liked mountains, jungles, exotic places; we preferred campfires to cocktail parties. So we were enthusiastic when we learned that he had been awarded funds to do research in Nepal. We knew living there would be a challenge, but we were not without experience. Our last two-year field trip had been spent with our daughters, Marion and Emily, in a village in north India, so we all were prepared for the rigors of field work. Only little Ben had been added to our family since then, and to leave him behind for this trip seemed unthinkable.

As always, relatives tried to dissuade us. They would look at year-old Ben and remind us of how fast dysentery can dehydrate a baby. But I would see a headline in a local newspaper, *Child Drowns in Family Pool,* and hope that—in some ways—we would be taking him to safety. We all had very real needs that could be met only if we stayed together. The children needed a father. Two years apart would bring John home a stranger; none of us would be able to understand what he had been through or what he was thinking or writing about. To me, this would not be a marriage.

There was another need that only those who have lived through long stretches of life in the field can understand—the need to have, among strangers, loved ones of your own. It was important to John that someone else cared whether a village headman would talk or not, that someone got as excited as he did when progress was made—or listened with understanding when the week seemed lost in unfulfilled hopes. And so our decision was made.

The journey from Los Angeles to Nepal, the long, narrow kingdom sandwiched between India and Tibet, took less than two days by jet. A slower trip would have made the shift less dramatic. But bridges from the world we knew to the world unknown already had been built. Many Westerners have found their way to the capital city of Katmandu—our first destination—through mission work or government service. Jeeps and old cars are an accepted part of the scene. Telephones and electricity, of sorts, are available in many homes. The latest miracle drugs can be purchased at the local pharmacy.

We stayed in Katmandu for several months while John selected his interpreters and laid the groundwork at the government offices to clear travel permits. During those months, eight-year-old Marion and Emily, who was ten, attended a school for girls as day students. In December we took them out of school, and the five of us began our trip into the field.

John's goal was to study Nepalese peasants—a people linked to us through our Babylonian ancestors, who lived some three thousand before Christ. Unlike their city cousins in Katmandu, Nepalese peasants have changed, in many ways, very little. Their crops, cattle, plows, and much of their way of life are still basically unaltered. We knew we would have to share this way of life to begin to understand it. Yet, to be honest, we knew we would not be sharing it all the way. We would not have to face the bedbugs without DDT. We would be very sorry if the rains did not come to the cornfields, but we would not go hungry. We knew also that two years was not a lifetime.

Still, we never dreamed our sharing would be so complete.

We scouted the countryside for several weeks before we found a village that would suit all the demands of the research problem. For various reasons, it had to be small—a village belonging to a group called Magars, one of the tribes that have become the backbone of India's Gurkha regiments. Because it would be too high for cultivating rice, the village would also be very poor.

We finally discovered Ulleri. It clung to the mountainside high above a river, unable to hide its face of poverty—narrow, steep terraces for corn, huts clustered together to save land. John met with the village headman, the *mukiya,* to try to explain the purpose of our work. We were not sure how much the headman understood. He must have thought John's occupation—asking all kinds of questions and writing down the answers—a strange one for a grown man. But he was good-hearted and agreed to cooperate. A paper bearing the official seal of the king of Nepal helped persuade him that we could be trusted. Now all we needed was a place to live.

"We will finish our school soon," the *mukiya* told us proudly, pointing to four well-made stone walls without any roof. "Then you can stay there."

"But you are building that for your children," John answered, a little puzzled.

"*Hanh, Sahib.* But we cannot find a teacher. No one wants to come to such a poor village."

While John talked to the headman, I stepped to the door of the hut to get away from the smoke of the fire pit. Coming toward me on the trail was a man carrying the body of a child wrapped in a blanket. His face betrayed none of his feelings. Two men equally stoic, followed him, one with a burning torch that blackened the sky, the other with a bundle of wood. They were heading toward the river.

I turned away. There is one difference between these people and us, I thought. We expect our children to outlive us. Nepalese parents expect their children to die.

We moved into a temporary shelter the villagers built for us that afternoon in a cornfield. The shelter had grass sides, woven matting for a roof, and a shallow hole in the center for a fire pit. We set up our tent inside the hut to keep out the wind, but we soon found that no clothing or down filled sleeping bag could really hold back the cold.

Every morning, after our breakfast of cornmeal mush, vitamins, and tea, John and Hem, a young high school teacher who was John's assistant, went up into the village to begin their long day. Krishna, my Magar helper, scoured the pots and set off down the trail to wash the clothes in the spring. He was a simple unspoiled hill boy who, like all good Gurkhas, was tough and adaptable. He carried water from the spring, roasted soybeans for the children, lugged camera gear, did all the laundry, and ground the corn.

Even with all Krishna's help, however, the girls and I were never idle. Our biggest concern was little Ben. We took turns being his nanny. Even while he slept, we stood watch, alert to avoid his suddenly awakening and toddling unseen over the terrace wall or into the fire pit. The wall, the fire, and dysentery— these were our greatest dreads.

But the days were not spoiled by our anxieties. We had arithmetic to do and socks to mend. We learned how to get along without supermarkets and stores, pulling sewing thread from a shirt-tail, pouring wild honey on our cornmeal mush to make desserts.

Often John came back to camp to tell us about something interesting he had seen in the village. Then all of us made a special trip to see it—women weaving, men building houses, a shaman driving evil spirits from a sick buffalo. Sometimes we helped John by taking pictures, holding a microphone, or recording distances when that would be useful.

At night the villagers came to chat and sing by our fire. Little Ben was their greatest joy. Few of them had ever seen such a blond child before. He was jovial and very affectionate with all of them. "Ben *Bahadur*," they called him—Ben the Brave. Always their arms went out to him, and in his energetic, little-boy way he shared himself with everyone.

One day, I took the children to the school to watch the workmen shaping the heavy slate shingles that would someday keep the winter rains from our heads. They were working near the edge of the terrace. Suddenly I held my breath—the drop was terrifying!

"How could they think of building a school there?" I asked John. "If a child made one misstep, he would fall a hundred feet. What about the girls—and Ben?"

"I know," John answered calmly, "but there's plenty of bamboo. I can hire several men to make a good fence. And I have been thinking of something the villagers would like even more," he added. "We can't pay people to spend time talking to us, but when we finish the school, perhaps I can spare Hem for a few hours a day. In six months all the children would know how to read."

Each day blended into the next. A month after we had arrived in Ulleri, John announced one morning that he and Hem needed a change of pace. They wanted to take a photograph from the highest peak before the snows covered the valley. The trip was too far for the rest of us in one day, so the girls and I decided to hike to a Buddhist shrine we had heard about. It was on a high ridge above the village.

I carried Ben in a pack. He seemed drowsy for midmorning, but by the time we reached the cluster of prayer flags that marked the shrine, he was wide awake and calling to the crows that soared over the valley. We honored the holy spot with our handful of flowers and sat down in the warm sun for lunch. Ben stretched his legs in the grass and trotted back to each of us in turn for a bite of unleavened bread and an apricot. We were very happy.

When we returned to the house, Krishna had supper waiting for us. The girls fell asleep before they finished their tea and Ben dozed peacefully in his father's arms in front of the fire. We decided the work would progress faster if we had more days like this one. That night we all slept so soundly, we did not mind the cold.

The next morning, when we awoke, our little boy was dead.

We had already lived through moments of life as they were lived millenniums ago. Now we were to learn in a very real way what it meant for Nepalese fathers to outlive the promise of their sons. The differences the centuries had made between us no longer mattered; the mysteries and frailties of life never change. The bond of sorrow that connected us to the Ulleri villagers joined us to all parents who have suffered loss, back through time to the beginnings of civilization.

John carried the small body to its forest grave. The women would not let me go with him; it was not a woman's place. Grief-stricken, I sat on a mat outside the hut with my little girls, surrounded with all the understanding anyone could hope to have at such a moment. The older village women came to sit with me, expressing their sorrow in the common language of tears. One of them held up three gnarled fingers. She had lost three sons; another at her side had lost five.

One mother wept, "All my babies are dead," and held her ten fingers in front of me. As I took her outstretched hands in mine and held them to my cheeks, I wondered: Could I have known such grief ten times and still weep for another?

What had happened to Ben? I searched my memory for answers, for some explanation of our inexplicable loss. Perhaps we would never know. Now we had only the answer from the medicine man. "An evil spirit shot an arrow from that tree," he said, pointing into the jungle. "The hut will be torn down and no one will live in this cornfield again."

We could not expect our girls to stay in Ulleri now, nor could we move anywhere in the village without constant reminders of our life as it had been with them and little Ben. In two hours we were packed and ready to leave for Katmandu.

An old woman came forward as we were turning into the trail, tears streaming down her wrinkled brown face. She opened the end of her ragged apron and held up two little eggs and a cluster of small potatoes. "Take them," she whispered. "For your girls."

I rested on her shoulder for a moment, needing all the strength her frail body could spare. In terms I had always known, she had nothing to give—but what gift from anyone who could give more would ever equal this!

After we left Ulleri, John and I reenrolled the girls in their Katmandu school and went out together to find another village. We chose this one, Musuri, with its bowl shaped valley and sweet spring water. When we had worked in Musuri for over a year, we felt ready to visit Ulleri once more.

It had taken us a long time to make a decision. We wanted to do something in memory of Ben, and we wanted it to have meaning for the people of Ulleri as well. We finally chose to build a *chautara,* a tree-shaded stone platform beside the trail, where travelers could place their loads and escape the heat of the sun to rest.

The trails of Nepal are dotted with beautiful *chautaras* built by a son or daughter to honor dead parents. But this one would be different. It would honor a child, honor all children—and say, if it could, that those who are left behind to weep belong to one another.

The headman of Ulleri seemed pleased to see us again, and joined us in our search for a good site. On our way up through the village, I began to feel confused and disoriented. Something was different.

"*Mukiya Sahib,*" I addressed him, "Where is the schoolhouse?"

"It is gone, *Memsahib,*" he replied.

"Gone? Where? Why?" I asked, incredulous.

"In the night," he answered, raising his hands in a gesture of helplessness, "during the monsoon. There was such a heavy rain, and while we were asleep it fell into the valley."

I stared at the gaping scar across the land in front of me that marked the place where the schoolhouse once stood, a monument to hope, built by men who wanted a better life for their children.

That would have been our home.

Words would not come, but the questions raced across my mind. Why the schoolhouse? Why Ulleri? Why Ben? Why not all of us? As if in answer, the *Mukiya* turned toward the trail with a look that seemed to say, "Come, *Memsahib,* we have a *chautara* to build. We could spend a lifetime trying to answer such questions. The important thing is to know that someday, somehow, people will find the strength to hope again."

The tree stood alone against the northern sky, shading the trail far above the village. It would be a welcome resting place after a long, hot climb.

Everyone worked hard. Krishna carried slabs of stone none of the other men could lift from the ground. Hem's every rock was equal tribute to the child he had learned to love. These young men were our sons now—these and another, Bihari, who had gone to a nearby town and returned with a large stone plaque to stand beneath the tree.

A stone carver had labored long to shape the Nepali words, and then again to copy the letters he could not read himself:

BENJAMIN JENNINGS HITCHCOCK
"BEN BAHADUR"
ONCE, OH SWEET, BRIGHT JOY
LIKE THEIR LOST CHILDREN
AN ULLERI CHILD

RENATE FERNANDEZ

8   Children and Parents
in the Field:
Reciprocal Impacts

Parents who take their children "into the field" have confronted applause, questions, and condemnation: "Aren't you scared they will succumb to infection? The doctors can't be nearby, can they?" "Won't the kids miss out on school? How can they keep up with their competitive classmates back home? Won't they get bored or lazy when they're without them?" "How does the shift to a foreign language affect their development?" And if parents of teenagers are asking the questions, "How does the shift in language affect their verbal SAT scores? Don't American teenagers resent parents who disrupt their lives, take them away from their friends, and jeopardize their standing in the school's tracking system?"

185

A popular view holds that the field is some distant community where an American child's health, psychological development, and pursuit of happiness are in serious jeopardy—and this may also be true for the family as a whole. Another view holds that the field is an arena in which the kids, parents, or both, display bravery, fortitude, commitment, all in the name of potential but uncertain benefits. These may accrue developmentally to the child. Or they may accrue professionally to the parents by providing the raw material on which ethnographies—and hence professional careers—are built. More disinterestedly, the benefits may accrue to anthropological theory and methodology, or, more remotely, to world understanding.

Before taking our children into the field some twenty years ago, I entertained some of these questions and oscillated between these views myself. And others contemplating going to the field have asked them of me ever since. General reflection on parenting in the field leads me to no clear-cut answers even now. Reflections on specific incidents that took place in the field do lead me to the following conclusions about the impact that children have on the central anthropological engagement.

1. Our children influence the choice of field site and bias us toward certain human resources. They nudge us toward certain communities and individuals, and rule out others.

2. Our children accelerate the ongoing social dynamics in the field community—the village, in our case—and contribute to our and the villagers' interpretation of events.

3. Our children forge the links on which our longitudinal studies are built.

4. The needs of our children prompt us to expand the proposed inquiry into the society and the bureaucracies that lie beyond the boundaries of the village.

5. A child's encounter in the field, witnessed by the parent, may create an emotional charge powerful enough to redirect the investigation.

In the first part of this paper I offer incidents on which each of these conclusions is based. They all have to do with the impact of children on their parents' fieldwork. I became an anthropologist only as a result of doing fieldwork, and mostly as a result of doing it with my children in the field. Therefore, I should say that it is primarily the impact of children on the fieldwork of their mother that I present here. The incidents involve matters of health and hazard, of schoolwork and play, and of language growth and its apparent arrest. The incidents, apart from providing the basis for the numbered conclusions, point diffusely toward developmental hazards and opportunities, which in this short space can be explored only briefly. I present these incidents in enough detail so that readers can interpret them differently than I do, if they so wish.

In the second part of the paper I discuss practical aspects of fieldwork and relate them to the long-term influence of the field experience on our children. Since I do not believe that we can ever closely tie character and achievement to experiential antecedents, except possibly for ourselves, I discuss the children's outcome with hesitation, even where, from my point of view, early experience seems to have imprinted itself boldly. The children have been invited to make their contribution to this volume. If they have not written for its pages, it is because, right now, activities other than writing about fieldwork have greater priority. They have read what I have written about them and agree to its being shared in this format. They do not feel that my words preempt what they might want to write in the future. They know, as does my husband, that these stories, although generated by a family's experience in a mountain village, are elastic and conform as much to the needs of the teller as to the perceived needs of the reader.

The Impact of Children on Fieldwork

Our Field Site and Our Children's Role in Choosing It

In 1965, my husband and I began a sequence of fieldwork in which our children played an important part. We were both in our thirties, he a professor of anthropology in a New England college and I a full-time mother with no didactic training in anthropology. I was beginning to itch under the veil of the feminine mystique. Prior to marriage and family, I had been an occupational therapist, working with disturbed children in a psychiatric setting. This made me take child development even more seriously than most of the women who shared the mystique. Like them, I felt that life's experiences made the critical difference in development. It was up to mothers to assure offspring the best-possible life experiences. This view was reinforced by my professional training. The field experience might be physically trying, I thought, but it could provide rich experiential fare for our children's growth. Perhaps it would immunize them against complacency, a defect especially visible to me on the academic sidelines. I had observed that some of the most thoughtful students of the 1960s were becoming critical of American complacency, and I hoped my children would also be thoughtful critics of whatever they chose to engage in as adults. To have the experience of living abroad, with people unlike themselves, would afford them a privileged perspective, and I hoped would contribute to such a thoughtful stance.

Before we had children, my husband had gathered field materials on revitalization movements in Africa, work in which I had collaborated to a limited extent. To contrast with those materials, we wanted to establish a field site to which we could return often, in the company of our children. It turned out to be in Spain, in the northern province of Asturias.

We knew that some parts of Asturias were undergoing rapid economic change. People who had been cattle-keeping subsistence farmers were going into mining, and we thought that accompanying processes of devitalization and revitalization would reveal themselves to our method of participant observation. But in order to feel free to participate in the life of the village, our family would have to feel welcome and be assured of a good water supply, for our family then included two children of preschool age, Lisa and Luke.

Among several proposed sites was Escobines, a village of some seven hundred inhabitants, located in the uppermost reaches of a steep, mountainous watershed where plowland is scarce. The trout stream passing through Escobines drains a coal-mining area not many kilometers downstream. It is an area from which Escobinos are drawing new wealth. Escobinos have traditionally made a living by raising stock for market and growing cereals and vegetables for local consumption. Their new wealth comes not only from miners' wages but from the tourism—banquet halls, lodgings, cafés, and bars—an industry developed largely by the women of the village. Tourist establishments cater to people getting away from the sooty towns downstream and to urbanites from the provincial capital. We decided that the water in Escobines, in contrast to that of the communities downstream, would be safe for our children.

But would we be welcome? During our survey of the villages, we sent out a probe: our son, Luke, a fast-moving and curious two-year-old towhead. In villages where he was ignored, we felt a

stolid indifference that would make our kind of fieldwork un-
necessarily difficult. This was not the case in Escobines, where an
elderly villager suddenly scooped up Luke a small distance away
from us. Unbeknown to us, Luke had discovered a swift-running
millstream that bisected the village. The watchful villager had
simultaneously discovered Luke. The village elder's reaction to
this fearless child allayed our fears.

A house was found, and the children and I settled into a pilot
study that we pursued that summer and the next. My husband,
having set us up in the field, then went off to conclude his fieldwork in Africa. The entire family returned for a formal and
funded eighteen-month investigation in 1971–1972, by which
time our offspring had increased to three. At the beginning of
this field trip, Lisa was ten, Luke seven, and Andrew had just
turned two. We returned to Asturias over a number of summers
in the 1970s, and spent a sabbatical year there in 1977–1978.

We have a photograph that recalls the kids at the time of that
formal beginning in the spring of 1971. They are perched on a
rail fence. Luke seems to be attending to the call of the snowy
peaks, just outside the frame. Lisa is smiling; she has managed to
force her short hair into braids like those of the local girls, and
seems quite satisfied with the stubbly results. (During that field
period, we could count on Lisa to apprise herself of local norms
and persuade us to comply with them.) Her arm around Andrew
keeps the cheerful toddler from falling plump off the the rail. He
appears jubilant because he has just managed to imitate the call
of the goats, and they have answered back. We also see signs on
his brow of his characteristic emphatic action—the day before
the picture was taken, he had seized the scissors and chopped off
the front of his hair. He was upset with the language shift imposed on his life. Failing to understand what his ears were hearing, he had apparently decided to improve his vision.

According to our grant proposal, a shift in expressive life would accompany the economic one; this expressive shift was the focus of our investigation. As background, I was to gather data for the basic ethnography, for such activity at this field site was compatible with traditional childrearing. It was also compatible with my inclinations, if not with my formal paramedical training. Thus, in the field summers of the 1960s and 1970s, I and one or more of the kids accompanied the villagers on their rounds. For us, it was a varied routine. We went to the grazing uplands, mapped the streets and the fragmented landholdings, and were invited into many homes where we came to know the family members and took down genealogies.

The harvest of data was always greater when we pursued the topic as villagers themselves pursue a topic: by digression. They embroider human detail and allude to black sheep along circuitous routes. The digressions were rich, expressive materials, but in combination with village-naming practices, created a problem for me that the children helped me solve.

Only a few last names are in use in the village, and these names are not used for identifying adults, except by the postmistress. Moreover, only a few first names are commonly given. Nicknames and relationships to persons and places are used to identify people. The results were confusing to me. I wrongly thought of Rosa and Rosaura, both "of the mountain chapel," as sisters, when actually one was born of Maria and the other of Mari Rosa. Genealogies based on such misunderstanding were useless. Here, as everywhere, *salud, dinero y amor,* "health, wealth, and love," were the chief topics of discussion. And where wealth depended on patrimony and love on matrimony, to get identities and relationships wrong was to misunderstand everything. The villagers tried to set me straight. They would recount the stories of events out of which a nickname arose. There was, for example, *La Galla,* the Rooster Woman, who had once been caught stealing a bird. They fixed her clearly in my mind when they pointed to a baby, her sister's granddaughter, being wheeled by Lisa and her friends down the cobbled street in a carriage. Many individuals remained obscure to me until the villagers provided me with a common referent: my kids and theirs, and the offspring of their affinals and collaterals, who were identifiable as my children's companions. By way of the children—visible in the street, under the storage houses, or by the millstream—I got the hang of the genealogies.

Children Reveal, Accelerate, and Interpret the Social Dynamics of the Village

In 1971, Lisa's emerging friendship with the granddaughters of an unwed elderly woman, Hermitage Mary, afforded insight into the dynamics of families that have little genealogical breadth, families that, for good reason, tend to be taciturn and on the defensive. Through Lisa, we gained insight into the preoccupations and strategies of the land poor in communities where, until recently, land was *everything*.

In this friendship, Lisa's study habits, imported from an Ivy League environment, propped up Hermitage Mary's granddaughter's waning dedication to study. The granddaughter, Mari Luisa, was bright, but good study habits are hard to establish in a crowded kitchen, the only warm place in a village dwelling, and her grades were falling.

Studying in tandem with Lisa, Mari Luisa's academic performance began to improve and in turn gave Mari Luisa's father, Santiago, the courage to reapply *himself* to the math he would have to learn to obtain a miner's promotion. He needed the promotion badly to support a growing family that was dependent exclusively on his wages. He had been disinherited when, over parental objections, he married Hermitage Mary's daughter, Mari Pepa, the sixteen-year-old girl he had impregnated. Between them, the teenage couple (such a *young* parental couple is a demographic anomaly in rural Asturias) had no land on which to grow the potatoes the family needed for survival. Mari Pepa, an illegitimate child, had of course received no patrimony; and Santiago had been cut off from his, having chosen love over land.

The family took heart when Mari Luisa, the eldest daughter, reversed her academic decline during her fifth school year. Secretly, Mari Luisa began coaching her father in math. We learned about Lisa's role as catalyst in this happy reversal only on a subsequent field trip, after Santiago had been promoted to *capataz.*

Our children and their friends are more than mere actors in such a sequence of events. They form the audience to whom the essential elements and morals of the emerging story are told, and the children themselves become its reinterpreters, as do the anthropologist parents who listen to them.

What we see in the story is not unusual, a seizing of opportunity in the ranks of those at the bottom—people deprived not only of land but also of relatives (the paternal relatives whose resources are denied them)—and the reversal of that status in times of economic and social expansion. What we also see is how the fortuitous friendship of the anthropologists' children can both accelerate these dynamics and illuminate them. As Hermitage Mary told her story to Mari Pepa, and Mari Pepa in turn told it to Mari Luisa and her sister when they were little, they told it also to Lisa—catching her up, as it were, on the family history in order to include her within its bosom. In its telling, the story acquired a new momentum and new possibility. For Lisa was not only a receptacle into which they poured the family tale but a resource for adding to that tale a happier ending.

Children Link Us Longitudinally to the Village

Luke, by contrast, experienced the intimacy of a family of great genealogical depth and breadth. In 1971, after several months in the village, he still had not made much progress in speaking the language of the villagers. As a second language, it was difficult to learn because the spoken language—one of the many archaic derivatives of Latin and Romance that continue to be spoken in the northern mountain region—corresponded neither to the Castilian Spanish he was taught in the village school nor to what he could decipher in the translation of *Peanuts* and other comics we had bought for him in the provincial capital. Nor, at first, did the words he heard correspond very often to the things he could see before him, for he was out in the street with boys who were speaking of action: of hiding, of losing animals, of defying bears, and of searching for mythical creatures. The words that Lisa heard, by contrast, referred to things and people close by, in a kitchen, or on the street visible from the kitchen window. It seemed to us that the greater domestic confinement of girls made it easier for them to learn the new language.

Luke seemed to take note of the contrast in progress. Did sibling rivalry appear in a new guise? At any rate, Luke began to withdraw from street play where he was continuously mobbed (with enthusiasm) and where words were hard to tie to their referents. During some of the pleasantest weather, he stayed inside by himself, reading Spanish editions of *Tin-Tin,* the Belgian adventure comic. It was during this period that the parish priest stopped by, inviting Luke to accompany him for the afternoon. The priest was driving into the uplands to say Mass in an outlying alpine chapel. Luke accepted. That evening, Luke did not return with the priest. We got word that he, at age seven, had been invited to stay and help with the tasks of an extended, cattle-keeping family. Some of its members were based temporarily on an outlying upland pasture, tending the youngest crop of calves and making the last of the summer's hay. Luke shared their "great bed," stuffed with fern, and when it got crowded with yet another guest, he moved off to sleep in the stable under the same roof. He ate beans and homemade sausage out of a common pot. When he was not making hay, he and another boy played at building dams. Together they diverted the thin, silver streams that fed the upland meadows. When, after two weeks, he descended to the village, he was ragged—a cow had eaten, or so he said, part of his acrylic sweater. Replete with parasites of that stable environment, he was gloriously happy. We were happy too. He had begun to speak a language that was understood locally, although he spoke only in the indicative mode.

We never did find out exactly how the working-guest arrangement came about, whether the priest had seen Luke's need to get away from a vocal crowd of street boys or whether Luke, by some gesture, had expressed to the priest a longing to remain in the relative freedom of the less-crowded mountains. Perhaps it was Obdulia, the head of the extended family that offered the mountain hospitality, who had sought the arrangement.

Obdulia had recently been widowed and had come into her own as the manager of the family herd and land, which she ran from the kitchen bench in her home in the village, confined as she was by mourning. The new responsibilities were added to those she had assumed in developing a widespread network of relatives and friends. On such a network of *amistades* (family friendships), she had advanced the careers of three of her six offspring. The three were now living and working elsewhere, in the industrial sectors of Spain and Belgium. They habitually came home for baptisms and marriages, and for haying. Obdulia had probably schemed with the priest to incorporate Luke, and thereby us, into her network. The initiative was to our mutual benefit, and the relationship developed over the years into a warm friendship.

In the late 1970s, for example, when Luke was fifteen, he and two biking companions cycled through northern Spain. They arrived, unannounced, in Escobines, and Obdulia fed the young men's hearty appetites. As Obdulia and I had shared a boy's company and labor for part of the summers of 1971 and 1972, and as she shared her meal a few years later with him and his companions, when now I visit her, *we* share a single piece of fish "like sisters," she says. Then we talk about our descendants, who are "as cousins of the flesh to each other." Luke's early social discomfort on the village streets, Obdulia's resourceful intervention, and the developments thereafter led to what I call our affective kinship. Such kinship rests on our parental interest in our own and each other's descendants.

As a consequence, Obdulia's grandchildren and their cousins are people whom we now keep track of in the village, although the latter were only peripheral contacts during our longest stay in Escobines. Of all her descendants, Obdulia advises us to keep track of her grandson Juanin, in whose promising leadership the future of Escobines may be vested:

> He works hard; harder than those twice his age. He's been
> pitching hay ever since Luke and he made a game of it that
> summer in Fechero [the name of the family's parcel of land in
> the uplands]. He was smaller than the scythe when he
> insisted that the men teach him to mow. He's skilled not
> only in country ways like his father; he's savvy. He works part
> time down at the bar run by his second cousins, that bar
> where outsiders mix with locals. There he overhears
> conversations and weighs what people say.

Sitting beside her in her kitchen in 1981, I remember having heard her voice tail off like this before. After a pause, she resumes speaking about an earlier time, for the thoughts of one generation lead to thoughts of another. She reaches for a photograph of Juanin and Luke that she has kept handy in a drawer under the kitchen bench, the *escano,* where now, in old age, she spends most of her day. A decade ago, I had taken the photo in the uplands. She looks at the photo. Talking about and looking at our mutual descendants has evoked her sense of generation. She speaks now of an ascendant generation, of her father: "He was a self-taught man. The judgment of no man in my generation, not even my husband Juan's, has ever equaled that of my father." She makes me attentive to the implicit comparison that is coming: "When our parish cooperative dissolved after *our* [civil] war, my husband was charged with the debts of others, for he had been the leader of the cooperative here. He shouldered the debts, but the resentment he allowed himself to feel ate away at his guts, and produced the ulcer that killed him." She pauses and looks again at the photograph of the descending generation, of Luke and Juanin. She sees two youngsters sharing a wineskin, dribbling red wine from their chins, and grinning. "Juanin," she says, "isn't only a good worker, brave and judicious, he's got a sunny disposition." I am to infer that the missing trait in Juan, her husband, was a sunny disposition. Courage *and* good disposition, in Obdulia's eyes, are required of a real leader. Through Obdulia, four generations of personalities and village politics come within the anthropologist's scan, prompted by a photo of our descendants.

She notices that I am no longer the young mother I was when first we met. She wants to share with me another part of her wisdom before she passes on. "Listen now, Renate. Your daughter is of age to soon be marrying, so I will tell you about my change of life." From her experience of several generations, she draws conclusions concerning a delicate gynecological subject. I see then that entrance into marriage and exit from reproductivity are seen by her as parallel transitions. The subject could not have been raised without the common trust based on our mutually reiterated motherhood, our "common" children and grand-children.

Years earlier, but under similar circumstances, Obdulia told me how she had tied her family into the world beyond the confines of the village. But more than Obdulia or any single villager, it is our own children who prompted us to expand our awareness into the region's bureaucratic institutions, within which all the villagers are embedded. The needs of our children inevitably pulled us out of Escobines and into the larger Asturian and Spanish compass, in this way obviating any possibility of our being faulted—as community studies correctly have been faulted—for ignoring the larger context.

Children Move Us Beyond the Local Community

Back in 1965, soon after settling into Escobines and soon after my husband's departure for Africa, when my powers of communication in the village were still very limited, I discovered that, just outside my range of view, Luke's irrepressible curiosity had driven him to open a small medicinal bottle and swallow an undetermined number of aspirin. Somehow, in a village then without motorized vehicles, a cab was gotten, and Luke was rushed to the hospital, two hours of winding roads down the mountainside. In all the commotion of that departure, I forgot his shoes. Barefoot, in a country where for over two decades bread and shoes had been promised to everyone, and, indeed, delivered to the vast majority, he was unwittingly admitted into the hospital as a charity case. I learned of our status only later, when I inferred it from the fact that Luke's pumping out and the overnight stay it entailed was followed by no bill. In this way, I was introduced to the national medical system. (Years later, a more serious illness assaulted Luke in the field and gave me insight into the class system of which our international biomedical system is also a part, an understanding that has a bearing on my current work, discussed below.)

If Luke's experiences introduced us to the health-care bureaucracy, Lisa's experience enlarged our understanding of the system of higher learning. During our sabbatical year in 1978, Lisa chose to go to boarding school in France, rather than attend a high school in Asturias or elsewhere in Spain. On previous field trips, village and city friends had told her how stifling the *institutos* were, how short of labs and sports, how routinized the learning. She imagined a French *lycée* to be different, if only because teachers in France did not have to contend, as did those in Spain, with the legacy of Franco. What she got in France was much less different than what she had anticipated. When Lisa came back to Spain over Easter vacation and reported on the "stuffy teaching" at the *lycée,* we saw that we would have to look beyond easy political explanations to explain the similarity in educational methods employed in France and Spain.

Lisa also introduced us to a less formal institution, whose dynamics were veiled from middle-aged scrutiny. On her last summer in the field, she helped with preparations for the annual village fiesta. Its organization is a task that young unmarrieds of the village arrogate to themselves. Through Lisa, we learned how not only villagers but young people from both sides of the mountain range, and from two provinces, take part in the fiesta's planning and execution, and in the writing of fiesta speeches. We noticed how formulaic were the references to locality woven into the fiesta's *pregon,* the keynote address. Lisa's contribution underscores how the expressive culture is annually reforged with external elements as well as with authentically local ones, and the important role that young outsiders play in that reforging.

A Child's Encounter Animates a New Inquiry

Finally, I want to speak of the incident that generated the emotional charge energizing my present investigation. Its source lies in Andrew's adverse reaction to Asturian voices when he was small. To be fair to Asturians, before I present the revelatory incident, I must brief the reader on Asturian vocalization.

In northwestern Spain, the atmosphere is normally damp; the region is known as "wet" Spain. Moisture rolls in year round from the Bay of Biscay and is forced up the mountainside where it is cooled and precipitates. Sheets are damp. Bronchitis is endemic; pneumonia, until recently, was a frequent cause of death; and black lung afflicts coal miners, causing fears of early incapacitation, premature retirement, and death.

No wonder, then, that the most reliable folk indicator of health is the respiratory and vocal system. Its cultural expression is the splendid Asturian "deep song," which evolved from desires to communicate across deep Asturian chasms and loud, rushing streams. Even now, "canned" popular songs have not driven the *asturianada* out of the region's bars. Annual competitions in the genre draw new compositions and competitors from city and countryside alike, and attract a large, vociferous audience that shouts its critique. Voice announces one's vitality, as long as one still has it.

Villagers were convinced that I had come to Escobines in order to obtain a cure for whatever ailed me, for in my American tonal range they perceived no vitality. By their standards, my voice was weak, and my health needed restoring. Back in the early mornings of 1965, I used to be awakened by what I thought were street quarrels. When I jumped from my bed to the window, all I could discern in the dim dawn were scenes of greeting. Asturians have their reasons for valuing pulmonary capacity and vocal cords.

In 1971, I saw that Andrew, then just turned two, was experiencing not only linguistic but auditory shock. He would cling to me and hold his ears when villagers paid attention to him. At my request, friends and neighbors learned to soften voice and gesture—a concomitant of speech—when directing themselves at him. As a favor to me, they stopped striving to elicit from Andrew the intense interaction that they valued but he was not inclined to give.

I could not control everyone in the environment or anticipate and deter every shock. A townswoman, the friend of a village friend, went on a picnic with us and took notice of Andrew's full baby cheeks and fair skin. In an especially piercing voice and effusive manner, she chortled at him and pinched his cheeks, hoping to receive a hug in return. Asturian kids learn to reciprocate with hugs; but my boys did not. When Luke was small, he escaped Asturian endearments even if that escape took him far from his mother. Andrew, in 1971, was still too attached to me for that. The strange woman's voice hurt his ears, and her gesture frightened him; he backed off and directed a deep, guttural sound at her. Repelled, and taken aback by this negative reaction, she plumped herself down on the grass, struck her hands as if to clean them, and condemned him loudly: *"Ay, que nino mas repugnante!"*

I realized that Andrew's temporary speechlessness had brought on the incident. And I regretted that, regardless of how much I had tried in Andrew's presence to maintain spoken English in our village home, local sounds had drowned it out as we became absorbed in local life. Under those circumstances, Andrew had lost the few words of English he had acquired before our departure and was left for a time without words, resorting to more primitive defenses against intrusion. It was these primitive defenses that the woman labeled "repugnant."

I often pondered the woman's exclamation. I see now that what Andrew experienced at the picnic was a kind of cultural test in

which, according to the woman's lights, he demonstrated a hope-
less animality, perfectly justifying her uncordial response. I wondered if, in earlier times, this outcome might have fixed Andrew's
assignment for life.

I also recalled that I had seen respectable village elders behave
as brusquely toward idiosyncratic villagers: toward a woman,
young in years but precociously aged, who wandered the streets
reciting ballads; toward a man of sluggish movement and bulg-
ing eyes; toward obese women with peculiar dermal formations;
and toward the several deaf mutes in the village. I determined to
understand how the unmitigated rejection I had seen could pass
as socially acceptable adult behavior. Questions arose as I searched
for understanding.

What was it that diminished the capacity and respectability of
such a conspicuous number of villagers? Was it a single affliction
or multiple? If multiple, how did villagers distinguish between
those who deserved courtesy and those who did not? How long
had the affliction(s) been endemic enough so that a whole social
code regulated the expression of courtesy toward the afflicted?
Under what conditions were villagers willing to revise the assignment of category that so often was accompanied by signs of
affliction?

How many children had been wrongly appraised, and for lack
of positive social reinforcement failed to thrive? What was the
level of village affliction? Was it higher than would normally be
expected in a pastoral Cantabrian community? Whatever the
level, was affliction due to causes *other* than those locally postu-
lated as "bad blood" (the Asturian believe in familial transmis-
sion of defective traits)? How did cultural practices play a role in
inflating the number of afflicted?

I had a hunch that children who were unusually sensitive or
shy—children like Andrew, who, by Asturian standards, failed
to communicate in the accepted manner at the expected time—

could quickly become labeled and marginated, relegated to the pool of the able-bodied permanently assigned to the most lonely and labor-intensive tasks, far from the social core of the village: goatherds, gatherers of firewood, smokers of others' hams, distributors of manure. And as I participated in the daily round of the village, I also got the hunch that environmental, rather than familial or genetic, factors posited locally (and not only locally, I was later to learn) could account for much of the affliction and behavior surrounding it. I resolved to pursue these hunches in a future investigation, to transform my parental shock into understanding.

Hazards and Rewards of Taking Children into the Field

When we took our family into the field, we exposed our children to hazards we thought we could manage. Unforeseen hazards of auditory assault and humiliation were far more difficult to overcome. Undoubtedly, these made more of a lasting impression on me than on Andrew.

He has recovered from the malediction. Now in high school, he excels at cross-country skiing and computer programming. As he did in the village, he refrains from intensely interpersonal interaction. Freshman English, with its analyses of grammar and character, is his dreariest subject; biology, with its animal behavior, neural evolution, and behavioral genetics, interests him considerably. When electives are offered, he chooses Basic and Assembly language over Spanish or any spoken language. Andrew's current mix of interests and strengths reflect the toddler's traits— and the problems and opportunities they created for his mother in the field.

I cherish the motive force given me by that woman at the picnic. I needed it to come to terms with the causes and cultural consequences of affliction in the village. Following my hunch I found that the cause of much affliction was an unrecognized deficiency of iodine. Accordingly, goiter and cretinism were endemic in isolated communities such as Escobines, where, until recently, people grew most of their own food and chose marriage partners from a small pool of relatives. Ignorant of the cause of the affliction, they attributed it to "bad blood." Now as villagers begin to "marry out" and cease to rely exclusively on locally grown crops, the deficiency fades, but cultural consequences linger: The community remains on the alert to categorize children into either "ordinary people" (the majority) or "those we exclaim about" (*el ay!*).

In a labor-intensive economy, the latter were destined to perform the most routine tasks. Such allocation once made sense in terms of the limiting resources: land and labor. It also made sense in terms of limited maternal patience. In Asturias, where good land is scarce and where, before the present generation, fertility rates were high, all able bodies, including women's, were needed to convert rocky slopes into cropland. Under such conditions, few women had either the time, imagination, or resources to devote to developing "the greatest potential" in their offspring. Had Andrew been born in Escobines, he might easily have been one of those designated early, and for a lifetime, to carry out routine and lonely tasks, far from the core of the village. While in the field during his toddlerhood, I apprehended this destiny only vaguely. Yet, however vague, it was unsettling.

My recovery took longer than Andrew's. It led, by way of graduate school, to the subject of my doctoral dissertation.[1] In it I explored the obstacles accounting for the long delay in implementing iodine prophylaxis, obstacles not unlike those delaying prophylaxis elsewhere. I would never have addressed this topic had Andrew not been assaulted at the picnic, had I not vicariously experienced his pain.

Balance Sheet

Our children in the field lead us to enrich our observations. They help us overcome the limitation built into us by our professional training: to become too intensely focused on a single, predetermined problem. Children also generate unforeseen tensions that are painful and that redirect our inquiry. Our children tie us to the social structure in a longitudinal way and bring us into contact with institutions to which we might not otherwise relate. What is predictable about children in the field is that their breadth of experience will be valuable and their depth of feeling will sometimes be inconvenient, even hazardous. Such contraries pose severe tests for anthropologists and their offspring, and force us to seek deep explanations. These can emerge as rich ethnographies.

The Impact of the Field on Our Children

Residing in the Field

We rented several houses over the field years discussed here. The houses varied our perspectives of neighborhood and affected the children in a variety of ways. Our first house was newly built and cold with damp plaster. Plumbing had been installed, but the infrastructure was missing, so water was fetched in buckets from a nearby spigot. I never succeeded in firing up the cast-iron stove with either wood or coal, so I cooked over a small fire on the kitchen hearth. Lisa, Luke, and I ate around it quite cozily. The damp, penetrating cold of the house induced me to type my notes with the Olivetti on my lap, keeping my fingers warm and flexible by the fire. The fire concentrated our indoor life into a small

radius. There were several rooms upstairs, but we rarely inhabited them, making our life in the kitchen and on the porch, with
the muddy or dusty lane and all its activity just beyond. We
learned, as the villagers did on entering a house, to park our
wooden shoes beside the doorstep, keeping on only the slippers
worn inside them. Escobinos work hard to maintain scrubbed or
polished floors, and wooden shoes that one can kick off easily are
crucial to that effort. Luke found, however, that the clogs impeded his fast getaways, and he never accepted the adaptation. What
with the attraction of cattle and carpenters, the thumping of a
butter churn in a nearby portal, pigs to circle around, and chickens to frighten—all within a few steps of our doorway—he was
constantly in and out. And I was forever sweeping, without ever
obtaining the requisite Escobines polish.

Later, the same wooden footgear allowed Lisa to be reasonably
comfortable in very cold schoolrooms. She quickly discarded the
rubber boots she had brough from abroad. Not always to our
physical advantage, we selectively adopted the local customs
evolved over centuries of adaptation to the wet climate. The se-
lectiveness was apparent when, for example, the older children
refused to wear the warm undershirts in which village parents
envelop children even in summer. These garments protect children from the quick chill that always threatens in the mountains.
Apparently, it was important for our children to maintain certain
material distinctions invisible to the eye of the village adult.
They were asked to conform in many ways to village norms, and,
largely, they complied. But they also endeavored to maintain
their own identities.

The house of our second summer was old but pleasant with
aged wooden planks, a floor-to-ceiling upstairs window, and a
filigreed iron railing. We could survey much of the upper end of
the village from that vantage point, and the sun shone in, making it a pleasant place for Lisa and her playmates. The front yard

was enclosed, and the owner kept an option on it so as to be able to corral his animals there from time to time. Luke and boys bigger than he played there with the Tonka truck he had brought from America. It hauled manure, corncobs, rocks, and small boys without ever breaking down. Across from this house ran the mill-stream from which we fetched water for bathing and scrubbing. We had to go much farther for drinking water, but the fetching put us on the same wet footing as the villagers.

The kitchen in this house had been designed with servants in mind, so it was dark and located in the back, cut off from the life of the village. This had unforeseen consequences for us. Georgina, the girl who helped us that summer, contrived to spend little time in the kitchen. The weather brought an uncommon drought, and we picnicked almost daily in the haying fields, often in the company of Georgina's family, who taught me to build a well-proportioned haystack and the criteria of balance by which both stacks and people are judged. Over the summer I learned that something as seemingly insignificant as the location of a kitchen can systematically affect the entire household. It can affect what we eat and with whom, and what we learn along with that consumption.

Our third house was again new, pretentious, and cold. It was a third-story apartment, built over a stable and hayloft. We learned to fire up the cast-iron stove and succeeded in making the kitchen comfortable. We converted the pantry into a tiny bedroom so that Lisa, who was by then a schoolgirl, could have privacy from her brothers, who shared a room. We fit in a custom-made bed just twenty-two inches wide. In the course of these arrangements, I learned that during our first summer in Escobines, Lisa was considered to be a deprived child—deprived of human warmth—because she slept in a room of her own. The villagers' observations on our unusual way of arranging for our children's comfort (observations shared with us only after watching us over several visits) gave

me valuable insight into the villagers' views of how living arrangements subserve development goals. We vacated that third home in
the village when the landlord requested the flat for his newlywed
daughter, who was about to establish a home.

Our fourth house put us at the center of village activity. This
house was eminently suitable for ethnographic purposes, and it
was advantageous to Luke and Lisa, who were already well integrated into village life. But village life still made daunting demands on Andrew, who in regard to villagers remained very reti-
cent. This location at the center of things heightened those
demands.

The apartment balcony hung over the bubbling millstream.
The spinsters knelt there washing, and boys dared one another to
jump over the stream and over the piles of laundry. Next door
lived a ninety-year-old woman, who sunned herself on the patio,
singing softly to herself. Across from us, a private chapel accom-
modated candlelight vigils on weekday nights. Next to it, a con-
struction worker regularly dumped his pile of sand. Beyond the
house, but visible from the kitchen, was the newly inaugurated
preschool. When the school's door was open, which was usually
the case, we could see toddlers practicing their letters at long
benches. At recess, the boys played chasing games or follow-the-
leader, obliterating the pictures girls made in the sand and
prompting them into circle games led by older helpers. Andrew
would look out on the school from the kitchen window, but
balked at attending it. Beyond the school was a popular miners'
bar and grocery store. I learned to know the time of day by the
daily sequence of benchsitters. A clientele of cattlemen and con-
struction men collected regularly in the bar underneath our
apartment.

The house was perfect for most of the family and for fieldwork;
but the noise from the first floor and the constant activity eventu-

ally drove my husband to seek a quiet study elsewhere, and drove me at least once to shout out the window at a late-night reveler. We were as much on display to the villagers as they were to us, and frailties and humanity showed through on both sides. In this house the boundary between village and family life became increasingly permeable, exposing us to previously unfathomed dimensions of its activity—and exposing Andrew to more faces and voices than he was ready for.

Household Help and Child Care

We always recruited help. Girls from Escobines rarely studied beyond the eighth grade, becoming employable at age fourteen. Adult women were not available for hire. The girls' heaviest labor was the wash, and during our first summer we had more wash than most households. Luke had arrived in the village ready to abandon diapers, but village generosity set back his toilet training. It was the custom to give small, locally grown hazelnuts in friendship, and Luke became an eager recipient of these offerings. He cracked them open between rocks to get at the sweet meat. Whether it was the rocks and dirt or the shells, or even the incompletely chewed nuts, some local factor accelerated peristalsis so that he had to remain in diapers until we left in the autumn. Although village infants learn to use the potty before the end of their first year, Georgina did not seem to mind doing the wash on Luke's behalf. His physiological distress allowed her to spend many hours with girls like herself, kneeling at a wash station distant from that of the spinsters and matrons. During the 1960s village girls were allowed to get together with friends only on Sunday, unless, of course, they found a way to assemble in the course of their duties. Their assemblies took place at the wash station. The diapers provided Georgina with an unusually sociable summer, and she sang her way through it. Her attitude, partly a result of all that happy washing, rubbed off on the children and on their relationship with her family.

Luke was content to stay with Georgina's mother and father, while Lisa, Georgina, and a daughter of Obdulia's accompanied me on an automobile trip through the province. Luke undoubtedly shared Georgina's parents' matrimonial bed, although Georgina showed me how she had placed his portable crib in a room of "his own" across from that of her parents. Luke holds an image in his mind of the few days he spent in Georgina's house when he was two: "It was very dark in that house and in the kitchen. I was very little; I guess I couldn't see out the tiny window up above the kitchen counter. We sat around that black hearth. They sat me down and gave me cups of black coffee." His memory is probably accurate. Georgina had noticed that our children did not drink coffee, and she knew that I did not approve of it. Her parents seized the opportunity to make up for what they saw as Luke's deprivation, and delighted in telling me of the pleasure he had taken in a substance forbidden under other circumstances. All children have some experience with forbidden pleasures when outside their parents' control. When our children served as proxy children to the parents of "our girls," they probably experienced both more pleasure and more pain than they would have experienced at home.

The demand for heavy rural labor slackened in the 1970s as mechanization supplanted human energies and fields that used to be sown in grain were turned to meadow. So in 1971 when we five were all together—my husband and I and our three children—we took on two girls: Graci and Mari. I did most of the cooking; they did the wash and the dishes. As for child care, Luke and Lisa hardly needed it, and Andrew for a long time refused to be left in the girls' company. Andrew's resistance was finally overcome with the help of Graci's little brother. Feliz occasionally came to our house to be watched over by his sister in the course of her duties with us, and attracted Andrew into playing "cows and calves" with him. Soon after, Andrew went off for hours to play with Feliz in the manger across from his mother's kitchen, and eventually Andrew trusted himself to enter that kitchen without my company.

Feliz's mother had a comfortable way about her—and a comfortable kitchen floor, made in another century of hand-hewn chestnut planks. Objects did not clatter, and voices did not echo the way they did in the newer kitchens with their floors of stone or cement. Several of the small children in the neighborhood went there to play. As Andrew came to spend happy hours in that setting, Graci's mother felt free, from time to time, to ask us to release Graci for some hours of work in the family fields. Through the growth of such exchanges, our families became important resources to each other. Goods and services, as well as youngsters, flowed between us, and as the flow intensified, so did the flow of ethnographic and expressive material. During those years, it would have been difficult—and certainly useless—to distinguish between my roles of mother and fieldworker.

The hired girls' labor freed me from much of the work that plumbing and appliances relieve us of in America, work that would have kept me housebound or kneeling and pounding at the wash station and unable, because of the rushing water and unaccustomed physical strain, to avail myself of its daily news. (The "daily news" is not a metaphoric invention. The word *prensa* refers to the daily press, *presa* refers to millstream. Villagers, knowing what an important source of communication is the center wash station on the millstream, humorously slurred their speech when speaking of the destination of a woman heading down the street with a washbasket.) But beyond the contribution of labor, the girls' presence in our home integrated us into the village and made their homes, at some distance from the center, far more permeable to us than would otherwise have been the case. Moreover, their laughter and conversation in our kitchen helped all of us to bridge the language gap sooner.

I recognize that the entry of the twosome into our home and family life occurred at a critical point in Andrew's early development and contributed to his acute sense of disruption. The best field situation for him would have been quieter, a house not centrally located but pressed against the hill, next door to a family like the one we acquired through our girl Graci.

Living Intertwined with Investigation

The girls rarely did the daily shopping. Lisa or I did it, for the round of errands in the village belongs to Escobinas. Lisa and I also dedicated ourselves to the child care that, in America, we see as so important: drawing, reading, or playing on a one-to-one basis with a child not yet in school. My husband, like the men around us, attended to his work beyond the walls of our house; he could be found in conversation with miners or cattlemen, or in his study in the next village, a kilometer down the road. After our 1971 spring and summer in the village, Luke and Lisa began to attend school. Along with the younger village boys, Luke sat quietly at his desk in the somber village schoolroom, and burst out of the classroom at recess to play "kick the donkey" (a kind of leap-frog involving penalties) and soccer. Lisa, along with the older village girls, rode the school bus to a consolidated school in the county seat. There, she and her friends, all in their wooden clogs, kept apart from the "townies."

As a family, we made excursions by car and on foot, sometimes with and sometimes without the company of villagers or urban friends. On occasion my husband would set out for the highest peaks, taking Luke and a friend, and sometimes Lisa and me; or he would join a party of climbers having roots in the village but livelihoods in the city. The demands of routine physical exertion made such recreation unattractive to villagers. Our lives were entwined with the locals, but distinguishable.

My activities differed from those of local women in one notable way. Their sedentary activity was needlework, mine was typing. They knew that their activities, and above all their words, were the raw material of my daily product. Just as a small boy for many months was my constant companion, so was a small notebook. Just as they fed him hazelnuts, they filled me with commentary to write in its pages.

The family fieldwork discussed here took place during years in which my husband was the principal researcher. I provided much of the raw material and he the theoretical perspective and research plan during our first funded field trip in Spain. He was then, and remains, a firm believer in "grounded fieldwork," and I provided much of that. Once the children were relatively settled, and much of the ethnographic context was delineated, he and I worked municipal and historical archives together, to give us depth in text and time.

I did not experience the role of principal researcher until 1976 when, for a short summer, only Lisa and Luke accompanied me to Spain. We lived in a lovely apartment in the eastern part of the province at the foot of the Peaks of Europe and within easy distance of Covadonga, a religious shrine and Spain's first national park. Luke and Lisa were then in their teens, and I could leave them for a few days at a time to go back to Escobines and other villages to make intensive inquiries on breast feeding under the auspices of the Human Lactation Project.

It was a group project carried out in a number of field sites. The sites, except for mine, were located in "developing countries." Fieldworkers were asked to follow a list of questions set out in a thick handbook. The protocol required me to pursue data in a more specific way than I had done before, when my roles were intertwined. The fact that my informants knew me well from before, and knew me as a mother who had lived among them, immensely facilitated my task. I already had the rich ethnographic background into which I could fit their specific replies and see the significance of their answers, which I could immediately follow up with more questions or type up as data without delay.

It was much easier to do this highly focused work without preoccupations about Andrew, who had remained with his father in the States, visiting his grandmother. The fieldwork was intense and the write-up in the apartment equally so. Neither of the children became sociable with the "townies" in that setting; indeed, they remember it as a dull summer, and Luke recalls it as an unhappy one. As teenagers, they seemed to need a common denominator, such as a classroom or a haying event, to breach the social barrier. As a consequence, Luke spent the summer biking and training for cross-country on steep country roads, and Lisa helped transcribe and process some difficult parochial archives, carrying out the task with a meticulousness I could not match. Both of them helped me photograph sculptures of the nursing Virgin Mary in remote chapels of the province. I liked being free to concentrate on my work and found I could be productive, alternating work with recreation in the splendid setting the location afforded. It was then that I decided to apply to graduate school to get the theoretical training that would focus my future inquiries. I could see that the maturation of my family was beginning to make such a course possible, and that the years of doing fieldwork in the company of children had sensitized me to topics worthy of inquiry.

Note

1. Renate Fernandez, "Ethnography of Nutritional Deficiency in a Spanish Mountain Village: Analysis of Public Health's Delay in Preventing Iodine Deficiency Disorders (IDD)," Ph.D. dissertation, Rutgers University, 1985.

9 A Children's Diary in the Strict Sense of the Term: Managing Culture-Shocked Children in the Field

In an early essay, "The Anthropologist as Hero," Susan Sontag refers to anthropology as a "total profession," one that demands a psychological and spiritual commitment equal to that of the artist, and a physical stamina equal to that of the explorer or adventurer.[1] The requirements of the discipline are such that we sometimes think of anthropologists as born and not made, as altogether rare individuals who voluntarily choose periods of homelessness, alienation, and physical discomfort in the radical pursuit of the experience and understanding of "otherness." As the demography of the profession has changed, however, the model of the solitary fieldworker (epitomized in Malinowski's original Trobriand work) has given way to a teamwork model in which spouses and children of all ages accompany the ethnographer. These family members may or may not share the anthropologist's affinity or enthusiasm for "basic strangeness," and the children especially may have been more often drafted than have willingly volunteered for the "foreign service."

This essay explores some of the cognitive and developmental limitations that children face in respect to their abilities to cope with the cultural and behavioral diversity encountered in the course of fieldwork. Based on a case study of my own children's psychological responses to recent and demanding fieldwork in Northeast Brazil, I argue that what we euphemistically refer to as "culture shock" takes on far more serious dimensions and consequences for the child and early adolescent, who may be, developmentally speaking, unable temporarily to suspend moral judgments and view difference with *la belle indifférence* of the disciplined ethnographer. I also include some concrete suggestions for guiding children through the inevitable shock, confusion, and anxiety that accompany traditional fieldwork with its emphasis on that paradoxically distanced and detached form of engagement called *participant observation.*

The by now voluminous literature[2] on the subjective aspects of fieldwork suggests that the requisite stance of cultural relativism by which the ethnographer presumably avoids negative value judgments and skirts ethnocentric biases and assumptions (and thereby also avoids considerable anxiety and depression) is by no means easy to achieve, even among professionally trained and well-seasoned anthropologists. Problems of projections, transference, and countertransference loom large, and the naive ethnographer may find himself using the field site as a huge Rorschach test in which to project and work out his own neurotic conflicts or rebellious fantasies. The shock and embarrassment caused by the publication of Malinowski's diary, which revealed the behind-the-scenes and unattractive attributes of the "genius of cultural relativism" at work as he battled (often unsuccessfully) with his own parochialism, chauvinism, racism, and hypochondriacal responses to cultural difference, is a classic case in point.[3]

The fieldwork experience is a highly fabulated social reality, a complex "as if" phenomenon. The Peltos speak of the "bargain" struck between the fieldworker and the people studied.[4] The anthropologist agrees to view as credible, reasonable, and correct many beliefs (e.g., sorcery) and behaviors (e.g., subincision) that the local people know the outsider does not really subscribe to at home. On their part, the local people agree to treat the outsider "as if" she were a member of the community, often "adopting" her into a clan, lineage, or family. Both sides recognize their behavior in relation to each other as metaphorical, a social fiction. But are the children of the ethnographer able to grasp the subtleties of this contract? Or are they able to "play the game" of participant observation in dead earnest only because their investment in the present moment, their being-in-time, is more immediate and complete than that of the adult? What is it like for children to struggle with radical otherness as they are, simultaneously, struggling with an emerging sense of self, identity, and social self-identity that are, to say the least, still fragile and vulnerable?

Growing Up Absurd

We have been anthropological refugees and fugitives as long as we have been a family. Rapidly orchestrated moves across country and across countries in pursuit of employment, as well as research, are part of our annual liturgical cycle. So much so that my elder daughter, Jennifer (thirteen at the time of the Brazilian research), has lived in more houses and attended more schools and preschools than she is years old. The same is true of my middle child, Sarah, who turned ten years old in Brazil, and my son, Nathanael, who was eight. We count the years and significant events and traumas in terms of place. That happened, we say, in the year of the Irish, or the year of the Boston "crazies," or during Fort Burwin summer. We recall that Nate took his first steps on Irish soil, that Sarah stopped speaking for several months when we put her into a bilingual, Tex-Mex day-care center in Dallas, that Jennifer (who has taken more than her share of lumps) had a broken arm both in Ireland and in Brazil and that she was knocked unconscious in a playground in Ranchos de Taos, New Mexico. My husband, Michael, and I were dumbfounded when, on one occasion, Sarah asked if we would be living in Amarillo, Texas, although it was only an overnight stop for us in a cheap motel on our way to the field site in New Mexico. On another occasion, when we asked Nate where he thought he was from, he said, "I guess I'm just an on-the-road boy."

In short, we are an anthropological family, and I thought, in the summer of 1982, that we were ready for the "real thing"—field research in the heart of the Third World—a market town in the interior, sugar-plantation region of Northeast Brazil. For me, it represented an opportunity to return to the same community and work in the same *morro* or *favela* (hillside shantytown) I had lived in as a Peace Corps community organizer and paramedic twenty years previously (1964–1966). This time, I would be initiating the first stage of a longitudinal study of the effects of extreme deprivation and exploitation on women as workers and as mothers, and on their children. I would be looking at infant and childhood mortality partly in terms of maternal behavior and selective neglect, and I would be studying the psychology of childhood survivors of these adverse conditions. The first stage, during the summer of 1982, was devoted to interviews and reproductive histories with seventy-two *favela* mothers, rural migrants, and residents of O Cruzeiro, largest of three shantytowns encircling the market town I call "Ladeiras."

Since I had been contacted by Dr. Cassell with respect to her proposed volume on children and fieldwork, I spent time in Brazil observing and recording the children's responses to the field, and I asked them to keep diaries and copies of letters sent to family members and friends at home. With their permission, I am going to share selected portions of their journals and letters with you. Although each child responded in a different way (based on individual differences, as well as sex, age, and birth order), I stress some of the common features of their experience and what was most problematic about it for all of them. While the oldest and youngest ultimately emerged not only unscathed but with positive feelings and new strengths, the middle child, Sarah, remains somewhat traumatized and scarred by the adventure, with effects and consequences still felt in our household today.

Settling In

The initial challenges the children faced in Ladeiras were rather straightforward and mundane: accommodating to cramped and uncomfortable living quarters, and a new diet of coffee, cola, beans, macaroni, rice, dried beef, and chicken that was eaten in an outdoor and *very public* café. In addition, for the first time, they had to behave conscious of the germ theory of disease. Here are excerpts from their first letters, or communiqués, out of Ladeiras.

> *Nathanael to his best friend:*
> Well, here I am in Ladeiras with nothing to do. It's a stupid place. One reason why it's stupid is our house. I hate it! It's

the worst house I've ever had to live in. Our roof is made of sticks and a lot of crud falls down into our stuff. Once a piece of junk fell on Dad's toothbrush.

Jennifer to her grandparents in New York City:
I'm having a rough time adjusting to Brazil. Here are a list of problems: We have to buy our drinking water. Our toilet doesn't work—it flushes right out into the back yard, so every morning we use the toilet at the bus station. The food—Yuk! *Straw* mattresses! Mom says her hammock is more comfortable, but she's afraid I'd fall out at night and break my arm again.

Sarah to her best friend:
Ladeiras is just *not* my kind of town. It's small, very poor, and very unmodern. Our house is crummy. Our water you can't drink, and there are rats, big spiders, and lizards all over the place. There's hardly any furniture, and the furniture we have is not so hot. Our floor is so dirty that we really, truly must wear shoes all the time so that we don't get little worms in our feet. And I can't wait til I can have a decent American meal without five million flies and 200 people watching us eat it.

Sarah's entry was complete with a drawing of a very mournful-looking Sarah eating at a table surrounded by, in her words, "rude, staring people."

Dealing with Difference

After the first few days, the complaints about physical conditions, while not ceasing, were overshadowed by difficulties in understanding and dealing with differences in behavior, expectations, and of course communication, linguistic and otherwise.

The children initially suffered from what they saw as a loss of privacy, autonomy, and calm, as their days became increasingly crowded with people, music, talk, and a general tone and intensity in human relations to which they were unaccustomed. The following are diary excerpts:

Jennifer:
There are always kids hanging around, and there's never any peace and quiet. Always noise, noise, noise (even at night). People never knock. They just walk right in. I mean *total* strangers. It feels like we're being attacked or something.

Sarah:
People are always *barging* in on us. They follow you right inside to where your bed is. Stupid people! They laugh at you because you can't speak Portuguese. [Picture of laughing heads looking through a window.]

Nathanael:
Jenny's the one who lets the kids in our door. Next time she does that I'm going to bop her one on the head. I went across the street to get a piece of candy and when I came back there were *still* thousands of kids in our house. I went into my room and closed the door. Too small, hard to breathe! This is going to be hard to go through.

Again, Nathanael, several days later:

At first just a few people were in our house. But in a little while there were Millions and Millions and Millions of people. I played ball outside with the kids while Jenny and Sarah went inside and threw up. The people spended *{sic}* about ten hours in our house. It was raining and we had to stay in our little room. Jenny was sick, Sarah was sick, and I was sick, but we had to stay with all these people in a squashed up room.

About two weeks into our stay, Sarah woke with a nightmare, while she later recorded for me. It captures her feelings of being overwhelmed:

> I dreamed that a huge soccer ball was chasing me in a motionless city. As I ran on through the city everything started to move again. I ran up to a person on the street to ask what was going on. As he turned his head I saw that it was a soccer ball. Then I ran to more people, and all of them had soccer ball heads and they started to chase me too. As I ran away a skinny hand grabbed me hard by the arm. I struggled and tried to bite the hand that held on to me.

The skinny hand in this dream is a particularly poignant image, for it conjures up all those encounters that Sarah, especially, found upsetting and shocking: the degree to which "strangers" touched her and played with her hair; the frighteningly thin arms of so many of the babies and young children of the Alto; the persistently outstretched (and sometimes grabbing) hands of the young street *molekes* (abandoned minors) and of disabled old beggars. For, in addition to dealing with *cultural* difference, the children were exposed for the first time to the social realities of life in the Third World, where want is large and death is small.

Here is an entry from Jennifer's diary on the occasion of one of her first visits to the Alto, where I was conducting my research:

> As we were climbing up the Alto, a deaf-mute, retarded kid kept pulling on Mom, trying to grab her purse. He made terrible faces and awful sounds came out of him. There was also a lady without a nose that freaked me out, but Mom said she was an old friend of hers.

Nate wrote in his diary:

> After lunch we went up to the Alto to see a newborn baby.
> When we got to the house there was a drunk man there. The
> drunk man had a moustache and he squeezed me hard and
> kissed me rough. He asked Dad to climb into the hammock
> with the baby. Stupid! Then the man got real angry and
> started asking Mom for money. We got scared and Mom got
> us out of there quick. After we got home some kids asked me
> if I wanted to come out and play ball. I said, "Don't bother
> with me now." I really wanted to go away from Brazil real
> bad now.

Although I did not explain to the children in any detail what
my research was about, Jennifer frequently accompanied me to
the Alto because she enjoyed playing with the babies and toddlers
while I interviewed their mothers. It was insensitive of me, however, not to consider that the topic of the research during this
initial stage, a social epidemiology of childhood mortality, might
be anxiety provoking for my own children.[5] Certainly, dealing
with human mortality, sickness, and suffering was the most traumatic challenge they had to face. On the cover of his diary, Nate
wrote in large, bold, Magic Marker script: "BRAZIL 1982 by Nate
Hughes. WHY WE WENT: Trying to Find Out Why Children are
Dying. Main Idea." His drawings of Ladeiras always include the
cemetery. And on subsequent pages he records the following:
"We went up to the Alto where Mom is interviewing the women.
One of the mothers had 17 children and 11 of them died. One
had 5 and 4 of them died. One had 11 and 6 of them died." And
Jennifer writes: "We saw this four month old baby on the Alto
who was really small and thin. I wish that the girl who was
taking care of him would come down to our house so I could help
care for him. We could give him bottled water rather than the
dirty river water that makes them so sick." When she learned
that our good friend Antonieta's newest baby was adopted—left

in a basket on her doorstep—Jenny developed a fantasy that we might acquire a baby in a similar fashion.

Eventually it occurred to Michael and me that it might be best to maintain a more protective distance between my work and research on the Alto and Mike's attempts to provide a more familiar and less threatening round of daily activities for the children in Ladeiras: marketing, Portuguese lessons, organized games and sports with neighborhood children, and visiting with the several families of the community that had generously taken on Mike's and the children's welfare *and* entertainment as a personal charge. In addition, we decided that every ten days to two weeks we would schedule overnight "mental health" weekends into the city of Recife where the children could enjoy the beach and eat their fill of Brazilian versions of American food—hot dogs, hamburgers, and milkshakes at Bob's Restaurant. Finally, we discovered that allowing the children to care for pets both alleviated boredom *and* at first reduced their gnawing anxieties about the precariousness of life. First we acquired three chicks—Chicken Little, Chicken George, and Chicken Jim. These were followed by a succession of stray animals, including a pair of runaway goats that were kept in our backyard and a miserable, scabby cur of a street dog that was rescued on its last legs and restored to a reasonable facsimile of health with scraps of corn, bread, and biscuits.

Yet each of these accommodations carried its own risks. The thoroughly enjoyed trips to Recife seemed to make the return to Ladeiras all the more difficult. "We got a bus and went back to Ladeiras," writes Nate on July 15:

> Tired and sad looking at our house. I went inside upsetly. Sarah was upset too. Sitting on a hammock with mosquitos biting us. I said, "Did we have to come here to do this research?" Well, with the look on Mom's face I think we had

to. After that one question we all fell down and went to
sleep.

Inevitably, perhaps, the first of the three chicks died, arousing
far more anxiety, especially in Nathanael, than it might have
under different circumstances. He writes:

> July 23. A Horrible Day in Ladeiras When My Chicken Died
> of Horrible Death. In the morning at 8:30 something terrible
> happened. I was playing with Chicken George on my bed
> and he fell over, straight on his back. Cheaping {sic} like
> crazy he died. I laid on my bed with him and cried and cried.
> It was the best and the funniest of all the chicks. I couldn't
> believe it. One of mine died. All day long I was thinking
> about it and crying. That was probably the saddest day in
> Brazil for me.

When the second chick showed signs of keeling over, Nate
scooped up the remaining two and gave them, as he writes, "to
an old couple who could take better care of them."

Not long after the death of Chicken George, the owner of the
outdoor café invited us to one of the cockfights he held regularly
in the back of his restaurant. We foolishly attended it with the
children, which not only reopened the recent wounds with respect to *our* chicks but convinced the children to give up eating
chicken (a mainstay of our diet) for the remainder of our stay in
Brazil.

A second trauma had more far-reaching effects, resulting in a
serious depression in Sarah that was further complicated by a
three-day bout of high fever and dysentery. It also brought Mike
and me to our senses and to the belated realization that we had to
change our *modus vivendi* with respect to the children's physical
and emotional needs in the field. While taking an afternoon rest,
we heard a racket outside. A crowd had gathered across the
street, and Sarah and I permeated the circle just in time to see a

sickly and scabied dog (not the one we had salvaged) give out its last whine as it was stoned and stick-beaten to death by a jeering and laughing group of adolescent boys. Sarah swallowed a scream and turned on her heels, closing herself into the little space she shared with Jennifer, promising never again to set foot outside the house. She almost made good her promise, insofar as her refusal to talk, or to listen to my "rationalizations" about *why* the sick dog *had* to be killed (although there was no sign of rabies), was followed by a fever that, under the circumstances, caused *all* of us to fear briefly for her life.

Nathanael, our most faithful scribe, recorded the incident most fully:

> *August 6, 1982.* In the middle of last night Sarah had three terrible fevers. One was 102, one was 103, and the other was 104. In the morning it was pouring rain and Sarah was sick again—103. She was sick while cuddling up in my bed. The doctor came to see what was the matter. She was sick alright {*sic*}, the doctor said. She had to have some medicine quick. So Dad went right out to get it, and I went with him. While we were walking back to the house I was thinking that Sarah could die if we don't treat her. Worst of all it was her birthday and *I* would die if she had to die on her birthday.

With the help of antibiotics (and *no* chicken soup), Sarah did get better, but her depression did not lift ("If I had a knife in my hand I promise I would stab it into my heart," she wrote with reference to the dog-beating incident). We rapidly decided that enough was enough and that Mike and Sarah should fly home immediately. Sarah resisted this plan, however. She wrote in her journal:

> Mom said that if it doesn't work out any better Dad and I should fly back to the USA and that Mom, Jenny and Nate would stay here for the last month. I'm really going to try to

handle it better because what Mom said really disturbed me.
I couldn't be separated from them for a whole month. Right
now I'm feeling very confused.

The confusion was followed by a fear that Sarah shared with us
and that gave me a clue as to how I might begin to help her. She
said she was afraid to go back to America now because everything
was changed, everybody was different, maybe *she* was different
too. "What if," she offered, "now I might even hate the United
States and all its fat, selfish people?" She was expressing a fear of
loss of social identity and of the anomie that accompanies this.
Then, angrily, she accused me of taking away *everything* that
meant anything to her: her home, her friends, even her country.
She said that I was changed too, because I was always "defend-
ing" the Brazilians, even when they were "bad" or wrong about
things, like beating a dog to death or making chickens peck out
each other's eyes. Shades of the Peltos' comments about the ar-
tifice involved in the stance of "cultural relativism." Sarah was
right, of course. Everything had changed for her, and not even
her mother was dependable because she explained and condoned
behaviors in Ladeiras that she would never for a moment accept at
home. I had perhaps succeeded as an ethnographer, but I had
failed miserably as a mother. From that point on, I at least tried
to collude with Sarah in making moral judgments and evalua-
tions that were more consistent with her level of cognitive development and more in keeping with our usual household and family values. It helped considerably. Sarah came out of her room (if
not out of her depression), and she even made friends with a shy
and reserved girl who lived a few doors away. She never did master more than a few words of Portuguese, however, and her appreciation of Brazilian culture remained minimal. But we were able
to complete the cycle of fieldwork as a family, and that felt very
much like a success to all of us (especially to Sarah).

Meanwhile, Jennifer and Nathanael were making tremendous strides, Nathanael through the medium of soccer, and Jennifer by breaking through the language barrier, which for her seemed to occur in an exhilarating and heady rush all in one day. There were also some regressions, especially for Nathanael, who began to take great pleasure in the consumption of Brazilian sweets (of which there are a seemingly endless variety) and in "stockpiling" and hoarding cheap, plastic toys and gadgets from the weekly outdoor market stalls. He writes in his journal: "Eating and eating and eating. Here's a picture of me eating three *chorros* after lunch. Burp!"

Termination and After: Working It Out

As the time to leave Ladeiras approached, the children began to engage in the behavior so characteristic of those who feel they are in a sense "doing time." Calendars appeared on the walls, with the days spent marked off, and journal entries were dominated by the countdown motif: five more days, four more days, and so on. Metaphors of the captive appeared in drawings. Nate drew a series of pictures in which our house in Ladeiras is depicted as a zoo, a prison, and a torture chamber. Jennifer's diary entry on the the last day reads "THIS IS IT" in huge letters over a drawing of balloons being released into the air with the caption "OH HAPPY DAY!" underneath. But the presumed sense of relief at the release from the field did not come easily. During this brief but intense time out of normal time, the children became attached to friends and to one large, extended family in particular. "I think I really am going to miss them," writes Jennifer. Nathanael, meanwhile, painstakingly records each leave-taking:

"This was the last time we would be seeing our good friend Padre Orlando. I know he's going to miss us."

But there was another anxiety, vague at first and difficult to pinpoint, but that finally became transparent in the final few days. The children could not easily separate their own feelings from their projections, and they assumed that most people in Ladeiras and on the Alto must feel as constrained and captive as they had felt. This was exacerbated by a few *molekes* (street children) who had "adopted" us, and who *now* requested that we take them back to the States with us. An Alto couple asked if we could not, somewhere in America, arrange an eye transplant for their blind son. A few town adolescents asked if we could help them locate scholarships or employment in California. And almost everyone we knew made requests for us to send back everything from presumed cancer medications to spare parts to "disco" roller skates. The America to which we were returning grew in mythic proportions for the children, fueled by local conceptions and misconceptions. The children began to see themselves as the elect, the lucky and privileged few who were able to escape into a land of milk and honey. And they began to experience something akin to the existential dilemma that Robert Jay Lifton, Kenneth Keniston, and Elie Weisel refer to as the guilt of the survivor.[6] They were leaving, but others would stay behind. The children confronted the central contradiction involved in accepting social advantages and at the same time feeling angry about social injustices. "I am going back to the place without flies," writes Jennifer, "and where babies are fat and healthy," and her fantasy of rescuing an Alto infant to take home with us became more insistent and real. Nathanael, meanwhile, besieged by requests for *lembranças* (souvenirs) from his neighborhood friends, distributed his cache of hoarded plastic "junk" and then even his prized Star Wars men and his miniature electronic games. The toys had, I sense, become somewhat tainted for him. He writes in his journal of giving each of his friends in Ladeiras their "share" of *lembranças*.

Most remarkable to me was the transformation in the children's attitude toward beggars, especially the ubiquitous street children who hang about every outdoor café and public place in urban areas. Initially the children had reacted with shock, followed by anger, denial, and rejection. "Beggars," the children write, "are always bothering you, always pestering you to death." On our return trip to Recife, however, just before our departure, the children (Jennifer and Nate, at least), seemed to accept beggars as part of their common-sense social world. I recall a particularly poignant incident in Fred's American Bar in Recife. We were eating our requisite hamburgers and milkshakes when a street *moleke,* about the same age as Nathanael, signaled to him from the street and demanded quite mater-of-factly and unapologetically: "Give me some of your hamburger." (I pretended not to notice.) Nate looked down at his half-finished burger, shrugged his shoulders, hopped off his seat, and handed it to the *moleke* waiting outside. The response was motivated, I suspect, not so much in this case by guilt or pity as by a growing realization that there were, indeed, limited goods in the world and that those without had the right to request, as Nate put it, "their share."

Long-term Effects

It is now more than a year since we returned from Ladeiras. The return meant, however, not "home" in North Carolina, but yet another move across the country to Berkeley, California, where new schools and new friends awaited the children once again. Their skills in dealing with difference, acquired in Brazil, came in handy in Berkeley, and all three children remarked on seeing Telegraph Avenue for the first time: "It's just like Recife!" Sarah and Nate were each asked by their teachers to write the predictable essay on the opening day of school: "How I Spent My Summer Vacation"—quite a challenging task for the children to integrate all their experiences this quickly. Nate's essay captured his characteristic ambivalence—his continuing anxieties about "entitlement" *and* his sense of wonder at the inventiveness of Brazilians:

> I learned from my trip to Brazil that the people there eat in dirty plates and dirty bowls. That's what I learned because we never eat with dirt in our pots and pans so every time I am sitting down I think of the people in Brazil eating with dirty plates. But there are a lot of things in Brazil that should be in America. They have so many ideas for the world. For instance, they have candy stands with many different kids of candy. [Here he enumerates.] And in Brazil they have ice cream made from all kinds of fruits and raisens {sic}, even *corn* ice cream. Also, America needs a market every Saturday. I thought it was a good idea. They sold live chickens, live turkeys, Brazil shirts and soccer socks, note books, and best of all special herbs for every kind of way of being sick. And they have cute little chicks and tiny monkeys. Also in Brazil they have motor cycle wheel chairs. In front is a motor cycle and in back is a wheel chair. Now *that's* what we need in America.

Sarah, even a year later and following some necessary family therapy and counseling, remains adamantly "closed" to any reinterpretation of her Brazilian experience. It still depresses her to think about it, and she has frequently let Michael and me know that the possibility of any of us returning there (and in any combination) hangs over her head like a dark thundercloud. Here are excerpts from an essay she has only recently written:

> In 1982 we went to Brazil for two months. I couldn't wait til
> we got back to America. Two months was more than enough
> for me. . . . I got sick in Ladeiras and spent my 10th
> birthday in a messed up house lying on a sharp straw
> mattress. I've decided now that the only places I'd ever visit
> again outside of America are Scotland, Ireland, and most
> countries in Europe. I'm *never* going back again to
> Brazil. . . . I like America better so I'm just going to stay in
> it. If my Mom goes to Brazil again, it would prove she
> doesn't care for me or the family because she would be
> breaking up the family over her work. And if she *made* me go
> she'd know I would hate it. So she'd make me miserable.
> Anyway she has *already* made me miserable because if we
> don't go back to Brazil because of me then Jenny and her
> would think I was a stuck up princess and get angry at me.
> So I would have to go back even if I hated Brazil.

Obviously, things are far from settled in our household, and
each of us is caught up in some rather classic double-binds. It is
not clear how the dilemmas regarding future research in Brazil
will be resolved.[7] For now at least, we have to put it on hold. We
are convinced, however, despite Sarah's very real distress, that
children *can* benefit enormously from the confrontation with radical otherness, although they may need several months, or even
years, and a great deal of patience to unravel their mixed emotions. I could point, for example, to the markedly increased sensitivity of all my children with respect to cultural and class differences, and their empathy toward stigmatized and marginalized
children. Nathanael's best friends over the past year have been,
somewhat like himself, refugees. As much as the children might
want to participate fully in the norms and activities of their classmates, there is a holding back, a kind of droll distance from some
of what they observe, an "as ifness" in their social performances.
They have acquired a larger world perspective against which they
now evaluate some of the absurdities of urban and suburban

American life. One could debate, of course, whether these traits
are beneficial or psychologically healthy. I tend to think so. The
children are proud of their knowledge and awareness and view
their behavior in the field as courageous, which in many instances
it was. And like the "fearless lion" in *The Wizard of Oz,* my
children have a gold plaque to prove it. Hanging conspicuously
on our living-room wall, it reads:

FOR COURAGE IN THE FIELD

———

JENNY, SARAH AND NATE HUGHES

———

CLOGHANE, IRELAND
1974–1975

"LADEIRAS," BRAZIL
1982

Notes

1. Susan Sontag, "The Anthropologist as Hero," in her
   Against Interpretation (New York: Dell, 1966), pp. 69–81.
2. See, for example, Hortense B. Powdermaker, *Stranger and
   Friend: The Way of an Anthropologist* (New York: Norton,
   1966); and Paul Rabinow, *Reflections on Fieldwork in Moroc-
   co* (Berkeley: University of California Press, 1977).
3. Bronislaw Malinowski, *A Diary in the Strict Sense of the
   Term* (New York: Harcourt, Brace and World, 1967).
4. Pertti Pelto and Gretel Pelto, "Ethnography: The Fieldwork Enterprise," in *Handbook of Social and Cultural Anthropology,* ed. John Honigmann (Chicago: Rand McNally,
   1973), pp. 255–257.

5. See Nancy Scheper-Hughes, "Infant Mortality and Infant Care: Constraints on Nurturing in Northeast Brazil," *Social Science and Medicine* 19, no. 5 (1984): 535–546; and Nancy Scheper-Hughes, "Culture, Scarcity and Maternal Thinking: Maternal Detachment and Infant Survival in a Brazilian Shantytown," *Ethos* 13, no. 4 (1985): 291–317.

6. See Robert Jay Lifton, *Death in Life: Survivors of Hiroshima* (New York: Random House, 1968); Kenneth Keniston, *Young Radicals* (New York: Harcourt, Brace and World, 1968), esp. pp. 131–132; Elie Weisel, *Night* (New York: Avon, 1970); and Samuel G. Freedman, "Bearing Witness: The Life and Work of Elie Weisel," *New York Times Magazine,* October 23, 1983, pp. 32–36.

7. Since writing this paper, I have been awarded a Guggenheim fellowship that will enable me to return to "Ladeiras," Brazil, in order to continue the research on child mortality and begin writing a monograph entitled "Mother Love and Child Death in Northeast Brazil." All five of us have decided to return to Brazil, although Sarah and Nate will return home with my husband, Michael, after the summer months. Jennifer, my elder daughter, has decided to postpone entering college in the fall of 1987 in order to remain in Brazil with me as my field assistant for the duration of the research project. All three children are enthusiastic about the return to Brazil and are somewhat dismissive of their previous difficulties. I remain guarded on the prognosis.

CAROLYN FLUEHR-LOBBAN AND
RICHARD LOBBAN

10   "Drink from the Nile
and You Shall Return":
Children and Fieldwork in Egypt
and the Sudan

Two years after our marriage in 1968, we headed for our first
experience in the field, in Khartoum, Sudan, to conduct research
for our doctorates. We had each received grants to conduct separate studies, in Sudanese law for Carolyn and urbanization for
Richard. Once settled in Khartoum, after six months of language
study and cultural acclimation, we learned how difficult it was for
the people we encountered to accept our status, not as predoctoral
research students, but as a married couple with no children. It is
customary in Sudanese marriage for a couple to conceive a child,
ideally, within the first year of marriage; here we were, married
two and then three years, without children and without even a
hopeful sign that we would conceive anytime soon.

237

In the beginning, we gave honest answers in our simple Arabic about wanting to delay this personal choice, but after much shaking of heads and clicking of tongues in disapproval, we backed off from the frequently asked question by claiming that such things were in the hands of Allah and out of our control. Frequently, after discussing our childless state, someone would express curiosity and request information about birth control, and Richard became a sought-after counselor for newly married or soon-to-be married men on this topic.

During this first period of fieldwork, from 1970 to 1972, we learned from some candid friends that because of our childlessness, many Sudanese doubted the fact of our marriage. This was brought home one day when a friend saw our wedding picture in our Nile houseboat bedroom and remarked, "So, you really *are* married!"

We went on to earn our doctorates in 1973 and were both employed as anthropologists at Rhode Island College, where we achieved tenure and passed through the academic ranks together. In 1975, when we returned to Khartoum for a summer visit, our friends expressed disappointment when they learned that no children had yet blessed our union. Carolyn's female friends assured her that the problem was no doubt Richard's and no fault of her own.

Our years of childlessness in the field clearly made us somewhat anomalous in the eyes of the Sudanese, but this aspect of our Western behavior was probably no more curious than the clothes we wore and the small Italian Vespa motor scooter we used as "family" transportation. So, as far as our research was concerned, although our childlessness was a social liability, it seemed to have had little direct effect on the gathering of our field data.

Nearly ten years later, in 1979, we made the decision to return to the Sudan for our sabbatical year; Richard planned to conduct a restudy of the same communities in which he had worked in

1970, and Carolyn, to investigate the practice of Islamic law in metropolitan Khartoum. We were now tenured associate professors and had had our first child, Josina. Many of our anthropological colleagues had warned us against taking a young child to the field, and our Sudanese friends were astonished that we actually brought our daughter with us.

Josina left America at the age of two years and seven months, just two weeks after she was fully toilet trained. She spent one month touring Europe, visiting the ancestral villages and towns of her great-grandparents. By the time of her arrival in the Sudan, then, she had already learned that people speak different languages in different countries—German, Polish, and Ukrainian—and even different dialects of English in the British Isles. Now she was learning that the Sudanese speak Arabic, that her parents also speak this language, and that she was expected to learn greetings and polite expressions in Arabic in order to function in her new life.

Fortunately, Josina was an outgoing, articulate, if small person at the time. She kept us informed on a regular basis of reactions, likes, and dislikes in her new setting. Apart from casual encounters on the streets and in public places, Josina did not act as the social "ice breaker" that children are supposed to be, for our friendships and relationships had become well established through our stays in the Sudan between 1970 and 1979. We lived with old family friends in Omdurman, across the White Nile from Khartoum, for about six weeks until we found accommodations in Khartoum that were more conveniently located to the university campus.

New foods, "Asian-style" toilets, and burned feet from accidently walking on a metal manhole cover exposed to the hot sun got Josina off to a slow start in her appreciation of, and adjustment to, Sudanese life. Sleeping out-of-doors because of the summer heat was a fun thing to do, and Josina liked very much the

Sudanese tradition of offering sweets to children and not demanding that they eat "good" foods. She attached herself to an eight-
year-old boy in the household, Waleed, but wanted no part of the
two small girls, Selma and Suakin, who followed her around the
house. Chewing gum and candy, purchased locally, were shared
and helped to form bonds with the children. Within a few days,
Arabic and English expressions for "Come on" and "Yes" and
"No" were heard throughout the house. We spoke only Arabic in
the house, except in our own quarters, where we continued to use
English, but with some lessons in Arabic for Josina.

During this six-week introductory period, we began the initial
phases of research, and, more important from Josina's point of
view, we found that the American Club of Khartoum was still
operating. We took her there one day. The combination of hamburgers, swimming pool, and Western-style toilets was too
much, and she reveled in this oasis of American culture. We
realized at this point how much of an American culture-bearer
Josina was, even at the tender age of two years and nine months.

During this initial period, Josina learned the rudiments of
Sudanese culture from language to dress to food. The only thing
that continued to upset her was the difference in toilet facilities;
she took readily to Sudanese food and had fewer intestinal problems than her parents with their more conservative digestive
tracts. In the house of our close friends we did not practice sexual
segregation, so common through the northern Muslim Sudan.

Perhaps Josina's greatest shock came in the area of language, a
skill she was beginning to master. At two and a half, Josina was
able to express herself well in English, and she commented un-
hesitatingly about her likes and dislikes. From the beginning,
she resented her parents' use of Arabic, especially as this was the
only language spoken outside the family for the month we lived
in Omdurman and when we visited Sudanese friends in their
homes. Very soon, the novelty of Mommy or Daddy translating

what she wanted to say wore off, and the games she played with the two children were primarily action oriented, thereby reducing wordplay. Although she ultimately came to understand and was able to speak a good deal of Arabic in basic greetings and conversations, she did not get to the point of feeling positive or being at ease in Arabic.

We luckily found a flat in Khartoum's bustling Suq el ʿArabi (the Arab market) where our neighbors were ʿAhmed the yogurt maker, Mohammed the cobbler, and Osman the watchman of the building. The flat had a bathtub, Western-style toilet, and even a bidet, all of which delighted Josina. We quickly established our daily routine, with the two adults going about the business of our research projects and Josina attending an international day-care center staffed by Kenyan and Eritrean women. Lacking our own transportation at the time, we were out each day walking the streets to catch our *boks* (small Japanese trucks converted to carry people on the box on the chassis) to do our shopping and visit our friends. This vitality of city life stimulated Josina to give a rich variety of comments and imitative behavior. The first comments we recall dealt with Khartoum's beggars, who elicited a flood of probing questions and subsequent sympathetic behavior. Lepers, the blind, cripples, and small, poverty-stricken children were subjects of the deepest probing. "Where is their home? Why are they so poor? Mommy, Daddy, we have to give them some food or money." The sight of a small, "European" girl giving coins to the poor in a society that highly values generosity touched many a Sudanese heart, and she was often swept up and embraced for such good acts.

Next came comments about the traditional Sudanese practice of facial scarification for ethnic identification. At first, when people with facial scars approached, Josina would run away, saying that she was afraid and that people looked like "witches," her term for bad people. As time passed, Josina came to know that many of our friends had facial scars, and through social contact, they gradually became "human beings" and no longer "witches" for Josina. Finally, one day she reversed herself completely and announced that people with scars are "good people."

During the third to fifth month of life in Khartoum, Josina began to act-out for us what were, to her, the most interesting and entertaining aspects of Sudanese life. Each act was performed first for us at home and subsequently for select visitors to our home, but Josina rarely performed outside our flat. The first act was an imitation of a begger she had seen dragging himself on the ground, having only the use of his hands and arms. Josina had seen this man with Richard and had talked about him for several days before she imitated his affliction in her personal dramatization of his plight. Her compassion for his condition was evident, but she found it intriguing to move about the house in this fashion. A short time later, Josina gathered all her books and toys, spread them out very carefully on the floor, and sat down in front of them, calling, "I'm selling, I'm selling. Books for sale, books," in a market huckster's voice. We joined the game and found out that we had to bargain for her wares, as is required in all Sudanese open-air markets. The game of selling continued, although her goods varied from clothes to canned goods to dishes and pots, and they were always on the floor in the style of small-time entrepreneurs in the Sudan.

Josina next began to parade around the house with her security blanket acting as a head cover. The edge of the blanket was held fast in her teeth, in the way that many Sudanese women hold their head coverings when the wind or fast-moving traffic threatens to blow them off. Josina grinned, announcing, "I'm a Sudanese woman." Then she began to imitate the movements of the woman's "dove dance," which some other little girls had taught her.

Without any prompting on our part or any special discussion of Islam, Josina startled us one day with a nearly perfect rendering of the motions of Islamic prayer. She brought a small towel to the living room, spread it out carefully, took off her shoes, and intently began to stand, bend over, get down on her knees, and touch her forehead to the ground in a series of repetitive motions. Soon after, she asked, "Mom, what does the muezzin say?" I told her, *"Allahu Akbar"* (God is great), and she proceeded to cup her hands behind her ears, in good form, and perform the call to prayer. With this astonishing performance, we realized how much Josina was absorbing independently, without the "expert" guidance of her two anthropologist parents. We tried to discover how she could have learned the motions so perfectly and concluded that she must have observed the merchants in the market at dusk, praying just before the shops opened for the evening, as this was the time that we often went out after the afternoon rest.

Josina also independently learned several typical Sudanese gestures—indicating no with the hands, tongue clicking to signal the affirmative—and these she picked up without gaining any broad fluency in Arabic. In fact, her frustration at not being able to understand conversations fully in Arabic led to her forming her own gibberish language, which she would use with imaginary friends and occasionally with her parents. She did learn and would use Arabic commands, which were spoken not to the Sudanese but to her parents, whose favor she knew she could get by speaking in Arabic. Whenever she wanted us to listen and we were not giving her enough attention, she would switch to the Arabic ʿAsma, and we would stop whatever we were doing and listen to her. Long after our return to the United States, this special use of Arabic for gaining our attention continued; eight months after we had returned, Josina was asking for her drawing pens, and because Carolyn was not responding, she shifted from the English "Give me" to the Arabic *"Iddini"*—and then she got her drawing pens.

Josina found a unique solution to the common problem of Western children living in non-Western countries, that of high visibility. Josina is a fair-skinned, strawberry blonde who insisted on wearing her shorts and T-shirt on our excursions. Women, in particular, were attracted to the little girl and would invariably comment, *"Ya, sukkar"* (Oh, sweet one). Josina quickly tired of this routine and would frequently reply with perfect diction in Sudanese colloquial Arabic, *"Ana moosh sukkar, ana shata"* (I'm not sweet, I'm hot pepper). This exchange amused everyone even more. The women laughed, but Josina felt that she had gotten the last laugh. Her ultimate defense from constant attention was a cute-looking lion's mask from the People's Republic of China that she had received for Christmas. She often carried this, wearing it, on occasion, in high-visibility areas, such as the times she rode atop Richard's shoulders. When she wore the mask, people looked up, stopped, and laughed, but the mask did have the effect of curbing their interaction.

All was not a rejection of Sudanese culture by any means. Despite frightening bouts of malaria for all of us and a serious case of pneumonia for Josina, our daughter had certain distinct cultural preferences in favor of the Sudan. She enjoyed the habit of eating with one's hands, she liked the shorter schoolday (most offices and institutions closed by 1:00 in the afternoon because of the intense heat), and she loved the Sudanese custom of indulging children with sweets, even when they did not eat their meat and vegetables.

Once our research was under way, we became fully immersed in social visiting and having guests in our house. Josina was always in attendance. In the beginning, the separation of our social activities, Carolyn in the *hareem* section of the house with the women and Richard in the more formal *salon* with male members of the household and guests, was disturbing to Josina. She kept running back and forth, not really knowing where to be, all the while insisting that we sit together and eat together. Once persuaded that this separation was the custom and that we were going to follow it in the homes of friends, she settled into a pattern of moving back and forth, reporting to each group what the others were doing. Somehow, she understood that when we visited our very closest friends, the custom was not observed. But when Sudanese guests were entertained in our home, she insisted on the men sitting apart from the women, and at the end of the visit she would not permit her parents to embrace a member of the opposite sex to say good-bye. Men shake hands with women, and women shake hands with men; they do not usually embrace in this social context. Josina became a more rigid enforcer of the norms than her parents.

On our return to the United States, we were given fresh insights into Josina's experience. We knew what she had observed and, to a degree, we had inculcated the spirit of Sudanese generosity. She shared more or less freely with Sudanese children, took pride in offering our guests plates of food, and happily distributed toys that we could not carry with us to special friends on our departure. None of this was of much note to us until we returned to the States and witnessed a continuation of this behavior pattern, incongruous in the context of American values of individualism. Josina offered or gave personal items to relatives, friends, and strangers alike, and scrupulously reciprocated any gift she received. Drugstore clerks were amazed to see Josina open a pack of just-purchased chewing gum and offer them a stick; grandparents were pleasantly surprised when birthday presents were greeted with a return gift.

In the Sudan, Josina learned that she is an American with specific ties to Rhode Island, where she was born. Every time she heard the words "America" or "Rhode Island," she would cry out,

"Mom, Dad, they said America," or, "On the television they said Rhode Island." These words had come to signify home and the return to the culture of America that a two-and-a-half year old had learned and remembered.

With respect to the conduct of our research this second time around, we would say that the presence of a child affected our field situations in several ways. Our social acceptance was greatly enhanced, and having a child with us opened up new areas of Sudanese reality. Carolyn could discuss childbearing practices and learn how Sudanese feel about the benefits of male versus female children. Richard could have his friends and informants open up to him in new ways after interacting with and exchanging gifts with Josina. The overall effect on fieldwork and family was positive.

For those who are contemplating fieldwork with children, we would say that there are certainly risks if you want to identify them, but with American society filled with social problems for young people, we are also inclined to ask, "Are you ready to risk life in America?" Sudanese children face the possibility of getting malaria—but not drugs in school. Youthful suicide, joyriding, and drunkenness among young people can also be ruled out. The gains from time spent overseas are very great indeed, and our lives and those of our children have been enhanced, risks included.

Life in the developing countries can make some aspects of child care and domestic life easier. There is an endless debate about the ethics of hiring domestic servants and staff. As graduate students doing our doctoral research, and, later, as tenured college professors, our circumstances changed. With children, more social and professional responsibilities, and a tighter time schedule, we discovered the necessity of having others tend to some of the chores, especially where there are no massive shopping malls, easy transportation, reliable telephones, and convenience foods—and there is the unrelenting Saharan sand and dust. Having a cleaning person, a cook, or a house servant can solve some of these daily problems, although of course, it brings other kinds of complexities into your domestic life. Even here, it is often through employing household help that you can get more fully involved with the local community. This can be both rewarding and frustrating.

In many ways, the problems you face about the division of labor in the household, child care, cooking, cleaning, and so forth exist universally. The differences rest mainly in the kinds of human and cultural patterns and resources available to solve these problems. Here, the best advice is to be flexible, creative, and tolerant. If you insist, you will find some way to keep your old habits and solutions. Better yet, you will find new ways to meet your household and personal needs, and will learn more of the diversity of human solutions to human problems.

Our own approach developed over the years, from our first field trip in 1970 through our third in 1982–1984, with other visits in between. As young graduate students, with limited funds and a serious desire not to seem elitist, we disdained any help whatsoever: Shopping, food preparation, laundry, and cleaning were done by the two of us. This proved especially challenging after Saharan duststorms, which deposited fine, powdered dust on everything in our small houseboat flat, including interior drawers, closets, and even the ill-sealed refrigerator. By 1979, with our first child in tow, our financial situation had improved, but we were still influenced by a "do it ourselves" model of behavior; we believed it put less distance between us and our Sudanese hosts. With Josina's child-care needs handled by her nursery school, our major domestic tasks, including shopping and food preparation, were still carried out primarily by us. Since we both had research projects, as well as the added responsibility of taking Josina to and from school on the *boks* and caring for her after school, we finally found it impossible to keep ahead of the daily accumulations of sand and dust. Although we considered it a major concession at the time, it was a relief to hire someone to look after the increased amounts of laundry and clean the flat each day. Ultimately, our helper did a bit of basic shopping for bread, milk, and eggs, but the cooking and washing up remained a family chore. In Cairo, during our third long-term residence in the Nile valley, we had two small children, Richard held a full-time position at the American University in Cairo, and Carolyn had full-time work in her third postdoctoral fellowship at the American Research Center in Egypt. Consequently, our time was even more limited, but our compensation was greater. Since Richard had settled in before Carolyn arrived, a cook, Hafez, had been hired. Hafez shopped and prepared two meals a day for Richard, Josina, and niece Betsy, who constituted the "family" during this phase of our lives in Egypt. When Carolyn arrived with baby Nichola, Hafez was still needed, and he did most of the grocery shopping, as well as other errands, such as finding the latest source of *butagaz* (bottled gas for cooking) and similar household management tasks. From time to time, cleaning women were hired to help with the laundry. For much of the time, however, Carolyn did the laundry by hand with the family joining in on the cleaning. Or we sent out the laundry to the washing and ironing establishment two blocks away. Cloth diapers, still worn by Nichola, were boiled on the stove and washed by hand in the bathtub. Disposable diapers are available in the main urban centers in the Middle East and Africa, but at a considerable cost.

Nichola was born in 1981 in Rhode Island, but she spent her first year in Philadelphia where Carolyn was a Mellon Fellow at the University of Pennsylvania. Midway in that year, Richard assumed his position at the American University in Cairo, taking Josina and Betsy to Egypt with him as company. Carolyn planned to join them following her year in Philadelphia. Being a single parent in a non-Western setting was advantageous in some respects for Richard, since it was not a standard role in the Middle East (or in the United States, for that matter), and neighbors and colleagues "took pity" on him, feeding and housing him liberally.

The family was reunited in Cairo at the end of the summer of 1982. Nichola had turned one, while five-and-a-half-year-old Josina had completed a Cairo kindergarten and was entering first grade. Josina was a fieldwork veteran and enjoyed "teaching" her younger sister how to travel in airplanes, keep sandals on to protect her feet against hot asphalt, and say "lollipop" in Arabic. This sense of superiority over her sister gave Josina a more positive attitude toward Egyptian cultural differences. The major shift in attitude came with respect to Josina's use of Arabic. Her first-grade class at the Cairo American College studied Arabic language and culture twice a week, and Josina soon became the star of the class. The Arabic she spoke in the house with Hafez, in the market, and on social occasions became much more proficient; her stirring rendition of the Egyptian national anthem, "Biladi, Biladi," was an invariable showstopper. During this field trip, Josina's health problems were limited to chicken pox and Nichola suffered only a few bouts of gastroenteritis.

Josina's experience in Egypt build on her Sudanese background. For our younger daughter, Nichola, her first non-Western experience had a more profound effect. Nichola, at one year, showed no signs of the culture shock Josina had experienced in the Sudan when she was two and a half. From the beginning, Nichola accepted Egypt as "home." Perhaps because she had moved so much in her young life, from Providence to three addresses in the Philadelphia area, then back to Providence and on to Cairo; perhaps because the family was finally together; perhaps because a year-old child has not yet developed a sense of cultural attachment that living in a foreign nation may disrupt. Whatever the reasons, Nichola settled in with no signs of difficulty except for a brief disturbance in sleeping patterns caused by jet lag.

Nichola had not yet developed a speaking ability in English; this may be why she exhibited no shock or disappointment with our use of Arabic. Instead, she evidenced an openness to language, and the resulting mélange of English and Arabic entertained speakers of both languages. Interestingly, the assertion of self, the first-person pronoun, was expressed in Arabic as *Ana,* this being joined to sundry English and Arabic words to indicate states of mind and mood. Nichola's use of *Ana* for "I" continued months after our return from Egypt; her own name, "Nicky," at last displaced *Ana.* As of this writing, just after her third birthday, she still has not made the correct transition to the use of "I" and other pronouns in English.

As Nichola's vocabulary grew during the year in Cairo, her apparent ability to understand both languages was matched by her use of words in each language. When she wanted to learn a word for an object, we would give it to her in English and Arabic. Normally, she chose the easier version to pronounce; *dik* not "chicken"; but "car," not *arabiya.* "Important" words, such as those for candy, sweets, and ice cream, were spoken only in Arabic, no matter how difficult. These items were usally begged for in the market or from the hands of generous neighbors. Another important term, this one for Nichola's security blanket, a white cloth diaper she clung to then and clings to still, is *futa,* although she does know the English word "diaper." Her sister teaches new babysitters this important word, and, if necessary, Nichola will instruct caretakers herself: "That's my *futa,*" pointing out her diaper to the sitter.

Nichola surprised us, not with her mimicry of Egyptian culture, as her sister had done some three years before, but with her total absorption of the culture. Egypt was not foreign; it was home. She took in all the sights and sounds as normal: the ducks and chickens in the garden, the open-air markets, and the constant reminders of the practices of Islam. Here, especially, Nichola fell in with the rhythm and routine of life in Cairo. The call to prayer, which had fascinated Josina in the Sudan, captivated Nichola in Egypt. As those who have lived in Muslim societies know well, no place of residence is ever far from a mosque and the call to prayer, *"Allahu Akbar, Allahu Akbar,"* in welcoming tones five times a day. This is the reminder to the faithful and a marker of the passage of time during the day. At the beginning of the call, Nichola would perk up, stop whatever she was doing and start singing, "Allah, Allah, Allah." She would announce the moment to the household and, on occasion, perform her own version of the Islamic prayers. Her "window on the world" was the kitchen window, which overlooked an overcrowded boys' school; beneath the window was the open-air mosque where the middle-school boys prayed before school and during recess. Nichola watched these ritual performances with as much interest as she watched the soccer games the boys played, and on many occasions she displayed her considerable religious "abilities."

Carolyn cared for Nichola from breakfast time until she took her rather long, late-morning nap, which lasted until early afternoon. Hafez prepared a bottle of milk or a snack when Nichola awoke, and Richard was home very shortly afterward. This system worked well, since it permitted Richard to be at work early while following the Egyptian schedule of leaving relatively early for lunch at home. Carolyn's work, which often encompassed interviews and social calls in people's homes, was best conducted in mid-afternoon and early evening. This dovetailing of the routine worked out very well. Fridays were family days; Richard did not work on Sundays in order to accommodate the Coptic employees of the American University in Cairo. Carolyn had her second day off on Saturdays, when Richard was at work. In short, the adjustment to having a preschool child was not serious; indeed it followed a somewhat normal pattern for dual-career or academic couples, wherever they might be.

Children are a focal point of attention, even adulation, in Egypt, and whenever we went out, both girls received a great deal of genuine affection. Josina took this more in stride the second time around, while Nichola enjoyed the give and take that is the Egyptian way of constantly joking in conversation. Her biggest and best part in the conversation came in the form of a loud, assertive *"La"* or "No" in English to just about every question, no matter how ridiculous the meaning might become. After Nichola had "warmed up" the inquisitive stranger, Josina would finish the act with a near-perfect example of some colloquial Arabic saying. Our Egyptian hosts were invariably pleased and amazed at this use of their language.

When we left Egypt in the early summer, spending a week's vacation in Wales on the way home, the United Kingdom was more of a foreign country to Nichola than Egypt. On arriving in Rhode Island, which we announced was "home," Nichola had no reaction. She was unable to comprehend her sister's delight at being back in the land of Hershey bars, McDonald's, and Saturday cartoons. Throughout the first year of our return to America, Nichola continued to have difficulty with the concept of home. To her, any long car trip was a trip "home," to Egypt. This was exacerbated by the fact that Richard remained in Cairo to complete his two-year contract there. Once her father returned, Nichola's attachment to our home in Rhode Island became stronger. Yet Egypt remains a vivid image in her mind and is recalled every time she sees pictures on the television from almost anywhere in the Third World. The showing of a television miniseries on Anwar Sadat was a grand occasion in our home, with both children excitedly pointing to familiar street scenes, and Nichola looking for Daddy on the screen.

On her first day in an American school, Josina raised her hand when the teacher asked the children to recite the American Pledge of Allegiance. Josina told the teacher that they did not have to say that Pledge of Allegiance in Egypt but that she did know the Egyptian national anthem. The teacher asked her to sing it for the class, which she did, causing a minor sensation. A few days later, we learned that Josina was teaching the words of the Egyptian anthem to children at the bus stop. This curiosity about other languages and places was underscored when we visited Josina's class, where she "lectured" with slides about life in the Sudan and Egypt. The children wanted to know about everything from irrigation techniques in the desert to television programs in Cairo.

Josina also "lectured" before a small anthropology seminar at Wheaton College in neighboring Norton, Massachusetts. Dr. Christine Obbo, one of Africa's few female anthropologists, extended this invitation to Josina after the two met and shared experiences. Josina may have set the record for the youngest Wheaton College lecturer. She was candid about her likes and dislikes in her matter-of-fact exposition about her visits to the pyramids and her study of Egyptian history, the Arabic language, and Islamic culture; about malaria and intense heat; and about sleeping out-of-doors when you are in your house in the Sudan.

Although Josina may tell you that she never wants to leave America again or see another airplane, she enjoys programs and books about other cultures. But we should say that when we mentioned the possibility of another long trip to Josina, she said, "Maybe, just maybe, I would be interested to go." She immediately made plans for which of the Barbie dolls would come along. Moreover, she seems essentially free of cultural bias and has a positive view of the diversity of other cultures. Josina is able successfully to field questions about the images of lions, jungles, and huts in Africa, for she has seen Africa and the Middle East firsthand and knows the difference between myth and reality.

Josina is also effectively free of racial prejudice—indeed, until Michael Jackson, she was not really sure what a "black" American is. Her experience in the Afro-Arab societies of Egypt and the Sudan certainly went a long way to retard the development of an American style of racial consciousness, and her ability to make racial categories is, by these standards, poor to this day. When pressed by Wheaton College students to distinguish between the sometimes lighter-skinned Egyptians and the sometimes darker-skinned Sudanese, Josina mentioned almost every variable except race, including the style of dress, type of headgear, and the presence or absence of facial scarification. Perceptions of race are so ingrained in our society that we suspect that the Wheaton students were simply unbelieving that Josina did not categorize the world in the same way as they.

With these experiences, in two countries, with and without children, we feel confident in making some generalizations about children in the field. Despite the difficulties of traveling with small children, it is perhaps easier for youngsters to accompany their parents into the field during the stage of early childhood. Our children's intestines seemed less susceptible to alien bacteria; their tongues were more flexible in response to acquiring foreign languages; their abilities to absorb and incorporate cultural diversity were not blocked by too great a knowledge of, or attachment to, their own culture. Surely we had greater freedom of movement without the children; we were able to take long trips and, if we wished, work long hours without worrying about their welfare. But our social status in an Islamic setting was undoubtedly enhanced by being together as a family. Carolyn's acceptability as a female researcher was certainly improved and legitimized by the fact that she was in the Sudan, and later Egypt, with her husband and children. Richard's visits to the communities he studied in the Sudan became more meaningful, involving social occasions that led to increased knowledge, because of the presence of his family. Despite health problems of malaria, pneumonia, and diarrhea, there is no doubt in our minds that the children had a positive effect on our field situation and that they, in turn, were positively affected by their experiences.

JOAN CASSELL

Conclusion

Despite differences in anthropologists' temperaments, experiences, family constellations, and research sites, the ten narratives in this book have a common characteristic: like Wordsworth's definition of poetry, each stems from emotion recollected in tranquillity. Fieldwork is a profound and emotional experience. Reaching out to "the other," we move deep within ourselves; learning foreign ways, we illuminate our native culture; studying strange assumptions, we confront our unexamined preconceptions. The anthropologist Rosalie Wax, who wrote a book on doing fieldwork eventually called just that, *Doing Fieldwork,* first titled it *The Risk of Self.*[1]

In parenting, we also risk ourselves. Children are fragile links between our past and future, fears and hopes. We wish our children to be more than we, to have more, to learn more; we fear that they will be, have, learn less. In seeking their growth, we expose them to challenge and the possibility of failure.

We are doubly at risk, then, when our children are in the field. In attempting to learn and grow, we risk failure and sorrow, our own and theirs. In exposing ourselves, we expose them.

The Observer Observed

The contemporary Western split between the personal and the professional cannot be maintained when the researcher's children come to the field. Our children make us as accessible to the people we study as they are to us. As a result, the anthropologist and those on whom anthropology is practiced cannot neatly be divided into observer and observed.

Researchers who were parents before becoming fieldworkers may take this reciprocity for granted. This situation seemed natural to me when I arrived in Jamaica as a novice fieldworker; it was clear that my children and I were far more visible to the villagers I was supposed to be studying than they were to us. (My hope was that I would eventually learn some of the techniques for observing them that they knew from the beginning for observing us.) Renate Fernandez was in a similar position when she arrived in a Spanish village with two toddlers; to find a suitable place to carry out anthropological observations, she observed the elderly villager observe her two year old, and act when necessary (pages 189–190). Infinite regress: We observe them observing us observing them. Perhaps there is always some element of a hall-of-mirrors in fieldwork. Children, however, increase the ricocheting images.

Anthropologists who carried out research before they had children may have mixed feelings about the self-disclosure generated by children; personal information can no longer be rationed or "managed" when one's family is in the field (page 168). Although some may have an ambivalent reaction to this, as Dreher points out, it is surely a more egalitarian way to conduct research. The relationship between those who study and those who are studied becomes less interrogative, more *dialogic.* This mutual disclosure, where each is encouraged to observe, judge, and interpret "the other," can lead to more profound understanding and, consequently, to better social science.

The Effect of Children on Fieldwork

Whether the presence of children helps or hinders the researcher's task depends, in part, on family constellation.

Not surprisingly, a spouse who takes primary responsibility for child care simplifies research. If that parent also aids in data collection and, as some anthropological wives do, types her husband's field notes, the task is further facilitated. This book describes the experiences of three female anthropologists, four male anthropologists, and two professional couples. Of these, five couples followed the "traditional" pattern: Nancy Scheper-Hughes was accompanied by a nonanthropologist husband, who assumed primary responsibility for child care; the four male anthropologists were accompanied by wives, all of whom took responsibility for the children; Renate Fernandez helped her husband carry out fieldwork as well.

The conduct of research may be hindered by the lack of a nonresearcher spouse to help with child care. Melanie Dreher and Christine and Stephen Hugh-Jones, for example, found that their family responsibilities impeded their fieldwork. The Nichters and the Lobbans mention no such difficulties; like the Hugh-Joneses, they seem to have shared child-care responsibilities, but their field situations were less arduous and dangerous—and in India and Egypt, unlike the Amazon, domestic help was available (it was probably available in the Sudan as well, although the Lobbans did not at first employ a helper). I did have someone to help me with the housekeeping (so, too, did Dreher); in fact, I knew no other way to conduct fieldwork. I had no previous fieldwork habits and techniques and no standard of comparison against which to weigh my research experience. (I now realize it was far easier to conduct research during my final month in Jamaica when my husband was present; I was able to leave my children for as long as necessary without worrying about their well-being; moreover, for the first time, I could conduct research at night.)

The Nichters list four benefits from their child's presence:

1. It was easier for the villages they studied to relate to a family unit; the child was the subject of conversation and a guarantee of good intentions. Wylie, Fernandez, Klass, and I had similar experiences.

2. When the subject of study related to children or families, the researchers learned more. Klass, for example, describes the information on childbirth and childrearing that villagers volunteered when his daughter was born. Moreover, his status among the East Indian villagers changed dramatically: He was now a householder, or "family man," with whom other mature family men might converse.

3. The child was a source of pleasure and entertainment, and the child's presence made the researchers more welcome. I found this to be true in Jamaica: I believe "Mistress Cassell" was more warmly welcomed in Mango Ridge with her "pickneys" than she would have been by herself.

4. The presence of a child taught the fieldworkers about their own, previously unexamined, cultural biases and assumptions.

Thus, my nine-year-old daughter's proud entry in her field notes, comparing American tourists who see only the Jamaicans who serve them with our family (who "are like citizens, we do our own things, get grocerys {sic} and LIVE!") and Wylie's wry account of his family's Thanksgiving visit to the American army base, highlight anthropologists' and their families' quiet feelings of superiority to those "other Americans"—tourists, missionaries, army officers, Peace Corps administrators.

As anthropologists, we perceive ourselves as somewhat marginal members of our own society, taking pride in understanding and fitting into the host cultures. The presence of her children, however, made Dreher realize that, despite her assumption that she is in some ways culturally neutral, her children are archetypical middle-class American "culture carriers," and when it came to a choice, she rejected rural Jamaican childrearing methods for them. It is easier for an anthropologist to be value neutral and practice cultural relativity in regard to other people's children; one can risk one's "self" more freely than one's children. (As an anthropologist, my passionate commitment to the welfare of my children is my Achilles' heel: As an upper-middle-class intellectual, I define their welfare in extremely culture-specific— some would say ethnocentric—terms.)

Challenging her unperceived cultural assumption, Fernandez learned that a private bedroom for a child can be considered deprivation; even a separate bed for a baby, as Dreher discovered, may be considered a kind of deprivation. (It is not surprising that those reared with "my room," "my bed," and "my toys" have a strong sense of themselves as separate atomistic individuals and of their possessions as an integral part of their "selves"; when such individuals become anthropologists, they are likely to think possessively of "my people.")

My cultural assumptions were also challenged: I discovered that a strict schedule is an American or, perhaps, postindustrial invention and that children do not curl up and die, or even fail to thrive, if they are not fed or bedded at the same time every day.

This is learning, indeed. Gut learning, when it pertains to one's children.

The Effect of Fieldwork on Children

A number of factors influenced the way fieldwork affected the children in these narratives: among them are housing, food, child-care arrangements, the age of the child, and the "fit" between the family (and the individual child) and the culture.

Most important, perhaps, is the parents' philosophy. Fieldworkers can be divided into *protective* (or *timid,* depending on one's viewpoint) and *macho* (or, alternatively, *brave*) parents: those who attempt to shield their children from the physical and emotional rigors of the field, as I did, and those who, like Scheper-Hughes (page 234), are convinced that "children can benefit enormously from their confrontation with radical otherness." How radical the "otherness" depends on the field situation; the extent of shielding depends on the parents' temperaments and beliefs.

The gulf here may be deeper than it first appears. Our relation to our children condenses and symbolizes our relation to our social (and political) worlds. They are our hostages to fortune—and misfortune. Those who are most committed to bridging the terrible division between the haves and the have-nots may feel that protecting their children from the rigors other children are forced to endure (and from the "radical otherness" of the world of the have-nots) is an act of moral cowardice. Others may be torn between belief and parental nurture. Some will opt for protection. Others, more conservative or less courageous, depending on one's stance, may wonder "what right parents have to subject their children to dangers and discomfort in the pursuit of the parents' preoccupation"—as did a reviewer for the manuscript of this book.

Living and eating arrangements are affected by this division between protective and macho parents. Finding an appropriate dwelling for a family can be difficult, as the Nichters, Wylie, and I learned; these difficulties may be compounded by the researcher's definition of the family's basic requirements. Thus, despite the time and worry it took to find a suitable dwelling, I flatly refused to live with another family (as my childless co-researchers in Jamaica did) because I believed my children and husband would find such an arrangement uncomfortable.

In similar fashion, whenever possible, I drove to the city of Kingston to buy supermarket food. Food *was* difficult to purchase in the village I studied, but another factor influenced my behavior: My ethnic group equates feeding with love, and I unquestioningly assumed that familiar meals would help my children feel at home. In the same way, Dreher learned that canned tuna, peanut butter, and marshmallow fluff can buffer culture shock.

The Hugh-Joneses were willing and able to live in an Amazonian longhouse with their children and subsist on local fare; they report no physical or psychic ill effects. Each parent spent considerable time and effort, however, shielding their children from physical and emotional difficulties.

Scheper-Hughes, in contrast, was unable to locate a house with a stove, which meant that her children had to eat strange foods in a public environment; this seems to have exacerbated their culture shock. (Why did Scheper-Hughes's children react so differently from the children of the Hugh-Joneses? One cannot know the entire story, but I would hazard a guess that not all the children in the Brazilian market town lived as Nancy Scheper-Hughes's family did, while the Hugh-Joneses saw no children in the field who lived otherwise.)

In a personal communication, Scheper-Hughes told me that she was not discomfited that the only house her Brazilian friends were able to find had no stove; cooking, buying, and keeping food in a hot climate with limited electricity and no refrigeration are enormously difficult and time-consuming tasks, and Scheper-Hughes does not believe in employing domestic help. With a stove, she would have felt compelled to prepare meals, which would have interfered with her research. And any domestic help would have had to be recruited from the poorest segment of the community—the shantytown dwellers she studied—and she felt it was morally unacceptable for her to set up a relationship of employer and employed with them. The mother's ideological and emotional identification with the *favela* residents affected the way her children lived. The Lobbans, as graduate students on their first field trip, also questioned the morality of hiring domestic servants (page 247). Apparently, the couple were able to balance and share child-care and research responsibilities; yet they report that when they returned to the field some years later with two children, they were more open to the idea of employing someone to help out.

Domestic help and housing, then, are matters of both ideology and convenience. Family constellation also affects how much one needs help. A single researcher accompanied by one or more children, or two researcher parents in a site where household and food arrangements are arduous and time-consuming (e.g. Nichter, page 68), has more urgent need of help than a researcher parent accompanied by a spouse who takes primary responsibility for child care, or two researcher parents with a single child.

The age of the children apparently influences their welfare. Wylie and Scheper-Hughes note that older children seem to have more trouble adjusting to a foreign situation. (The elder Hughes daughter, however, had fewer difficulties than her ten-year old sister; individual differences cannot be discounted.) The Fernandez children were introduced to the field site when they were very young; as teenagers, they were familiar with the village, the people and the language.

Younger children need more supervision and, as the Nichters learned, are more vulnerable to the physical hazards of the field. (The anthropologist David Maybury-Lewis describes how his one year old contracted dysentery and almost died when the family lived with an Indian tribe in Brazil. [2])

Schooling, one of the issues parents seem to worry about most before bringing children to the field, did not seem to cause serious difficulties for any of the researchers who describe their experiences in this volume. The Fernandez and Wylie children attended local schools, while the Fernandez teenager chose to board at a *lycée* in France for a year. None of the children seems to have found local schooling traumatic. Jonathan Wylie, in fact, apparently enjoyed the French village *école* he attended with his brother more than the "enlightened" American schools he went to before his stay in France (pages 99–100). No child's academic progress seems to have been permanently retarded.

When no schools existed, the Hitchcocks and Hugh-Joneses tutored their children. The writers mention no serious problems associated with doing this.

The fieldworkers' sorrow and guilt when something did go wrong is apparent: Simeon Nichter's positive reaction to a tuberculosis skin test, for example, or Sarah Hughes's illness and depression. The death of the Hitchcock baby is, of course, the stuff parents' nightmares are made on. Yet the cause of the baby's death remains unknown; conceivably it might have occurred in the United States as well.

Culture and Temperament

Almost every narrative describes patterned difference in temperament, behavior, and expectations between the anthropologists' children and those of the host people. These differences highlight the kinds of behavior valued and encouraged by upper-middle-class academics, as opposed to those encouraged by the rural, tribal, and/or deprived peoples most frequently studied by anthropologists.

The researchers' children are described as independent, active, curious, and verbal. They are frequently far less well behaved than the local children. Dreher, for example, reports that rural Jamaican children are "polite . . . quiet in the company of adults, do as they are told, speak when spoken to, say good morning and good evening on entering a room, eat all the food on their plates, are too mannerly to ask for more" (page 165).

Of course, rural Jamaican children who are disobedient are "flogged." Jamaican children are raised to follow orders with little or no questioning, schooled by rote, and removed from school to help out when their labor is needed; at the same time, their mealtimes and bedtimes are flexible, and they share adult festivities as well as work. The kinds of adults such an upbringing produces have the ability and flexibility to survive in the tragically limited adult circumstances of rural Jamaica. (Dreher's story of her children's petted, pampered puppy, which was torn apart by the ferocious village dogs the night before they left, is thought provoking. Could our petted, protected children survive in such a harsh environment?)

Interestingly, when social mobility is feasible—as in the Spanish village studied by the Fernandezes, where new economic opportunities were unfolding—the anthropologists' children may teach the local children new and useful behaviors (pages 192–193).

Dualities Confronted

The presence of children may emphasize aspects of the field situation that the fieldworker might otherwise ignore. Gillian Gillison, for example, an anthropologist who brought her family with her when she studied a highland New Guinea tribe, reported that the way the people she studied treated her children during the family's second visit to the field illuminated disturbing aspects of the relationship of fieldworkers to the host people. Gillison and her husband brought their six-year-old daughter to New Guinea for two years; ten years later, they returned with the girl, now sixteen, and her six-year-old brother. In a tape-recorded interview I conducted with her, Gillison said of her daughter's acceptance during their first visit:

> Aside from the fact that she was a cute kid, she was also a White Princess. She was, for one thing, a route to us, she was a way of getting to us without confronting us—you could make a request and use Samantha as a conduit. And she was also an outsider that they could have for their own; they could get a look at us through her. So she was an object of fascination in herself; she was also an object of use to them. And that had something to do with why her own experiences were so pleasant. She was always given food. She didn't have to contend with a lot of the conflict and difficulties the other children had to contend with. She was a little celebrity, really. . . .

It was an idyllic life, but still it was inescapably tied to
who we were and why we were there. . . . We had enormous
power; it's hard to conceive of how much power you have in
that situation. And wealth. Unimaginable wealth. I
sometimes compare it to people I know . . . enormously
wealthy people, and when they talk to me . . . I'm not
judging them like I judge other people . . . if they're a little
boring and they talk about themselves, I am more inclined to
suffer their self-indulgence and suffer their interests. . . . I
think people put up with us and catered to us.

Gillison reports that she never questioned this state of affairs until ten years later, when she returned to the field with two children. Unlike her sunny, outgoing daughter, her son is intense
and shy:

Instead of being relaxed and enjoying the adulation, he felt
very self-conscious, very angry, and couldn't really fathom it.
And his bewilderment made me see how extraordinary the
situation was. Because he was right: This was incredible! It
was an unusual, bizarre situation to be in. Through him I
began to reexamine some things I had taken very much for
granted. . . .

When my son rejected children, nobody was offended,
nobody held it against him . . . they suffered him in
whatever way he might have behaved and catered to him and
tried to cajole him. . . . And I guess it was the experience of
bringing my second child that made me realize that I, too,
am treated the way my children are. . . . It's very flattering
to live with people who have that much respect for you.

She continued:

I don't mean to give the impression that I was a *"bwana"* and
was able to get what I wanted by waving a magic wand. I
still did intense fieldwork and had to work very hard at it.

> But there is this other thing. And I think when you have
> children, it is much more obvious than when you don't.

Gillison's recital has an uncomfortable ring of truth when I recall our experiences in Jamaica. Were my children popular and beloved, not so much because of their intrinsic lovability, as I fondly believed, but because we were wealthy, powerful representatives of white culture? How does this apply to the reception of all researchers' families in poor, rural, and tribal settings—and to the reception of anthropologists themselves? Anthropologists traditionally "study down"; we investigate people less powerful, less fortunate than ourselves—certainly less powerful and fortunate than the group our hosts perceive us as belonging to. (Our feelings of marginality, of not quite belonging to our own culture, tend to protect us against this disturbing insight.)

I am at present engaged in "studying up." I am doing fieldwork among a group of people more powerful than I am. Here, I am not flattered, beloved, welcome; frequently, I am barely tolerated. The surgeons I am now studying would be bored by my kids—the children hold no intrinsic or symbolic interest; they represent no access to power, wealth, or a dominant culture. In this field situation, my children represent nothing but themselves.

I am not intimating that anthropologists exploit the people they traditionally study. Nor am I saying that one should enter the field with a feeling of guilt, a need to make reparations to the host people. Such an approach would, I believe, be simplistic and false. Nevertheless, the presence of our children in the field, and their reception, does more than resolve dualities between the personal and the professional, between those who study and those who are studied. The presence of our children can also illuminate aspects of our situation within the world, in our own social structure, and among those we study, that we might otherwise over-look or ignore.

Notes

1. Rosalie Wax, *Doing Fieldwork* (Chicago: University of Chicago Press, 1971).
2. David Maybury-Lewis, *The Savage and the Innocent: Life with the Primitive Tribes of Brazil* (Cleveland, Ohio: World, 1965).